Hippocrene Language and Travel Guide to

FRANCE

For information, address:
HIPPOCRENE BOOKS, INC.
171 Madison Avenue
New York, NY 10016

Library of Congress Cataloging-in-Publication Data

Klein, Elaine.
    Hippocrene language and travel guide to France / Elaine Klein.
      p.   cm.
    Includes index.
    ISBN 0-7818-0080-3
    1. France—Guidebooks. 2. Paris (France)—Guidebooks. 3. French
language—Textbooks for foreign speakers—English. I. Title.
DC16.K54 1993
914.404'839—dc20
                                                      93-13498
                                                         CIP

To Mildred, ma mère

Contents

Maps

Introduction

Like most countries, France has been gratified with descriptive clichés. *Rebellious* and *romantic* are two of the most usual. And like all clichés, they are not completely true nor totally false. The image of rebellion, at the least the idea that its people do not quite stay "in line," is a persistant one. The 1968 student revolt, the Paris Commune, the French Revolution, the Reformation—Calvin was a Frenchman—are just a few "rebellious" events that are now part of world history.

The notion of the romantic Frenchman also sticks. There is a lot to be said about the French . . . *l'amour* and *le sexe* . . .

For the French themselves their country is *la douce France*, gentle France. While it is not the whole story, I like that image. It evokes rolling hills, poplar-lined fields, orchards and flower gardens, sleepy villages down leisurely slopes and country lanes, slow-moving rivers, calm seas and a mild climate.

But France is much more: it is an elegant land of refinement; it possesses an incalculable number of fabulous castles and monuments as well as superb museums and galleries and impressive vestiges of the past. And it is a place of taste: there is a certain way of decorating shop windows, arranging the dinner table, or simply knotting a scarf with a toss of the head.

France is a country which excites the imagination. It also fills the eyes, titillates the senses and whets the appetite!

CHAPTER 1

Practical Information

Accommodations

Suggestions for hotels and other accommodations are provided at the end of each itinerary. Pricing corresponds to the following categories (Restaurant categories under **Restaurants** later in this chapter):

Inexpensive: under 150 francs
Moderately priced: from 150 to 300 francs
Medium-priced: from 300 to 500 francs
Moderately expensive: from 500 to 700 francs
Expensive: from 700 to 1000 francs
Luxury prices: over 1000 francs

For bed and breakfast accommodations, information can be obtained from Café Couette, 8 Rue d'Isly, 75008 Paris, tel: 4294-9200. There is a 100-franc membership fee.

A *gîtes ruraux* or rural housing guide can be obtained from the French National Federation of Rural Housing, 35 Rue Godot-de-Mauroy, 75009 Paris, tel: 4742-2543.

Agriculture and Tourism, 9 Avenue George-V, 75008 Paris, tel: 4723-5540, maintains a list of farms receiving tourists.

For château housing, Château-Accueil, c/o M. de Chenerilles le Gerfaut, 37190 Azay-le-Rideau, tel: 4745-4016, distributes a brochure of addresses.

NOTE: For hotel suggestions in Paris, see the *Insiders' Guide to Paris* published by Hippocrene Books.

15

Airlines

Major airlines operating between France and North America (Paris offices):

Air Canada: 31 Rue Falguière, tel: 4320-1200.

Air France: 119 Avenue des Champs-Elysées; Invalides Air Terminal, Quai d'Orsay, and others, tel: 4535-6161.

American Airlines: 38 Rue du Mont-Thabor, tel: 4296-2061. Toll free number from anywhere in France: 0523-0035.

British Airways: 12 Rue de Castiglione, tel: 4778-1414.

Continental Airlines: 92 Avenue des Champs-Elysées, tel: 4225-3181. Toll free number from anywhere in France: 0525-3181.

Delta Airlines: 4 Rue Scribe, tel: 4768-9292.

Northwest Airlines: 16 Rue Chauveau-Lagarde, tel: 4266-9000.

Tower Air: 11 Boulevard Montmartre, tel: 4013-8080.

TWA: 101 Avenue des Champs-Elysées, tel: 4720-6211.

United Airlines: 34 Avenue de l'Opéra, tel: 4897-8282.

US Air: 85 Avenue Emile-Zola, tel: 4579-6868.

Airlines operating within France:

Air France: see above.

Air Inter(*): 49 Avenue des Champs-Elysées; Invalides Air Terminal, Quai d'Orsay, and others, tel: 4546-9000.

(*) reductions on off-peak flights for youth and students, senior citizens and families.

Airports
Paris-Orly:

Orly Airport is divided into Orly Sud and Orly Ouest. Transatlantic traffic leaves and arrives at Orly Sud. Orly Ouest handles European and domestic flights. Orly is located south of Paris. By car, taxi or bus, normal driving time is roughly one-half hour. Give yourself extra leeway in case of heavy traffic. The RER (line B4), with OrlyVal automatic train link-up to the terminals from the Antony stop, also takes about one-half hour.

For international departures, plan to arrive from 90 to 120 minutes before flight time. For Western Europe, 60 to 90 minutes in advance of flight time. For domestic flights, be at the airport 45 minutes before flight time.

Taxi fare: approximately 150 francs.

Air France buses Orly-Invalides terminal: 29 francs.

RER-OrlyVal to or from Paris: 42 francs. The RER can be boarded at the following stations, among others: Gare du Nord, Châtelet, Saint-Michel/Notre-Dame, Luxembourg, Denfert-Rochereau.

City bus 215 to or from Denfert-Rochereau: 23 francs or six bus tickets.

City bus 183A to or from Porte de Choisy: three bus tickets.

Roissy/Charles-de-Gaulle:
Air France, Air Inter and UTA flights leave from Terminal 2. All other flights leave from Terminal 1.

For Terminal 1 departures, arrive from 90 to 120 minutes before flight time. For Terminal 2 departures, from 60 to 90 minutes ahead of flight time.

Roissy/Charles-de-Gaulle is located north of Paris. By bus, car or taxi, normal driving time is 45 minutes. During the morning and evening rush hours, give yourself an extra half-hour.

The RER (line B3) with a bus link-up to the terminals takes about 45 minutes. The RER can be boarded at the following stations, among others: Denfert-Rochereau, Luxembourg, Saint-Michel/Notre-Dame, Châtelet, Gare du Nord.

Taxi fare: from 180 to 230 francs.

Air France buses Roissy-Porte Maillot or Etoile: 36 francs.

RER with bus link-up to terminal: 33 francs.

A new bus line to Roissy/Charles-de-Gaulle operates from Rue Scribe, at the corner of Rue Auber, alongside American

Express (métro: Auber or Opéra): departure every 15 minutes, 30 francs.

City bus 350 to or from Gare de l'Est and Gare du Nord: 23 francs or six bus tickets.

City bus 351 to and from Nation: 23 francs or six bus tickets.

Buses (Paris)

Individual tickets purchased on a bus cost 6 francs per ticket. Ten-packs can be purchased in métro stations for 36.50 francs and are good on both métro and buses. Tickets must be punched in machines just behind the driver or in the median area on double buses. Short rides cost one ticket, longer rides cost a maximum of two (check with driver).

Day, week and one-month passes can be used on both métro and buses. **Important:** Transportation passes should not be punched. They are simply shown to the driver.

Parisian bus lines begin operating at 7 A.M. The last bus leaves the end of the line at appoximately 8:30 P.M. Lines with black numbers marked on white discs operate on Sundays. Some of the latter operate until 12:30 A.M. The noctambuses run all night. They leave their terminals every hour on the hour from 1 to 5 A.M. There are 11 different departure and arrival points at the Paris *Portes*. All buses go to and from the Châtelet stop in the center of town. Departures from Châtelet are on the hour also. You can get on or off at any point along the way.

Car rental

Ada: (Paris) 4293-6513/4572-3636
Avis: (Paris) 4609-9212 or 0505-2211*
Budget: (Paris) 4686-6565 or 0510-0001*
Eurodollar: (Paris) 4938-7777
Hertz: (Paris) 4788-5151 or 0505-3311*
RentaCar: (Paris) 4522-2828 or (France) 4959-8989

*French 05 numbers are the equivalent of American 800 numbers.

Credit cards

American Express, Diners, Masters accepted widely
Visa accepted everywhere
In case of loss, call:
American Express: 4777-7200/4777-7000
Diner's Club: 4762-7500
Master's: 4567-8080/4567-5353
Visa: 4277-1190

Driving

Practically all French and European cars are equipped with hand shifts. There are generally four or five forward gears plus reverse. If you have never used a clutch, practice before setting out.

Remember that in France the driver on the right always has priority, even when coming out of a side street (if there is no stop sign). So the general rule is "eyes right." French drivers enforce their priority. Road courtesy is the exception rather than the rule. You will not need an international drivers license. Foreign driving permits are accepted in France.

Speed Limits

There are no speed limits on turnpikes, parkways and highways, except where indicated. Slow down to the limits posted at the entrances to villages and towns.

Electrical Appliances

Voltage in France is 220. If your electric shaver or hair dryer is not equipped with an adapter or a European "male" plug, these can be purchased in Paris at the following department store basements:

Samaritaine, 19 Rue de la Monnaie, métro Pont-Neuf or Louvre.

Bazar de l'Hôtel de Ville (BHV), 52 Rue de Rivoli, métro Hôtel-de-Ville.

Embassies and Consulates

Canada: 35 Avenue Montaigne, tel: 4723-0101.
Ireland: 4 Rue Rude, tel: 4500-2087.
U.K.: (Embassy) 35 Rue du Faubourg Saint-Honoré, tel: 4266-9142; or
(Consulate) 16 Rue Anjou, tel: 4266-9142.
U.S.A.: (Embassy) 2 Avenue Gabriel, tel: 4296-1202; or
(Consulate) 2 Rue Saint-Florentin, tel: 4296-1202.

Emergencies

Police, tel: 17.
Fire department, tel: 18.
Ambulance service (called SAMU), Paris tel: 4567-5050.
In case of poisoning: Paris tel: 4037-0404.
Medical assistance (called SOS Médecins), Paris tel: 4337-7777/4707-7777.
All night drugstore, Paris: 84 Avenue des Champs-Elysées.

English

While we hope you will be speaking French during your trip, you should know that English is spoken widely, especially in establishments dealing with tourists, such as hotels, restaurants, tourist offices, train stations, travel agencies, banks, etc.

Currency Exchange

Banks and the post office generally pay better rates than exchange offices and hotels. Beware of high commissions and service charges. Foreign banks in France often pay the best rates.

Banks in Paris are open from 9 A.M. to 4:30 P.M., Mondays through Fridays. Outside of Paris they usually close from 12 to 2 P.M.

Medical Services

In case of illness, first see a pharmacist. They provide much more medical advice than in the United States. They, as well as hotel personnel, can direct you to doctors, dentists and hospitals if needed.

For extreme situations, see **Emergencies** above.

Métro

The Paris métro starts operating at 5:30 A.M. The last train leaves the end of the line at 12:30 A.M. Smoking is prohibited in the trains, on the platforms and in the stations. Tickets are sold individually (6 francs) or in ten-packs, which are cheaper (36.50 francs).

Passes valid for both the métro and buses are available:

2-day pass: 60 francs
3-day pass: 85 francs
5-day pass: 135 francs

A one-week pass for Monday through Sunday (photo required): 57 francs; one-month pass from first to last day of month (photo required): 201 francs

After putting your ticket in the turnstile, it will pop up. Pick it up and keep it until you are through the exit at your destination. Métro agents often check tickets to control payment of fares.

Museums

Many cities, Paris included, issue museum passes which enable you to visit several museums with one ticket at a discount. Museum passes are sold at the museums and, in Paris, in métro stations and travel agencies. One advantage of the passes is the possibility of immediate admission, with no waiting.

Most national museums close on Tuesdays, and most municipal museums close on Mondays. On Sundays, entrance to most museums is free or at reduced prices. Many museums offer reduced rates for senior citizens and children.

Pickpockets

Pickpockets exist. It is best to keep money, credit cards, driver's license and passport where they cannot be reached. One possibility is the hotel safe, another is a money belt or good inside pocket. Beware especially of over-zealous assistance in railway and subway stations.

Post Office

In Paris, post offices are open from 8 A.M. to 7 P.M., Mondays through Fridays, and from 8 A.M. to 12 noon on Saturdays. Outside of Paris, post offices are often closed from 12 to 2 P.M. Stamps are also sold at tobacco counters in cafés. Operator-assisted long distance telephone calls can be made from post offices. The main Paris post office, located 59 Rue du Louvre (métro Louvre), is open day and night.

Mail can be addressed to you, care of American Express, 11 Rue Scribe, 75009 Paris (métro Opéra).

Rail Travel

In Paris there are six railway stations:

Gare d'Austerlitz
Gare de l'Est
Gare de Lyon
Gare de Montparnasse
Gare du Nord
Gare Saint-Lazare

Information for all stations:
4582-5050 day and night.

Reservations for all stations:
4565-6060 from 8 A.M. to 8 P.M.

Reservations:

Reservations can be made by telephone. You will be given a time limit for pick-up. Reservations made within a few days of travel can be picked up just prior to departure time.

For the TGV *(train à grande vitesse)* or high-speed train, there is no standing room. Seat reservations are required. They can be made up until departure time.

Fare reductions:

French railroads have created time zones for travel. Cheaper fares (blue zone) apply from 12 noon on Saturdays to 3 P.M. on Sundays, and from 12 noon on Mondays to 12 noon on Fridays. The other periods fall within the white or red time zones, the red corresponding to days of particularly heavy traffic, generally at the beginning and end of school vacations. A 25% reduction applies for round trip or circular trip tickets covering 1000 kilometers and including a Sunday if travel takes place in "blue" periods. The Couple Card, free-of-charge and valid one year, entitles you to a 50% reduction on one of two tickets. Travel must take place on "blue" days.

The French Vacation Pass for non-residents permits you to travel on French railroads for 4, 9 or 16 days (within a two-week or one-month period). This pass is also valid for one or two days free travel on buses and the métro in Paris, as well as reduced rates for car rental, museum visits, etc. It can be purchased in UTA offices and through travel agents outside of France and at Roissy and Orly airports, as well as at the following railway stations: Gare du Nord, Gare Saint-Lazare, Gare de Lyon (all in Paris), and Nice, Lille and Strasbourg.

Special reductions are also available for children under 16 years of age and young travelers between 12 and 25 years of age.

Bicycles are for rent in many railway stations outside of Paris.

Punch your tickets *Compostez vos billets*

Tickets must be punched before you get on trains at orange punching machines situated at the entrance to train platform areas. Tickets not punched are subject to fines, although conductors are usually lenient, in particular with visitors from abroad.

Restaurants

Suggestions for restaurants are provided at the end of each itinerary. The asterisk * preceding an address indicates that the establishment offers a fixed price menu for 100 francs or less. Restaurant pricing in this guide corresponds to the following categories for a full meal and one-half bottle of wine:

Inexpensive: under 100 francs
Moderately priced: from 100 to 200 francs
Medium-priced: from 200 to 300 francs
Moderately expensive: from 300 to 400 francs
Expensive: from 400 to 600 francs
Luxury prices: over 600 francs

NOTE: For restaurant, tearoom, wine bar, pastry shop, etc. suggestions in Paris, see Insiders' Guide to Paris published by Hippocrene Books.

Seasons (can change slightly from region to region)

Super high season: July 13 to August 16
High season: July 1 to August 31
Mid season: May–June and September–October
Low season: November to April

Hotel prices can change considerably during low season, even in Paris. Around the country they can drop as much as 50%. In some regions, particularly in the mountains, the Christmas holidays are considered high season.

Shopping

For purchases over 1200 francs, it is often possible to obtain a VAT (sales tax) discount of approximately 15%. You will have to fill in forms and provide passport information. You then present these forms (and a stamped envelope provided by the store) to the customs authorities on your departure from France. Some businesses discount the VAT immediately; others reimburse you by check following receipt of your customs-controlled form.

Sound and Light Shows

Reserve in advance or early in the day during high season.

Store Hours

Department stores in Paris are generally open 9:30 A.M. to 6:30 P.M. Mondays through Saturdays. There is usually one 10 P.M. closing during the week. Shops in residential neighborhoods close from 12 to 2 P.M. and often on Mondays. Food stores and markets are generally open from 8:30 A.M. to 1 P.M. and from 4 to 7:30 P.M. and closed on Mondays, except for *charcuteries* which are open on Mondays. Supermarkets do not close during the lunch break. Bakery and pastry shops are generally open from 8 A.M. to 8 P.M. Many art galleries open afternoons only.

Outside Paris, except for major department stores, everything shuts down from 12 to 2 P.M. and all day Mondays. Markets and food stores usually close from 1 to 4 P.M. Most department stores have one late night closing in the week.

Taxis

Metered taxis accept a maximum of four persons: three in the back seat and, at the driver's discretion, one in front. There is a baggage charge for each piece of luggage.

Limousines are three or four times more expensive than taxis. A 10% tip is the general rule.

Telephone
From Paris:

To Paris and suburbs: dial 8-digit number.

To rest of France: dial 16, wait for dial tone, then dial 8-digit number.

To foreign counries: dial 19, wait for dial tone, then dial country code, area code, and number.

From elsewhere in France:

To Paris: dial 16, wait for dial tone, then dial 1 + 8-digit number.

To rest of France: dial 8-digit number.

To foreign countries: dial 19, wait for dial tone, then dial country code, area code, and number.

Country codes:
  Canada: 1
  Ireland: 353
  U.K.: 44
  U.S.A.: 1

Reduced Rates for Europe:
  9:30 P.M. to 8 A.M. weekdays;
  after 2 P.M. on Saturdays;
  all day Sundays and holidays.

Reduced Rates for Canada and U.S.A.:
  8 P.M. to 2 P.M. next day, Mondays through Saturdays; all
  day Sundays and holidays.

Collect calls abroad:
  Collect calls are called PCV in French: dial 19, wait for dial
  tone, then dial 33 + 11 for Canada or U.S.A.; dial 33 + country
  code for other countries.

Telephone Cards:
  In Paris, public phones rarely take coins; they are operated
  with *télécartes* which can be purchased in railway stations,
  post offices and at most tobacco counters in cafés. The lowest
  denomination is 50 francs. Elsewhere in France there are usually two possibilities: coins or cards. Operator assistance is
  available at most post offices.

Tipping

Generally speaking, there is no need to tip in restaurants,
cafés and tea shops. The tip is included on your check. If you
are pleased with the service, you can leave a few coins. For
stand-up eating or drinking, at bars or counters, tips are not
included on the tab. You may leave ten percent.

Hotels add a service charge to cover tipping. However, in
the more expensive establishments, the staff seem to expect
an additional something for carrying a bag, providing room
service, etc. It is really up to you.

For taxis, the normal tip is 10% of the fare.

Tourist Information

French regional and national tourist offices are well stocked with excellent brochures on their areas in English. The following list of addresses covers the regions included in this guide:

France: Maison de la France, 8 Avenue de l'Opéra, 75001 Paris.

Paris: 127 Avenue des Champs-Elysées, 75008 Paris.

Alsace: 9 Rue du Dôme, 67000 Strasbourg.

Bourgogne: 12 Boulevard de Brosses, BP 1602, 21035 Dijon.

Champagne, 5 Rue Jéricho, 51000 Châlons-sur-Marne.

Paris suburbs: 73 Rue de Cambronne, 75015 Paris.

Southwest: 54 Boulevard de l'Embouchure, 31022 Toulouse.

Western France: 2 Rue de la Loire, 44000 Nantes.

Picardy: 3 Rue Vincent-Auriol, 80026 Amiens.

Provence: Immeuble CMCI, 2 Rue Henri-Barbusse, 13241 Marseille 01.

CHAPTER 2

A French Accent

French stems from the modernization of Latin, the language spoken by the Romans when they occupied Gallic France in 52 B.C. The Celts and Gauls emasculated the conqueror's language, dropping endings, slurring and nasalizing sounds, simplifying it, in somewhat the same manner as various populations around the world have "murdered the king's English." The result, in all cases, is a unique, rich, expressive language, cherished by those who have grown up in it or acquired it.

To the beginner, French pronunciation may appear strange and difficult. More than one future linguist has arrived at this hurdle and turned back. This will not happen to you if you keep in mind that, contrary to English, French pronunciation follows rules. And there are few exceptions.

Let's begin by listening to the French.

Have you ever heard a French man or woman speak English? Speak this sentence and try to mimic a French accent. This exercise should produce roughly the following:

['av you evair 'erd ah Fransh man or voman speek Angleesh?]

Note that **h** is always silent. For example, **heure** (hour) becomes **err. homme** (man) is pronounced **om.**

The **w** (in woman) is pronounced **v. wagon** (carriage or

29

car of a train) although spelled with a **w,** becomes **vagon.** In French, our **w** is called **double v.**

The **r** is pronounced deep in the throat and is slightly gargled. Try **rêve** (dream) gargling once, and **rire** (laugh) gargling twice.

The **ch** (in the word **French**) would be pronounced **sh,** as in **show.** Pronounce **cher** (dear, expensive) in the French way with a soft **sh** sound.

an and **en,** as well as **am** and **em,** are both spoken and nasalized. The final **n** or **m,** barely pronounced, is your indication that the sound is produced through the mouth and the nose at the same time, lips pursed, something like a short grunt coming from the back of the mouth, not the throat.

Before proceeding, let's look at the major vowel sounds:

a, à, â   like the **a** in **part: bar, là** (there), **gâteau** (cake) The **eau** is pronounced **o;** on its own, **eau** means water.

e, è, ê   like the **e** in **met: excellent, grève** (strike), **fêter** (to celebrate). An **e** at the end of a word is mute: for example, **recette** (recipe) is pronounced **recet.**

é, er, ez   like the **a** in **date: café, marcher** (to walk), **parlez** (you speak).

i   like the **ee** in **meet: police, ici** (here), **idée** (idea).

o, ô   at the end of a word or a syllable, like the **o** in **rose;** within a syllable the **o** resembles the **o** in **ton: océan, hôtel, donner** (to give).

u   no English equivalent. Try pursing your lips and pronouncing the **u** like the word **you** without the y sound that begins it in English, in the upper part of the mouth. Practice with **une** (one), **avenue, lutter** (to fight, to struggle).

Stress

Now try the exercise sentence again, this time concentrating on its musicality. In French, stress is always placed on the last syllable of a word. Also, the end of sentences and even the end of phrases within sentences are given an additional lilt. The words **ever, woman** and **English,** having two syllables, would be stressed on the final syllable. The word **English,** completing the sentence, receives an extra push upward. You might try pronouncing other English phrases and sentences with a French accent before starting to speak French in the next chapter.

NOTE: Complete French pronunciation table in chapter 20.

CHAPTER 3

Let's Speak French

Bonjour   Hello, good morning, good afternoon

on as well as **om** are nasal sounds, pronounced against the upper palate, lips pursed. They employ the **o** of **rose,** to which a barely audible **n** is added.

The **j** is pronounced softly, like the **z** in **azure; ou** corresponds to the **oo** in **food.**

Bonsoir, madame.	Hello, good evening, good night (to a woman)
Au revoir, monsieur.	Goodbye (to a man)
Merci beaucoup, mademoiselle.	Thank you very much (to a young woman or little girl)

The **oi** in **bonsoir, revoir** and **mademoiselle** is pronounced **wa; monsieur** is special—pronounce it as though it were spelled **missye.**

Comment allez-vous? (How are you?)

Je vais bien, merci. Et vous? (I'm fine, thank you. And you?)

Liaison

Generally speaking, final consonants are *not* pronounced in French (this includes the **s** of plurals). The word **comment,** either standing alone or followed by a word beginning with a consonant, is pronounced **commen.** However, when it is followed by a word beginning with a vowel or an **h,** the **t** is pronounced and the two words are connected. This is called *liaison.* To the ear, the **t** sounds like the first letter of the next word: **commen-t'allez-vous.**

aller (to go) is an irregular verb (present tense):

je vais	I go, do go, am going
tu vas	you go, do go, are going
elle/il va	she/he goes, does go, is going
nous allons	we go, do go, are going
vous allez	you go, do go, are going
elles/ils vont	they go, do go, are going

As you will have noticed, the present tense is simplified. While in English there are three forms, in French there is only one, and it does not require an auxiliary.

Comment ça va?	Familiar for how are you? How's it going? How are things?
Ca va. Ca va très bien.	Everything's okay. All goes very well.

Note that the **ç** in ça (that) is pronounced like the **s** in **sun.** The **cédille,** or comma attached to the bottom of the letter, indicates that the sound is soft. Otherwise, the **c** is hard as in **candy: canard** (duck). When capitalized, the cedilla does not appear.

être (to be) is an irregular verb (present tense):

je suis	I am
tu es	you are (familiar)
elle/il est	she/he is
nous sommes	we are

vous êtes	you are
elles/ils sont	they are

The familiar form of **tu** (you), is used in lieu of **vous** when addressing children, members of the family, and friends. For others, **vous** is both singular and plural. The plural of **tu** is also **vous**. If you are just beginning French and only require a working knowledge for your trip to France, you might skip the **tu** forms.

Quelle est votre nationalité? (What is your nationality?)

Je suis américain. (I'm American.)

Mes amis sont canadiens. (My friends are Canadian.)

Don't forget the **liaison** in the second and third sentences: pronounce the **s** in **suis** before **américain,** and in **mes,** before **amis,** with a hard **z** sound. The **ain** et **ien(s),** as well as **im, in** and **ein,** are pronounced like the **an** in **and.**

Two other basic irregular verbs should be committed to memory at the very outset: **avoir** (to have) and **faire** (to do or to make).

avoir (to have) present tense:

j'ai	I have, do have, am having
tu as	you have, do have, are having
elle/il a	she/he has, does have, is having
nous avons	we have, do have, are having
vous avez	you have, do have, are having
elles/ils ont	they have, do have, are having

faire (to do, to make) present tense:

je fais	I do, make, do make, am making
tu fais	you do, make, do make, are making
elle/il fait	she/he does, makes, does make, is making

nous faisons we do, make, do make, are making
vous faites you do, make, do make, are making
elles/ils font they do, make, do make, are making

With the four verbs you now know, plus a few nouns and adjectives, conversation will be easier.

Avez-vous des bagages? (Have you any baggage?)

J'ai une valise. (I have one suitcase.)

Ma femme a un sac de voyage. (My wife has a travel bag.)

Nous faisons un tour de France. (We're doing a tour of France.)

Faites un bon boyage. (Have a good trip.)

And finally, three essentials:

Oui (Yes)   **Non** (No)   **OK** or **d'accord** (OK)

Practice your pronunciation with the sentences and verb forms above. Do not be afraid to drop final consonants and to nasalize all those endings with an **n** in much the same way. Learners often feel they will not be understood if they do not pronounce all the letters in a word. On the contrary, let yourself go French and you will make sense.

CHAPTER 4

Parlons français

Le français, French, like many other languages, gives gender to its nouns. They are either masculine or feminine. This is a basic fact of life. To my knowledge, no sectors of opinion, not even the most radical feminist organizations, have ever questioned French language gender.

Most nouns ending in **e**, **té** and **tion** are feminine. The definite and indefinite articles indicate the gender of nouns. **The**, for a feminine noun, is **la** or **l'** when the word begins with a vowel:

l'autoroute	the turnpike
l'avenue	the avenue
la gare	the station (rail or bus)
la moto	the motorcycle
la route	the road, the route
la rue	the street
la voiture	the car

For the masculine, **the** is **le** or **l'** before a vowel:

l'avion	the plane
le bateau	the boat
le bus or **l'autobus**	the city bus
le car or **l'autocar**	the bus (except for city buses)
le métro	the subway
le train	the train
le vélo	the bike

The plural of **la** and **le** is **les**: **les voitures** (the cars).

The indefinite article **a** is translated by **un** in the masculine and **une** in the feminine. The **un** is pronounced like the **an** in **and**.

un café	a café
un garçon	a boy, a waiter
un hôtel	a hotel
un magasin	a store
un restaurant	a restaurant
un verre	a glass
une boutique	a shop
une chaise	a chair
une chambre	a room
une épicerie	a grocery
une serveuse	a waitress
une table	a table

The plural of **un** and **une** is **des**, meaning some or any: **des voitures** (some cars).

Adjectives

Adjectives agree in gender and number with the nouns they qualify. Unlike English, they follow their nouns, except for a few short, frequently used adjectives which include: **beau/ belle** (beautiful), **bon/bonne** (good), **grand/grande** (big), **jeune/jeune** (young), **joli/jolie** (pretty), **petit/petite** (little), **vieux/vieille** (old). Numbers also precede nouns.

Un grand lit ou deux petits lits? (One large bed or two small beds?)

Les chambres sont grandes. (The rooms are big.)

Allons au petit restaurant. (Let's go to the little restaurant.)

NOTE: à (to, at) plus **le** (the) becomes **au**. The contraction for à plus **les** (plural of **the**) is **aux**. Both are pronounced **o**.

In most cases adjectives are made feminine by adding an **e**, unless the word ends with an **e**:

J'ai un sac noir. (I have a black bag.)

Ils ont une voiture noire. (They have a black car.)

C'est un petit hôtel agréable. (It's a pleasant, little hotel.)

Plurals of both nouns and adjectives generally take an **s**, as in English. There are some exceptions: words ending in **al** in the singular become **aux**; words ending in **au** and **eu** take an **x**. Words ending in **s** or **x** do not change in the plural. Examples: **le canal/les canaux** (canal/canals), **le château/les châteaux** (castle/castles), **le prix/les prix** (price/prices).

This may seem complicated but don't be discouraged. One of the charms of English-speaking visitors to France is their mélange of word endings and genders. No one minds. It can even be fun.

parler (to speak) is a regular verb. All verbs ending in **er** are conjugated as follows in the present tense:

je parle	**nous parlons**
tu parles	**vous parlez**
elle/il parle	**elles/ils parlent**

Here are a few other useful verbs:

acheter	to buy
aimer	to like, to love
manger	to eat
marcher	to walk

Parlez-vous anglais? (Do you speak English?)

Nous allons manger. (We are going to eat.)

Il va acheter des fruits. (He is going to buy some fruit.)

J'aime marcher. (I like to walk.)

NOTE: Complete Table of verb endings and major tenses in chapter 20.

CHAPTER 5

S'il vous plaît

One of the keys to getting along in France (and elsewhere) is knowing how to ask for things. Pointing is a start, but results will be better if you add **s'il vous plaît** (please).

You can avoid the necessity of a large vocabulary of verbs by using nouns plus **s'il vous plaît:**

Une bière, s'il vous plaît. (A beer, please.)

Un verre de vin blanc, s'il vous plaît. (A glass of white wine, please.)

Deux cocas, s'il vous plaît. (Two cokes, please.)

Les toilettes, s'il vous plaît. (The toilets, please.)

Here are some other helpful words indicating position or location:

ici	here
là	there
là-bas	over there
à droite	to the right
à gauche	to the left
tout droit	straight ahead

To satisfy your wants, you will also need the press reporter's **w**s:

qui	who	**Qui est là** (Who is there?)
où	where	**Où est-il?** (Where is it, he)?
pourquoi	why	**Pourquoi faire ça?** (Why do that?)
quand	when	**C'est quand? Quand est-ce?** (When is it?)
comment	how	**Comment faites-vous?** (How do you do it?)

NOTE: **est-ce** is pronounced **ess.**

Then, there is the question everyone knows: **Qu'est-ce que c'est?** [keske-say] (what is it?) and **combien?** (How much?) **Combien est-ce? C'est combien?** (How much is that?)

To understand the reply to that question, you will need to know numbers. Learn them by groups: 1 to 10, 11 to 20, 21 to 69, 70 to 99, 100 on.

    0 **zéro**
    1 **un, une**
    2 **deux**
    3 **trois**
    4 **quatre**
    5 **cinq**
    6 **six** [the x is pronounced s]
    7 **sept** [the p is silent]
    8 **huit** [the h is silent]
    9 **neuf**
  10 **dix** [the x is pronounced s]

  11 **onze**
  12 **douze**
  13 **treize**
  14 **quatorze**

15 **quinze**
16 **seize**
17 **dix-sept**
18 **dix-huit**
19 **dix-neuf**
20 **vingt** [pronounced like **vin**/wine]

21 **vingt et un** [pronounced **vin-té-un**]
22 **vingt-deux**
30 **trente**
31 **trente et un** [pronounced **tren-té-un**]
40 **quarante**
41 **quarante et un** [pronounced **quaran-té-un**]
50 **cinquante**
51 **cinquante et un** [pronounced **cinquan-té-un**]
60 **soixante**
61 **soixante et un** [pronounced **soixan-té-un**]

70 **soixante-dix** (60 + 10)
71 **soixante et onze** (60 + 11) [pronounced **soixan-té-onze**]
72 **soixante-douze** (60 + 12)
80 **quatre-vingts** (4 × 20)
81 **quatre-vingt-un** (4 × 20 + 1)
82 **quatre-vingt-deux** (4 × 20 + 2)
90 **quatre-vingt-dix** (4 × 20 + 10)
91 **quatre-vingt-onze** (4 × 20 + 11)
92 **quatre-vingt-douze** (4 × 20 + 12)

100 **cent**
101 **cent un**
200 **deux cents**
1 000 **mille**
10 000 **dix mille**

20 000	**vingt mille**
100 000	**cent mille**
200 000	**deux cent mille**
1 000 000	**un million**
1 000 000 000	**un milliard**

Within number combinations, the French use periods or full stops where we use commas, and vice versa: two thousand becomes **2.000,** not 2,000; 4.2% becomes **4,2%** in French. Spoken **four point two percent: quatre virgule deux pour cent** (**virgule** meaning comma).

La chambre quarante-cinq, s'il vous plaît. (Room forty-five please.)

Avez-vous la monnaie de cinq cents francs? (Do you have change for five-hundred francs?)

Mon garçon a douze ans. Ma fille a dix ans. (My boy is twelve years old. My daughter is ten years old.)

NOTE: **ll** is pronounced like the **y** in **yet. Fille,** therefore, becomes **fiy.**

NOTE: Table of Possessive Pronouns in chapter 20.

CHAPTER 6

Time, Please

Do you remember the old song "Your time is my time"? Well, that is not quite the story in France. French time is elastic: verbal invitations to dinner usually spread out the arrival time. For example, 7:30–8:00 o'clock usually means 8, even 8:30. While one should arrive on time for a business or doctor's appointment, it is rare to be ushered into the inner sanctum on time. Trains, however, are practically never off time.

Quelle [kel] heure est-il? (What time is it?)

Il est cinq heures. (It is five. It is five o'clock.)

(***NOTE** that, contrary to English, one cannot omit **heure(s)** and say **Il est cinq.**)

Il est neuf heures trente. (It is nine thirty.)

Il est neuf heures et demie. (It is half past nine.)

Il est quatre heures moins dix. (It is ten to four.)

Il est midi. Il est minuit. (It is noon. It is midnight.)

From 1 P.M. until midnight, the French use most often what we think of as military time. One P.M. is 13 **heures,** 9 P.M. is 21 **heures** and so on. An exception to this custom is **a quarter to** or **a quarter after** the hour, even when it is evening: 9:15 P.M. is **neuf heures et quart;** 9:45 P.M. is **dix heures moins le quart.** It is, however, correct to say: **vingt-**

et-une heures quinze and vingt-et-une heures quarante-
cinq.

Le spectacle commence à 20h30 [vingt heures trente].
(The show begins at 8:30.)

Le petit déjeuner est servi de 7h30 à 10h00 [sept heures
trente à dix heures]. (Breakfast is served from 7:30 to 10 A.M.)

Le train part à 16h45 [seize heures quarante cinq or cinq
heures moins quart]. (The train leaves at 4:45 P.M.)

The days of the week are not capitalized in French:

lundi	Monday
mardi	Tuesday
mercredi	Wednesday
jeudi	Thursday
vendredi	Friday
samedi	Saturday
dimanche	Sunday

Nous partons lundi après-midi. (We are leaving Monday
afternoon.)

Nous restons trois nuits. (We are staying three nights.)

Notre train arrive samedi matin à 9h20. (Our train arrives
Saturday morning at 9:20.)

J'ai rendez-vous avec elle dimanche soir. (I have a date (or
an appointment) with her Sunday evening.)

Le temps is both time and weather, and not the hour as
we have already seen.

Vous avez le temps. (You have time.)

Il est temps de partir. (It is time to go.)

Quel temps fait-il? (What is the weather like?)

Il fait beau. Vous avez beau temps. (It's lovely out. You have lovely weather.)

Il fait froid. Il fait chaud. (It's cold. It's hot.)

Il pleut. Il neige. (It's raining. It's snowing.)

A few other useful words of time are:

hier	yesterday
aujourd'hui	today
demain	tomorrow
avant-hier	day before yesterday
après-demain	day after tomorrow
semaine (f)	week
mois (m)	month
année (f) **an** (m)	year
il y a deux semaines	two weeks ago
matin (m)	morning
après-midi (f/m)	afternoon
soir (m)	evening
nuit (f)	night

f feminine noun
m masculine noun

Nous avons quitté les Etats-Unis il y a un mois. (We left the United States one month ago (literally, there is one month).

Il y a means both **there is** and **there are.**

Nous allons à Versailles demain. We are going to Versailles tomorrow.

Ils restent un an (or **une année**). (They are staying one year.)

Je suis allé au Louvre hier. (I went to the Louvre yesterday.)

Nous avons quitté and **Je suis allé** are in the past tense which corresponds to both the English **left** and **went** as well as **has** or **have left** and **has** or **have gone**. This past tense is composed of the present tense of **avoir** (to have) and the past participle of the verb. For a few important verbs, mostly concerning movement, **être** (to be) is used in place of **avoir**. Among the latter are:

aller	to go	**je suis allé(e)**	I went (have gone)
venir	to come	**tu est venu(e)**	you came (have come)
arriver	to arrive	**il est arrivé**	he arrived (has arrived)
partir	to leave	**elle est partie**	she left (has gone)
entrer	to enter	**nous sommes entrés**	we went (have gone) in
sortir	to go out	**vous êtes sorti(s)**	you went (have gone) out
rester	to stay	**ils sont restés**	they (have) stayed
naître	to be born	**ils sont nés**	they were born
mourir	to die	**elles sont mortes**	they died

e is feminine.
s is plural.

Elle est sortie. (She has gone [went] out.)

Ils sont arrivés hier. (They arrived yesterday.)

Ma fille est née en 1982. (My daughter was born in 1982.)

Son père est mort il y a un an. (Her [his] father died a year ago.)

NOTE: Read 1982 as **mille neuf cent quatre-vingt-deux** or **dix-neuf cent quatre-vingt-deux**.

CHAPTER 7

Pot-pourri

Originally a stew composed of several kinds of meat, **pot-pourri** today might be translated by **odds and ends.** Since we are all anxious to start traveling, let's clear away a few leftovers.

Possessives

As in English, there are several ways of saying something is yours or his or theirs.

C'est le mien. C'est à moi. (It's mine. It belongs to me.)

C'est ma valise. C'est mon sac. (It's my suitcase. It's my bag.)

Ils sont dans leur chambre. (They are in their room.)

Ce sont les leurs. C'est à eux. (They are theirs. It belongs to them.)

While it may not be necessary to memorize all these forms, it is useful to be able to recognize them. One set of the following is probably sufficient.

Possessive Adjectives

ma/mon/mes	**ma chemise/mon chapeau/mes chaussures** (my shirt/my hat/my shoes)
ta/ton/tes	**ta photo/ton passeport/tes billets** (your photo/your passport/your tickets)

sa/son/ses	**sa soeur/son frère/ses parents** (his, her sister/his, her brother/his, her parents)
notre/nos	**notre voiture/nos vélos** (our car/our bikes)
votre/vos	**votre hôtel/vos cartes** (your hotel/your maps)
leur/leurs	**leur ami(e)/leurs enfants** (their friend/their children)
	ma, ta and **sa** qualify feminine nouns

Disjunctive Pronouns

moi (me, mine)	**avant moi** (before me)	**c'est à moi** (it's mine)
toi (you, yours)	**avec toi** (with you)	**c'est à toi** (it's yours)
elle/lui (her/him, hers/his)	**pour elle/lui** (for her/him)	**c'est à elle** (it's hers) **c'est à lui** (it's his)
nous (us, ours)	**près de nous** (near us)	**c'est à nous** (it's ours)
vous (you, yours)	**après vous** (after you)	**c'est à vous** (it's yours)
eux (them, theirs)	**par eux** (by them)	**c'est à eux** (it's theirs)

This and That

French does not distinguish between **this** and **that.** They are both **ce** in the masculine, **cette** in the feminine and **ces** in the plural when used as adjectives.

Donnez-moi ce livre. (Give me that [or this] book.)

Je préfère cette jupe. (I prefer this [or that] skirt.)

J'aime ces chaussures. (I love these [or those] shoes.)

If you absolutely have to distinguish between this and that, these and those, add **-ci** or **-là** after the noun:

Elle préfère cette paire-là. (She prefers that pair there.)

Ce gâteau-ci, s'il vous plaît. (This cake (or pastry) here, please).

Ces bagues-ci sont belles. (These rings here are beautiful.)

And if you do not know the French equivalent of the noun you wish to use, you can avoid it by using **ceci** or **cela** or **ça.**

J'aimerais cela. J'aimerais ça. (I would like that.)

Elle aimerait ceci. (She would like this.)

This use of aimer brings us to the use of the conditional tense. It is formed by adding endings to the infinitive:

aimer (to like or to love) conditional tense

j'aimerais	**nous aimerions**
tu aimerais	**vous aimeriez**
elle, il aimerait	**elles, ils aimeraient**

NOTE: **ais, ait** and **aient** are all pronounced **é.**

Who, Which, That . . .
The best advice to beginners in French is to keep sentences short. If, however, you do get involved in one with clauses and require a relative pronoun to undo yourself, **qui** (who) and **que** (which or that) should work.

Je suis venu chercher les billets que nous avons commandés. (I have come to pick up the tickets that we ordered.)

J'aimerais voir la personne qui fait les réservations. (I would like to see the person who does the reservations.)

That all inclusive *they*
That great catch-all **they,** such as in **they say,** is **on** in

French. **On** is nasalized and also corresponds to **people** or **we** or **you** when used in a general sense.

On dit qu'on peut boire l'eau partout en France. (They say that you can drink the water everywhere in France.)

Excuse me
It is no more difficult to be courteous in French than in English. The simplest way is to say **pardon.** For heavy offenses, try **pardonnez-moi** or **excusez-moi** meaning **pardon me** or **excuse me.**

Being negative
Up until now we have only been positive and affirmative. To be negative is slightly more complicated than in English. You place **ne** in front of the verb and **pas** after it.

Je ne comprends pas. (I don't understand.)

Il ne sait pas. (He doesn't know.)

Nous n'avons pas son numéro de téléphone. (We don't have his telephone number.)

Apostrophe out
In French say **number of telephone** rather than **telephone number.** The same is true of expressions taking **'s** or of expressions in which a noun is used as an adjective, as in the first example below:

La clé de la chambre n'est pas là. (The room key is not there. [literally, the key of the room])

Avez-vous le nom du restaurant? (**du** is the contraction of **de + le**) (Do you have the restaurant's name? [literally, the name of the restaurant])

Les bijoux des femmes sont au coffre de l'hôtel. (des is the contraction of **de + les**) (The women's jewelry is in the hotel safe. [literally, the jewelry of the women and safe of the hotel])

CHAPTER 8

Built-in French

Little did you know that you actually have a ready-made French vocabulary. Hundreds of cognates—words that are similar in English and French—exist and facilitate progress in the language. Although there is sometimes a slight difference in spelling, words like the following are easily recognizable for what they are and what they signify:

accepter	to accept
adresse (f)	address
âge (m)	age
arrivée (f)	arrival
argument (m)	argument
baby-sitting (m)	babysitting
bagage (m)	baggage
camping (m)	camping
certain(e)	certain
correspondant	correspondent or -ing
départ (m)	departure
enveloppe (f)	envelope
exemple (m)	example
exercice (m)	exercise
gouvernement (m)	government
hôtel (m)	hotel
indépendant	independent
interview/entrevue (f)	interview
lettre (f)	letter
mariage (m)	marriage

miroir (m)	mirror
musique (f)	music
nom (m)	name
page (f)	page
parking (m)	parking lot or space
picque-nique (m)	picnic
police (f)	police
préparer	to prepare
prisonnier (m)	prisoner
pullover (m)	pullover
réserver	to reserve
salon de beauté (m)	beauty salon
sandwich (m)	sandwich
sûr(e)	sure
taxi (m)	taxi
théâtre (m)	theater
t-shirt (m)	t-shirt

Hundreds of words ending in **tion** are the same or similar in French. They are feminine in gender. The **t** in **tion** is pronounced **see**; the **on** syllable is nasalized, the **n** being barely audible. These are only some of the words that start with **a**:

action	action
adaptation	adaptation
addition	addition (or bill)
administration	administration
admiration	admiration
adoption	adoption
agression	aggression
ambition	ambition
appréhension	apprehension
articulation	articulation
attention	attention
attraction	attraction

| **attribution** | attribution |
| **automation** | automation |

A number of American expressions have been adopted by the French. Although the French sometimes endow them with a slightly different meaning, they are recognizable and useable:

> **cool**
> **in**
> **super**
> **wow**

A great many sports terms come directly from English. In some cases, a more proper French word exists or has been invented, but the English terms are more generally used and, in any event, understood. Most sports are masculine in gender, except where indicated (f).

baseball: French children are beginning to learn the game, though it is still far from enjoying the popularity and organization of even soccer, for example, in the United States.

basketball or **basket:** some of the most outstanding professional players in France are Americans.

boxe (f): **direct, knockout, match, round, swing, uppercut**

football (soccer): **corner, dribbler, goal, passe** (f), **penalty, shoot**

hockey sur glace (ice hockey)

ski: faire du ski (to go skiing)

tennis: lob, point de match, out, raquette (f), **service, set, smash, timebreak, volée** (f)

Before closing this chapter, we should warn you of a fre-

quent beginner's trap. Many words in English seem to have
a French equivalent; however, on closer analysis their mean-
ings are different, even contrary. For example:

actuel(le), **actuellement**	present day, at the present time
assister	to attend
cave (f)	cellar, wine cellar
collège	high school (*not* university)
formidable	fantastic, tremendous
gentil(le)	nice, kind
grand(e)	big, tall, large
hôtel de ville (m)	city hall
hôtel particulier (m)	private town house
introduire	to insert
lecture	reading
librairie	book store
magasin (m)	store
grand magasin (m)	department store
patron(ne)	boss, proprietor
raisin (m)	grape (**raisin sec** is raisin)
travellers (m)	travelers' checks (travelers are **voyageurs**)

CHAPTER 9

Bienvenue en France

You have arrived. This is France. You have just stepped off a plane from the United States, a ferry from England, a train from Switzerland or Italy. You are numb and bedraggled after a sleepless night or a choppy sea. You are in Paris or Nice or Calais. The first French person you see will probably be wearing a blue uniform and will be saying:

Passeports, s'il vous plaît. (Passports, please.)

Vous restez combien de temps en France? (How long are you staying in France?)

Environ deux semaines. (About two weeks.)

After police control, you will pass customs. On trains coming into France, the customs' officials open the doors to each compartment or carriage shortly after passing the border:

Bonjour, Messieurs Dames. (Good day, ladies and gentlemen.)

Douane française. (French customs.)

Avez-vous quelque chose à déclarer? (Have you anything to declare?)

Non, Monsieur, je n'ai rien à déclarer. (No, sir, I have nothing to declare.)

NOTE: **rien** (nothing) replaces **pas** in a negative sentence.

Taxis

If you take a taxi to your final destination, keep in mind that there is a handling charge for each large bag or suitcase. Generally speaking, taxis accept three passengers. At the driver's discretion, a fourth may be accommodated on the front seat. You should also be aware that, contrary to certain cities in the U.S., limousines are several times more expensive than metered taxis.

French taxi drivers have the reputation for being talkative, coarsely witty and perfectly knowledgeable about streets and sights. This is no longer true. Fighting traffic has made taxiing a tedious job as well as less rewarding financially; the hours are long and there are risks. As a result, a considerable number of newcomers to France and to the profession are behind the wheel now. They are generally quiet and discreet; unlike the oldtimers, they often refer to their maps. A tip is expected of roughly 10%.

Il faut combien de temps pour aller en ville? (It takes how long to go to town?)

Ca coûte combien jusqu'à l'hôtel? (It costs how much up to the hotel?)

Avez-vous un itinéraire préféré? (Do you have a preferred itinerary?)

Est-ce qu'il y a beaucoup de circulation? (Is there very much traffic?)

NOTE: In addition to the English way of asking questions— first the verb and then the subject—there is **est-ce que.** It indicates that this is a question and is followed by the subject, then the verb. Remember that **il y a** means **there is** or **there are.**

Accommodations

There are five categories of hotels in France: from one to four-star deluxe. Simple but attractive rural housing, called **gîtes ruraux** or **chambres d'hôte,** bed and breakfast **à la française** (French style) are inexpensive and more and more appreciated by foreign visitors.

Throughout the countryside are camping sites. In the provinces and the cities you will find youth hostels **(auberges de la jeunesse)** and, during school vacations, dormitory housing. In and around Paris and fashionable vacation areas like the Riviera or the Alps, it is possible to obtain short-term apartment, house or chalet rentals. A number of very beautiful châteaux and manor houses also receive guests.

Nous avons une réservation pour deux personnes. (We have a reservation for two people.)

Voulez-vous une chambre avec baignoire ou avec douche? (Do you want a room with bath or with shower?)

Il y a des WC dans toutes les chambres. [WC, pronounced **double vay say,** stands for **water closet**] (There are toilets in all the rooms.)

Je peux vous donner une chambre sur cour avec un grand lit. (I can give you a room on the courtyard with one large bed.)

Ou préférez-vous deux lits sur rue? (Or do you prefer two beds on the street side?)

Il faut quitter les chambres avant midi. (Rooms must be vacated before noon. [literally, it is necessary to vacate rooms before noon])

Le petit déjeuner est servi dans la salle à manger au premier étage. (Breakfast is served in the dining room on the first floor.)

NOTE: the first floor in France is equivalent to the second floor in the United States: one flight up.

Traditionally, tipping is not required in French hotels. A service charge is included on the bill. However, in the more expensive hotels, American practices are being adopted and a tip is expected for baggage handling, room service, etc. In most cases, ten francs should be sufficient.

ascenseur (m)	elevator
caisse (f)	cashier
concierge (m/f)	bell captain (in a hotel)
	superintendent (in apartment house)
environ	about, more or less (*not* environs)
femme de chambre (f)	chambermaid
hall (m)	lobby
il faut	it is necessary, you have to, it requires
jusque	up to, until
réception (f)	reception
rez-de-chaussée (m)	ground floor
sonnette (f)	bell
sur	on, over, above
sûr(e)	sure
veilleur de nuit (m)	night clerk

If no one has said "Welcome to France," let us be the first: **Bienvenue en France!**

CHAPTER 10

Paris, City of Light/ville lumière

Greater Paris encompasses ten million inhabitants, yet the city does not emit the pulsations of a teeming metropolis. The transportation system is one of the best in the world and one is almost never overwhelmed by billowing crowds pushing in and out of central stations linking cities and suburbs. Except for a few neighborhoods in which highrises were authorized in the sixties and seventies, buildings have a height limit of roughly seven floors. Honking is against the law and screeching police sirens are probably more frequently used to clear the way for a visiting head of state than to chase bank robbers, which is not to say that Paris has none of the urban problems of cities elsewhere.

The exception to this apparent tranquility is caused by cars. Compacts, sports cars, luxury sedans, motorcycles—dash, pass on orange and sometimes on red, brake urgently, careen, double park, sidewalk park—madness is total or so it seems. Driving in Paris can be daunting. The basic, fundamental, never-to-be-forgotten rule is **priorité à droite,** which in simple English means eyes-right. Even from a side street or a driveway, the car on the right has priority and expects you to give way, unless there is a stop sign. And French drivers exercise unremittingly that priority. Pedestrians must also beware. To be on the safe side, cross at crosswalks or lights.

The two halves of Paris and the two islands of the Seine are joined by bridges, each with a unique elegance and personality. The river does not hem the city in; rather, it has been tamed and dominated by its urban surroundings. The southern half of Paris is called the Left Bank **la rive gauche,** and the northern half the Right Bank or **la rive droite.**

There is nothing more gentle and romantic than a walk along the Seine at water level. On hot summer days the northern water promenade turns into a seaside beach for picnics and sunbathing. In true Parisian style, nonchalance is pushed to the maximum with the appearance of attractive topless creatures seemingly oblivious to the world around.

How long should one plan to stay in Paris? How many days, weeks, months, years? The city is wealthy enough to sustain the visitor for a lifetime: monuments and museums, shows and exhibits, theater, music, entertainment, sports fairs, happenings—day in and year out. Today, as I write, Paris is host to retrospective exhibits of Toulouse-Lautrec, Alberto Giacometti and Richard Parker Bonington, period shows of Modigliani and Rouault, *Les Misérables* and *Phantom of the Opera,* a jazz festival, a book fair and literally hundreds of temporary exhibits, concerts, plays, as well as the best in films from around the world.

Paris is often advertised as the city of light: **Paris, ville lumière.** Compared, however, to the neon metropolises of the world, Paris's lighting may actually seem quaint. But **ville lumière** evokes another, greater aura of this city: the light of beauty, of art, of learning. The phrase recalls the fact that Paris was at the heart of 18th century rationalism—**the Century of Enlightenment/le siècle des lumières**—when it was understood that reason or intellect was the true source of knowledge.

Since Napoleon's time, the city has been divided into administrative and electoral districts called **arrondissements,** of which there are now twenty. Other than two very chic and bourgeois neighborhoods—the seventh and sixteenth arrondissements—Paris has had a history of social heterogenity. Unfortunately, urban renewal, rental up-scaling and real estate speculation are chasing the working class population out to the suburbs, **la banlieue.** It is there that Paris's ghettos are located, in unnatural housing projects in "new cities" (**villes nouvelles**) or appended to old towns. Problems in the **banlieue** are compounded by ethnic division. Immigrants from Black Africa, North Africa, the West Indies and elsewhere have little by little moved from Paris proper, where they lived in relatively "mixed" neighborhoods, to more affordable housing on the outskirts. In recent times, unemployment and racism have given rise to poverty amidst plenty, isolation and racial tension.

Within the city, Indochinese (essentially Vietnamese or Chinese from Vietnam) have taken over parts of the thirteenth and twentieth arrondissements. Parisians now call the thirteenth Chinatown. North Africans still concentrate in the eighteenth, near Barbès-Rochechouart. In the mornings on market days (**Boulevard de la Chapelle** under the elevated subway) you can buy wonderful homemade, unleavened breads, sweets like baklava and halvah, fresh Algerian dates, and in the local restaurants you can feast on typical thick soups, couscous and lamb. In the twentieth arrondissement, in and around **rue de Ménilmontant,** you will find total ethnicity. Restaurant after restaurant serve their particular specialities: West, East or North African, Middle Eastern, kosher North African, Turkish, Greek, Indian, Pakistani, West Indian, Chinese, Thai, Vietnamese—and I have certainly missed some!

Now that your appetite is whetted, it is time to put on your walking shoes. The next chapter is for visiting Paris!

Some Useful Words and Phrases

Quelle est la station de métro la plus proche?	Which is the closest métro station?
Quel est le métro pour la tour Eiffel?	Which is the métro for the Eiffel Tower?
Quel bus devons-nous	Which bus should we take

prendre pour aller au Louvre?	to go to the Louvre?
Vous pouvez utiliser les mêmes billets pour le métro et le bus.	You can use the same tickets for the métro and the bus.

NOTE: **la plus proche** (closest) is the superlative of **proche** (close). The comparative is **plus proche** (closer). Another illustration of this principle is as follows:

Nous avons loué une *petite* **voiture.**	We have rented a *small* car.
Cette voiture est *plus petite* **que la vôtre.**	This car is *smaller* than yours. (comparative)
Cette voiture est *la plus petite* **du monde.**	This is the *smallest* car in the world. (superlative)

building (m)	highrise
cinéma (m)	movie house
exposition (f)	exhibit, show
film (m)	movie, film
foire (f)	fair
louer	to rent
immeuble (m)	building, apartment house
monde (m)	world
musée (m)	museum
pellicule (f)	photographic film
pièce (f)	play, coin (*not* piece)
salon (m)	trade show
spectacle (m)	show (theater, variety, etc.)

CHAPTER 11

Paris, City of Walks/ville promenade

I   Heart of Paris

Paris provides the visitor with endless pleasurable possibilities. They may be visual, gustatory, intellectual or emotional. They can be crowded into a few days or extended into weeks or months.

Everyone is aware of the classics: the Eiffel Tower (**la tour Eiffel**), Notre-Dame, Montmartre, the Louvre, Versailles. For vastly different reasons, each merits its reputation. But Paris offers much more. Those who wish to delve deeper into the city's life should set out on foot. While aimless wandering can provide surprises as well as enchantment, the following promenades will assist you in savoring the gifts of delight which the city offers. The itineraries are relatively short in distance and time, taking at the most a half day.

Notre-Dame/Ile Saint-Louis

Métro: Cité
Bus: 47, 24, 27, 21, 38, 85

Notre-Dame took 182 years to construct. Started in 1163 under Louis VII, it was completed in 1345. Following the French Revolution it was used to store food, wine and forage. Although Napoleon and Josephine were crowned here in 1804, it fell into disuse until Victor Hugo's *The Hunchback of*

Notre-Dame aroused popular interest in its repair. Notre-Dame survived, unharmed, the Paris Commune and World War II.

During the Middle Ages, the exterior stone imagery was painted bright colors against a gilt background. For a largely illiterate population, these representations were the story of the Bible in figurative form. The gallery of figures just above the portals are the kings of Judea. At the time of the French Revolution, they were mistaken for the kings of France and beheaded!

Notre-Dame was the first Gothic cathedral. The flying buttresses, introduced in the 14th century, bear the weight of the framework and the ceilings. This technical advance, in shifting weight from the walls to the buttresses, made it possible to lighten the walls and to cut large window openings in them.

Organ concerts are held on Sunday afternoons at 5:45 P.M.

Behind Notre-Dame, slightly to the left, a bridge crosses the Seine joining the Ile de la Cité and the **Ile Saint-Louis.** The latter was originally two islands until 1664 when the channel separating them was filled in. The style of the buildings, which date from that time, is called Classic. The principal architect was Louis Le Vau.

The **Hôtel de Lauzun** or **Lansan** at 17 Quai d'Anjou (northern side of the island) was, in 1845, the seat of the Haschich Club whose members included Charles Baudelaire, Alexandre Dumas and Eugène Delacroix. The **Hôtel Lambert,** 1 Quai d'Anjou or 2 Rue Saint-Louis-en-l'Ile, was once the residence of Michèle Morgan. It now belongs to the Rothschild family. **Berthillon,** 31 Rue Saint-Louis-en-l'Ile, is famous for its ice cream.

Sainte-Chapelle/Saint-Julien-le-Pauvre

Location: Sainte-Chapelle, Boulevard du Palais
          Saint-Julien-le-Pauvre, Quai de Montebello

Métro: Cité

Bus: 47, 24, 27, 21, 38, 85

In the Middle Ages the city of Paris was largely confined to the single Ile de la Cité. The Royal Palace was located on the northern bank of the island at the Conciergerie. Louis IX or St. Louis, a very pious king who reigned in the 13th century, purchased what was said to be the "true crown of thorns" in Constantinople from a French nobleman much in debt. To house the sacred relic, **Sainte-Chapelle** was constructed next door to the palace. The epitome of Gothic art, it was completed in record time and received the crown in 1248.

There are in fact two chapels: a lower one intended for the palace servants and an upper one for the royal family. The stained glass windows on the upper level retrace episodes from the Old Testament. They are read from bottom to top and from left to right. One of the windows recounts the story of the crown's voyage, from its purchase by two friars weighing out gold to the barefoot King Louis and his brothers carrying it on foot from Sens to Paris, seventy miles distant.

The Sainte-Chapelle is open daily from 10 A.M. to 5 P.M. Evening concerts are at 9 P.M. Outside the chapel, if you feel so inclined, you may enter the Law Courts (le **Palais de justice**) and attend sessions.

On leaving here, turn right on Boulevard du Palais and cross the Seine. Turn left along the quay where you can peruse the **book and print vendors' stalls.** After crossing over Rue Saint-Jacques, you will see **Shakespeare and Co.,** George Whitman's well-known anglophile bookshop on your right. It is open from noon until midnight, organizes poetry readings on Mondays at 8 P.M. and serves tea on Sundays.

On the block after the bookshop is **Saint-Julien-le-Pauvre,** one of several churches which lay claim to being the oldest in Paris. Started two years after Notre-Dame, it was finished in 1220. It was here that the Latin Quarter was literally founded in the 13th century when the church became the headquarters of the Latin-speaking clerics and seat of the newly chartered University of Paris. Monks came to live and study here. In the 16th century with its activities greatly reduced, students furiously opposed to a newly elected university rector smashed the place to bits. During the French Revolution it served to store salt and flour and its grounds became a fairground for wool merchants. In 1889, the unused church was given to the Greek Catholic community by the Archdiocese of Paris. Today Sunday services (10 A.M. and 6 P.M.) are in Greek; the liturgy is sung at 11 A.M. by the church choir.

In the little park is a false acacia or black locust tree, the Robinia, held up by cement props. It was planted in 1601 and is considered to be the oldest tree in Paris. Across the street from the church entrance, at number 14, is the **Tea Caddy,** founded in 1928 on her retirement by Miss Kinklin, English governess for the Rothschilds. It is open from 12 noon to 7 P.M. and closed on Tuesdays.

Three short blocks beyond Saint-Julien-le-Pauvre, you will come to **Rue de Bièvre.** At number 22 is the private, unassuming home of French President François Mitterand.

Some Useful Words and Phrases:

bouquiniste (m)	secondhand bookseller
seconde Guerre mondiale (f)	Second World War
première Guerre mondiale (f)	First World War
glace (f)	ice cream, ice
île or **isle** (f)	island
monde (m)	world
moyen âge (m)	Middle Ages
palais (m)	palace
pont (m)	bridge
reine (f)	queen
révolution française (f)	French revolution
roi (m)	king

salon de thé (m)   tea room
tribunal (pl. **tribunaux**) (m)   law court(s)
vitrail (pl. vitraux) (m)   stained glass window(s)

A quelle heure fermez-vous? (What time do you close?)

Vous ouvrez à quelle heure? (You open at what time?)

Deux places pour le concert, s'il vous plaît. (Two seats for the concert, please.)

A l'orchestre ou au balcon? (In the orchestra or the balcony?)

Un thé au lait, un thé citron et un thé nature. (One tea with milk, one tea with lemon and one plain tea.)

Est-ce une gravure ancienne? (Is it an old print?)

II   Saint-Germain-des-Près

Métro: Saint-Germain-des-Près
        Mabillon
Bus: 39, 49, 63, 70, 86, 87, 95, 96

The Church/Delacroix Museum/School of Fine Arts/ French Institute/Street Market/Cour de Rohan

The original church, constructed on the grounds of **Saint-Germain-des-Près** in 542, was a basilica of marble columns and gilded rafters. Golden mosaic and shining copper adorned its exterior; it sat in green fields and shown from afar. Thus it remained for 300 years when Norse invaders, who took all to be gold, reduced it to ruins.

Saint-Germain-des-Près (of-the-Fields) was rebuilt with some of the original marble columns, in the Romanesque style, between 990 and 1021. Today's tower and belfry date from that time, giving it claim, also, to being the oldest church in Paris. From then until the French Revolution, it was one of the most powerful Benedictine abbeys in Europe, owing allegiance to the Pope alone and rivaling the City of Paris. After the Revolution it was turned into a warehouse for salt-peter. In 1794 an explosion destroyed most of the abbey's buildings and shook the church to its foundations. Thanks to writer Victor Hugo, it was reconstructed in the 19th century.

The bust in the square to the left of the church as you face it is by Picasso and dedicated to his friend the poet Guillaume Apollinaire.

Leave the church through Rue de l'Abbaye. At number 10 is a sales outlet for posters, books, playing cards and gifts from French national museums. As you continue on this walk, you will notice that the quarter is especially well stocked in antiques, decorator's fabrics, wallpaper, art galleries, ethnic jewelry and specialized book dealers.

The first left takes you into Place Furstenberg, a romantic square in which musicians settle on summer evenings. In the far left-hand corner is the old stable entrance to the **Eugène Delacroix Museum,** open from 10 A.M. to 5:15 P.M., and closed on Tuesdays. This was the painter's studio in the last years of his life.

Leave the square at the opposite end of Rue Furstenberg, turn left into Rue Jacob. At the first street light, Rue Bonaparte, turn right. Across from the entrance to Rue des Beaux-Arts (second street on your right) is the **Ecole des Beaux-Arts** (School of Fine Arts). In the 16th century, when Marie de Médicis arrived from Florence to marry Henry IV, it was built as a hospital and was staffed with Italian doctor/pharmacist-priests. It remained a convent until the French Revolution, when it became a museum. In 1858 it opened as the School of Beaux-Arts.

After a visit of the various courtyards of the school, to the left, to the right and around, proceed into Rue des Beaux-Arts. At number 13 is **l'Hôtel,** the inn in which Oscar Wilde lived and died in 1900. **Le Bélier,** a restaurant inside the hotel, has an excellent fixed-price menu. The winter garden setting is eye-filling.

At the end of the street, turn left in Rue de Seine. Pass through the archway at the end of this street, cross at the light and go up to the **Pont des Arts** footbridge. There is most always something happening on the bridge. As you turn back to cross the street and re-enter Rue de Seine, the enveloping arms of the **French Institute** will greet you. Intended originally as a boarding school for sixty "sons of gentlemen" from different regions of France, it houses today the Institute and five academies. Among the latter is the French Academy which presides over the purity of the French language. Forty "immortals" meet here every Thursday to update the definitive French dictionary, of which the last edition appeared in 1935 and the next is scheduled for 2050.

In Rue de Seine, at the second corner on your left (Rue Jacques Callot) is an inviting sidewalk café, **la Palette,** frequented by people from the neighborhood. It is a classified historic monument.

At the corner of Rue de Seine and Rue de Buci begins a colorful **street market,** open every day except Sunday afternoons and Mondays. Most of the stalls are closed from 1 P.M. until 4 P.M.

On leaving the market, if you are facing in the direction of the Seine, take your right in Rue de Buci. You will arrive at an intersection of five streets. Take Rue Saint-André-des-Arts directly in front of you. Go past the Mazet café on your right and turn into the Cour du Commerce, an arcade. On your left is **A la Cour de Rohan,** a tea shop as one should be. Continue down the passageway. Turn left opposite the back entrance to the **Procope** founded in 1686; it was the first Parisian café to serve that "new" brew coffee. Turn into the **Cour de Rohan,** the remains of a 15th-century mansion. It was in the second courtyard that Dr. Guillotin did trial runs on his famous machine—on sheep!

Some Useful Words and Phrases

abbaye (f)	abbey
affiche (f)	poster
carte de jeu (f)	playing card
doré(e)	golden, gilt
église (f)	church
gothique	Gothic
livre (m)	book
or (m)	gold
roman(e)	Romanesque

La première messe est à 8 heures. (The first mass is at 8 o'clock.)

Il n'est pas nécessaire de couvrir sa tête pour entrer dans une église. (It is not necessary to cover one's head to enter a church.)

Le style roman est caractéristique des onzième et douzième siècles. (The Romanesque style is characteristic of the eleventh and twelfth centuries.)

Le style gothique caractérise la période du douzième au seizième siècles. (The Gothic style characterizes the period from the 12th to the 16th centuries.)

III Le Marais

The Marais or marshes were originally swampland and forest, traversed by an affluent of the Seine. In the 7th century kings and noblemen would leave their island city to come here to hunt. After drainage in the 13th century, wheatfields, kitchen gardens, vineyards, and windmills covered the area. Monasteries and churches grew up among them. Weavers and drapers set up shop near the Seine and wealthy families built "country" estates in the meadows. At the end of the 14th century, Charles V walled Paris, bringing the Marais within the city limits. The king himself settled here. His court and notables followed suit.

Hôtel de Sully/Place des Vosges/Carnavalet Museum/ Jewish Quarter

Location: Hôtel de Sully, 62 Rue St. Antoine

Métro: St. Paul
Bus: 69, 76, 96

The **Hôtel de Sully** is a lovely Renaissance château built in 1624. Admire the courtyard, then go through to the orangery. The entrance to temporary exhibits is on the left. Exit the back way at the far right-hand corner of the garden, and enter Place des Vosges.

Place des Vosges was Paris's very first square, commissioned in 1605 by Henry IV. The king was an amateur architect and an early urban renewal bug. His plan was to create an elegant center for the city built of brick and stone. Unfortunately, bricklayers were a rarity and the majority of the facades were simply wood frames, plastered over and painted to resemble bricks and mortar. The southern royal pavilion was too restricted a space for a king, and neither Henry IV nor his successors ever lived in it.

The square itself became the stage for all major public events: tournaments, pageants, receptions of foreign dignitaries, equestrian ballets, parades, fireworks and duels. The statue in the middle of the square is of Louis XIII, who inaugurated it with the celebration of his marriage to Anne of Austria. Shortly before its completion, his father Henry IV, on his way through the narrow streets of the quarter in an open carriage for his daily visit to the construction site, was stabbed to death.

There are a number of interesting shops and good restaurants around the square. Circle to the left. At number 9 is

Ambroisie, a three-hat restaurant according to the Gault Millau rating; the food is delicious and expensive. At number 28 is the **Pavillon de la Reine,** an attractive new luxury hotel.

Number 16 is a **synagogue** for eastern European Jews; if you enter from the back side, Rue des Tournelles, you will be in the oriental half of the synagogue, the domain of the Sephardic Jews, mainly from North Africa.

At number 10 is **Eurydice,** a small, pleasant restaurant for cakes and snacks.

The **Victor Hugo House** at number 6 was the writer's home from 1832 to 1848 before he left France and went into exile on the Channel isle of Guernsey. It is open from 10 A.M. to 5:40 P.M. closed on Mondays and holidays.

Leave Place des Vosges from the northwest corner, diagonally across the square from Hugo's house, and enter Rue des Francs-Bourgeois. At Rue de Sévigné, turn right for the **Carnavalet Museum.** The museum, devoted to the history of Paris, is varied and magnificent. Its original Renaissance structure dates from 1544; an addition was added by architect François Mansart in the 17th century. In 1989, the City of Paris annexed the Hôtel Le Peletier de Saint-Fargeau next door, reorganized and redecorated the two châteaux.

The Marquise de Sévigné, the famous author of letters vividly depicting life in 17th-century France, lived at Carnavalet from 1677 to 1696. The lion guards and statues of the seasons in the first courtyard are by Jean Goujon. In this part of the museum are collections covering the period up to 1789; in the Le Peletier half are collections from the French Revolution to the present day. Carnavalet is open from 10 A.M. until 5:40 P.M. and is closed on Mondays and holidays.

Leave the museum to your right, and take Rue des Francs-Bourgeois to the right. At the first intersection, go left on Rue Pavée, and then right to Rue des Rosiers, the entrance to the **Jewish Quarter.**

This quarter has had its ups and downs, ins and outs. Jews were expelled from the city in 1182, were recalled in 1198, and expelled again in 1306. Banishment from Paris lasted officially until the French Revolution.

Jews arrived here from eastern France in 1870, from Russia and Poland at the turn of the century, and from Germany during the rise of Hitler. More recently, in the 1950s and 1960s, Sephardic Jews from North Africa settled in Paris when Tunisia, Morocco, and Algeria won their independence from France, with whom they had sided.

All along Rue des Rosiers are vendors of *fellafel* and other Middle-Eastern dishes. Several bakeries specialize in breads and sweets from Central Europe. **Chez Daisy** and **Chez Marianne** are excellent, inexpensive sit-down as well as carry-out restaurants. Unfortunately, the special atmosphere of Rue des Rosiers is gradually changing as chic boutiques replace the traditional shops.

To leave the quarter, turn left at Rue Vieille-du-Temple. However, if you have the time and energy, a walk along the little streets which are beyond this one and parallel to it is also pleasant. In Rue Bourg-Tibourg you will find *Mariage Frères,* the oldest tea merchant in Paris with 300 varieties of teas and a lovely (expensive) tea room. At number 14 is **Le Coude Fou,** a good wine bar. At number 31, a nice **Greek restaurant** frequented on occasion by Robert Mitchum!

Some Useful Words and Phrases

bar à vin (m)	wine bar
bois (m)	wood
brique (f)	brick
construire	to build
défilé (m)	parade
feux d'artifice (m)	fireworks
juif/juive	Jew, Jewish
peinture (f)	paint, painting
peu	few
pierre (f)	stone

plâtre (m)   plaster
synagogue (f)   synagogue
tournoi (m)   tournament

A Paris, il y a peu d'immeubles en briques. (In Paris there are few brick buildings.)

Les maisons anciennes sont construites en pierre. (Old houses are built of stone.)

NOTE the use of **en** for materials.

Dans le quartier juif les magasins sont fermés le samedi. (In the Jewish quarter, the stores are closed on Saturday.)

Picasso Museum/Pompidou Center

Location: Picasso Museum, 5 Rue de Thorigny
           Pompidou Center, Rue du Renard

Métro: Chemin Vert
Bus: 20, 29, 65, 75, 96

If you go by métro to the Chemin-Vert stop, takes Rue Saint-Gilles. After Rue de Turenne this street changes its name and becomes Rue du Parc-Royal. Along here you will pass a row of 17th-century houses. Number 8, the former Hôtel Duret de Chevry, now belongs to the St. Raphaël aperitif company. The gates usually are open and you can wander into the courtyards.

Turn right at Rue de Thorigny. The Hôtel Salé or **Picasso Museum** is at number 5. This château was built in the 17th century by a man whose money derived from the salt tax. The local population nicknamed his mansion the "Salty House," and the name has stuck. The museum possesses a very complete collection of Picasso's works. From 1901 to 1975, there are masterpieces from every period of his art. Open from 10 A.M. to 5:15 P.M., until 10 P.M. on Wednesdays, the museum is closed on Tuesdays.

Turn right on leaving the museum; you will run smack into the **Key and Lock Museum.** This was the home, designed for himself, of Libéral Bruant, architect of the Invalides.

Continue on Rue Elzévir to Rue des Francs-Bourgeois. Turn right. At number 43 is **Les Enfants Gâtés,** a very comfortable tea and snack house. At Rue Vielle-du-Temple, turn left and take the first right. You are now on Rue des Blancs-Manteaux. Continue straight until you arrive at the Pompidou Center.

The **Georges Pompidou Center** has been the object of both violent attack and passionate defense. Parisians are definitely not indifferent to the modern "inside-out" structure designed by architects Renzo Piano and Richard Rogers. Whatever the case, the Center receives through its doors not only museum habitués but curious, first-time museumgoers. Its success is uncontested: it attracts six million visitors a year.

The center was inaugurated in 1977 and comprises the Modern Museum which contains the largest collection in the world of 20th-century art, a public library, a children's library and workshop, the Center for Industrial Creation, and all sorts of distinctive temporary exhibits. There is a wonderful view of Paris from the top floor.

But as you will quickly see, not all activity is within the Center. The famous slanting esplanade is invaded daily by myriad groups of musicians, dancers, portraitists, fortunetellers, jugglers, and poets. The Center is open from 12 noon to 10 P.M. weekdays and from 10 A.M. to 10 P.M. on Saturdays and Sundays. It is closed on Tuesdays.

Some Useful Words and Phrases

artiste peintre (f/m) painter
atelier (m) workshop, studio

coûter	to cost
danseur/danseuse	dancer
devenir	to become
étage (m)	floor
événement (m)	event
musicien(ne)	musician
oeuvre d'art (f)	work of art
poète/poétesse	poet
solder	to put on sale
vendre	to sell
vue (f)	view

Certains ateliers d'artistes sont devenus des musées. (Certain artists' studios have become museums.)

Pour les événements de la semaine, achetez l'Officiel des Spectacles. (For the events of the week, buy the Officiel des Spectacles.)

Il sort le mercredi et coûte deux francs. (It comes out on Wednesdays and costs two francs.)

IV   Mansions & Monuments of the Left Bank

From Rue des Saints-Pères to the Eiffel Tower lies the 7th arrondissement, the fashionable area in which the French bourgeoisie has quartered itself since the 18th century. There were at one time some 150 private mansions in this area which replaced the Marais, the "in" quarter of the 17th century. The general architectural pattern included a first formal courtyard behind the street wall and gate. Horse-drawn carriages entered here to leave their passengers at the main door. At the back of the townhouse is the formal garden as you will see if you visit the Rodin Museum.

Orsay Museum/National Assembly

Location: Orsay Museum, Quai Anatole France and Rue de
           Bellechasse
           National Assembly, 33 Quai d'Orsay

Métro: Solférino
Bus: 24, 63, 68, 69, 73, 84, 94

The **Orsay Museum** was originally a railroad station. Adjoining it was a luxury hotel. Dedicated on July 14, 1900, the station incorporated the main architectural highlights of the time: glass between steel girders concealed behind a classic Napoleon III stone facade. In the 1930s the Gare d'Orsay became obsolete and was closed. It did serve, however, at various times: as a center for returning prisoners in 1945, a shelter for the destitute and derelict during the bitter winters of the early 1950s, the scene of Orson Welles' film *The Trial,* and so on. In 1970 its demolition was authorized to make way for a giant deluxe hotel. The outcry this decision produced swayed President Georges Pompidou who had the buildings classified as historic monuments. A museum devoted to art of the second half of the 19th century then was projected and the task of transforming the station and the hotel into a museum palace was entrusted to Italian architect Gae Aulenti.

The museum covers the period from the Revolution of 1848—the overthrow of King Louis-Philippe—to the First World War in its variety of expression. In addition to painting and sculpture, photography (born in 1839), furniture design, objects of art, and architectural models are honored. It contains probably the most important collection of pre-impressionist and impressionist painting to be found anywhere.

There is a good restaurant and tearoom, handsomely decorated and moderately priced, on the mezzanine. Upstairs is a welcome coffee shop. From the deck there is a clear view of

Right-Bank Paris as far off as Sacré Coeur. The Orsay is open from 10 A.M. to 6 P.M., until 9:45 P.M. on Thursdays, and it is closed on Mondays.

On leaving the Orsay, take Rue de Lille to the right. Turn right onto Boulevard Saint-Germain and go one block to the **National Assembly** (Assemblée nationale). The Assembly or Chamber of Deputies (Chambre des députés) was originally the Bourbon Palace, which it still is sometimes called. The columns were added during Napoleon's reign to match those of the Madeleine Church across the Seine. Actually this is the back side of the mansion; the main entrance is on the Place du Palais-Bourbon.

This building as well as the Hôtel de Lassay, next door, were built in the 17th century by the Duchess of Bourbon, one of eight natural children of Louis XIV and Madame de Montespan. The Palais de Bourbon was her residence and the Hôtel de Lassey that of her young lover, the Count of Lassay. On Bastille Day 1789, her heirs, the Prince of Condé and his family, slipped out of the Palace and out of France. The mansion was soon to play host to the people's representatives. The Hôtel de Lassay is now the residence of the Speaker of the House.

Visitors are welcome at 3 P.M. on days the assembly is in session. The entrance is just to the right of the columned facade as you face it. Be there at 2:45 at the latest and have your passport in hand.

Skirt the Assembly to the left as you face it to see the elegant Place du Palais-Bourbon. Take a look at the fine entrance to the Hôtel de Lassay as well. The **Rollet-Pradier Bakery** to the right in Rue de Bourgogne is a pleasant snack and tea-room with a fixed-price luncheon menu.

Army Museum/Napoleon's Tomb/Rodin Museum

Location: Army Museum, Les Invalides, Quai d'Orsay or Rue de Grenelle

Napoleon's Tomb, Les Invalides, Avenue de Tour-ville
Rodin Museum, 77 Rue de Varenne

Métro: Invalides, Latour-Maubourg
Bus: 63, 69, 83

From the esplanade of the **Invalides,** the eyes may feast on the Alexander III Bridge and the Grand and Petit Palais on one side (all three were built for the 1900 International Exhibition) and the splendid facade of the Invalides on the other.

The Invalides comprises a hospital and a home for old soldiers, the Army Museum, two churches (one gilt domed), and Napoleon's Tomb. The project owes its existence to Louis XIV. In the 17th century permanent armies were small; wars were fought with mercenaries. The time of glory past, regiments were dispersed and the men, deprived of their pay, swelled the ranks of the poor. King Louis XIV attempted to form permanent units of the mercenaries and constructed military barracks for them. The Invalides project became something of a lay brothers' cloister or monastery for former mercenaries. The men organized workshops and supplied the city with objects and clothing of all sorts. Today, the Invalides houses some 600 patients and residents. Most of the living quarters are occupied by the **Army Museum** which displays relics and remembrances from the paleolithic to the atomic age. In addition to arms and armors of France and elsewhere are objects and documents from the two World Wars, a replica of the room in which the prisoner Napoleon lived on Saint Helena, flags and banners from the Napoleonic Wars, etc. It is open from 10 A.M. to 5 P.M. every day.

Napoleon's Tomb is located in the exquisitely proportioned, domed church built at the end of the 17th century by Jules Hardouin-Mansart. Napoleon's remains are enclosed in six caskets. He died at Saint Helena in 1821; his burial in this church took place on December 15, 1840. It seems that

Napoleon died with his boots on. When his tomb was opened some twenty years later for its transfer to Paris, his toenails had grown through his socks and the seams of the soles.

It was in this place that Lieutenant Colonel Dreyfus was decorated with the Légion d'honneur in 1906. Hitler knelt in front of Napoleon's tomb in 1940. General Montgomery received the Légion d'honneur here in 1945, Churchill in 1947. The tomb is open every day from 10 A.M. to 5 P.M.

Leave the premises through the side gate, cross over Boulevard des Invalides and turn left. Your first right will be Rue de Varenne. On the corner is the **Rodin Museum.** The building in which the museum is housed was built by 1731. In 1820, it became a boarding school for young girls. In 1908 certain master artists were granted permission to work here: Rainer Maria Rilke, Isadora Duncan, Matisse, and Rodin. In 1910 the French government bought the building and authorized Rodin to remain on the condition that he will his sculpture to the state.

Rodin's most celebrated works are on display as well as examples of the genius of Camille Claudel. The two were lovers for some fifteen years. When Rodin left Camille for others, she was so totally bereft that she forsook her art completely. In 1913, her brother, the well-known French writer Paul Claudel, had her interned for the last thirty years of her life. The gardens are also well worth a visit. Tea is served at the far end. The museum is open from 10 A.M. to 5 P.M., except on Mondays.

Leave the museum to the right on Rue de Varennes. At number 57 is the Prime Minister's Office, the **Hôtel Matignon.**

At the end of the street, turn right into Rue de Grenelle. At number 63 is **Dalloyau,** one of the best pastry shops and caterers in Paris. At number 61 is the new **Maillol Museum** of sculpture.

Some Useful Words and Phrases

automne (m)	fall
été (m)	summer
hiver (m)	winter
malade	sick, ill
printemps (m)	spring
recruter	to recruit
suivre	to follow

L'armée recrute des soldats. (The army recruits soldiers.)

L'hôpital reçoit des malades. (The hospital receives the sick.)

L'hiver suit l'automne. (Winter follows fall.)

Le printemps vient après l'hiver. (Spring comes after winter.)

Il fait chaud en été. (It is hot in summer.)

Les représentants du peuple siègent à l'assemblée nationale. (The people's representatives sit in the National Assembly.)

V   Right Bank Elegance

Opéra/Place de la Concorde

Métro: Opéra
Bus: 20, 21, 22, 27, 29, 42, 52, 53, 66, 68, 81, 95

The flamboyant style of the **Opéra** or Palais Garnier had its supporters and its detractors when the edifice was dedicated in 1875. For Claude Debussy, "it will always resemble a railway station; once inside, it can be mistaken for a Turkish bath."

The tremendous central chandelier, weighing seven tons, is the largest in the world.

While the stage can accommodate 450 players at a time, the hall now seats only 1800 spectators. Needless to say, ticket lines are long and form early. Now that a new opera house has been constructed at the Bastille, this one specializes in ballet.

Leave the Opera through Rue de la Paix. On the right are jewelers Dunhill and Cartier; on the left, Poiray and Boucheron as well as Burma's gaudy imitations. Around **Place Vendôme** are Van Cleef and Arpels, Chaumet, and Buccellati. The place, one of Louis XIV's projects was designed at the beginning of the 1700s. In its center was a statue of the king in Roman garb and a Renaissance wig. Following the revolution, the statue was overturned and replaced by a Roman-garbed Napoleon. During the Paris Commune of 1871, painter Gustave Courbet was authorized to flatten the column. Felled like a tree onto a bed of firewood, sand, and dung, the statue was reduced to smithereens before a cheering crowd. A few days later, the Commune was routed and Courbet summoned to pay for the monument's reconstruction; he was ruined, totally disheartened, and died soon after. Today, Napoleon is back on his pedestal in uniform.

On the west side of Place Vendôme stands the **Hôtel Ritz,** one of the most elegant in Paris. Eleanor and Franklin Roosevelt stopped here in 1919 when FDR attended the Peace Conference as U.S. secretary of the navy.

In 1956, Ernest Hemingway went in for a drink. The baggage captain, recognizing him, asked him to remove trunks he had left in the storage room in 1927! In them he found lost notes that became the basis for *A Moveable Feast.*

As you leave Place Vendôme, you come to **Rue Saint-Honoré** and **Rue du Faubourg Saint-Honoré,** the fashionable shopping street lined with the ready-to-wear shops of the top couture houses (to the right).

Continue on Rue Castiglione, past the Intercontinental

Hotel, to Rue de Rivoli. Shop after shop along this street is filled with gifts and souvenirs for tourists. There also are two excellent English bookstores: Galignani's at 224 and W.H. Smith's at 248.

On the other side of Rue de Rivoli, enter the **Tuileries Gardens** designed by the garden architect Le Nôtre in 1664. Their central promenade is an important link in the perspective which, beginning at the Louvre, includes the Carousel Arch, the Luxor obelisk and the Triumphal Arch of the Champs-Elysées.

To the right, overlooking Place de la Concorde, are two pavilions, the **Orangery** and the **Jeu de Paume**. The latter, on the right, now plays host to temporary exhibits of modern art. The Orangery, on the left, is permanently occupied by the very imposing Walter Guillaume collection of impressionist and post-impressionist painting, as well as by Monet's famous water lily murals on the lower level. It is open from 9:45 A.M. to 5:15 P.M. and closed on Tuesdays.

Some Useful Words and Phrases

couturier/couturière	fashion designer, dressmaker
fiançailles (f)	engagement

Le prêt-à-porter est moins cher que la couture. (Ready-to-wear is less expensive than couture.)

Le bijoutier va dessiner une bague de fiancailles. (The jeweler is going to design an engagement ring.)

Nous cherchons un cadeau pour notre fille de trois ans. (We are looking for a gift for our three-year-old girl.)

J'étais en France pendant la guerre. (I was in France during the war.)

NOTE that **étais** is the past or imperfect tense of **être**. For complete table, see Chapter 20.

Place de la Concorde/Arch of Triumph

Métro: Concorde
Bus: 24, 42, 52, 72, 73, 84, 94

Place de la Concorde is an 18th-century square conceived as the glorification of Louis xv, whose statue stood in its center. It was designed by Gabriel, as were the handsome buildings along its northern side.

In 1770 a fireworks display was organized here to celebrate the marriage of the future Louis xvi and Marie Antoinette of Austria. It was a grand occasion until the crowd panicked and 103 people were trampled to death. In 1792 the equestrian statue of Louis xv was felled and the following year the guillotine was set up on the square for the execution of Louis xvi. Before it was removed in 1795, 1343 other victims, including Marie Antoinette, were decapitated.

In 1830 the Egyptian sovereign Mohamed Ali offered three Luxor obelisks to France. A boat was constructed especially for their transport but only one ever made the voyage. Because of its weight and the technical problems involved, its arrival in Paris took two years. Parisians launched into passionate debate as to the most suitable spot to plant the monument. It was finally dedicated here in 1836 by King Louis Philippe. The female figures around the square represent eight great cities of France.

At the entrance to the **Champs-Elysées** are two exciting marble statues by Coustou: *Numidian Horses Being Mastered by Africans*. From here one gets a magnificent view of the Elysian Fields in total span, ever so slightly inclined upwards. The French have labeled it "the most beautiful avenue in the world."

We shall, however, begin our promenade, on Avenue Gabriel, the road which passes in front of the **American Embassy,** once the home of famous epicurean Grimod de la Reynière. On the left are a theater and the fashionable restaurant **Ledoyen.** In the 18th century, this was a modest country inn where you could obtain a glass of milk fresh from the cows grazing outside.

Further along on your right are the gardens of the British Embassy and then the Elysées Palace, the residence of the President of France. Entrances to both are on Rue de Faubourg Saint-Honoré, which runs parallel.

Turn left on Avenue de Marigny where an open-air **stamp market** for sales and exchanges holds sway on Thursdays, Saturdays, Sundays, and holidays from 10 A.M. until sunset.

On the other side of the Champs-Elysées are first the **Petit Palais,** then the **Grand Palais,** halls built for the 1900 International Exhibition. The glass-roofed steel and stone structures are now permanent edifices and the site of exhaustive temporary exhibits, often very complete retrospectives.

Check to see what is going on now. The same Grand Palais, entering from Avenue Franklin-Roosevelt, is Discovery Palace, a scientific, hands-on museum for children and planetarium. Continuing on the avenue, at the Rond-Point, behind the flower displays, are several elegant 19th-century buildings.

At the top of the avenue is the **Arc de Triomphe** (Arch of Triumph). Although this area is officially called Place Charles-de-Gaulle, for Parisians it remains l'Etoile (the Star) with its twelve points or thoroughfares.

It was Napoleon Bonaparte who ordered the construction of a triumphal arch in honor of the Grand Army. Work began in 1806. With his overthrow, the project was abandoned for thirty years and completed, under Louis Philippe, in 1836. On November 11, 1920, an unknown soldier was laid to rest under the arch. Every evening at 6 P.M., the flame of remembrance is lighted in the course of a brief public ceremony.

Some Useful Words and Phrases

enterrer	to bury
sous	under

Je voudrais acheter ce timbre à un franc. (I would like to buy this one-franc stamp.)

Combien de timbres faut-il pour les Etats-Unis? (How many stamps are necessary for the United States?)

Le 14 juillet est un jour de fête. (The 14th of July is a holiday.)

Le soldat inconnu est enterré sous l'arc de triomphe. (The unknown soldier is buried under the Arch of Triumph.)

Quel est le problème? (What's the problem?)

VI   Montmartre

Métro: Lamarck-Caulaincourt
Bus: 80

The history of Montmartre begins with a legend. Saint Denis was decapitated on the top of the hill in 250 A.D. for his Christian beliefs. He then tucked his lost head under his arm and footed it to the place now named Saint-Denis. Sometime later Mount of the Martyr became Montmartre.

Until just over one hundred years ago, Montmartre hill was littered with gypsum or chalk quarries, some dating from Roman times. In 1830 there were eighteen open sky quarries and thirty ovens for the refining of plaster. The mines were closed in 1860 when Montmartre was incorporated into Paris.

At that time it was still a country village adorned with vineyards and windmills. Parisians came to drink its wine and dance in the barns and gardens. Artists and writers were drawn here as well, especially during the years from 1871 to 1914. Literary and artistic life centered around the Lapin Agile, the Billiards en Bois cafés, and the Bateau Lavoir artists' studios.

Saint Vincent Cemetery/Museum of Montmartre/ Saint Peter's Church/Sacré-Coeur Basilica/Place du Tertre

Location: St. Vincent's Cemetery, Rue Lucien Gaulard
Museum of Old Montmartre, 12 Rue Cortot
St. Peter's Church, Rue Mont-Cénis

Start the visit of Montmartre at Rue Caulaincourt. Go left on Rue Lucien Gaulard which takes you immediately into **Saint Vincent's Cemetery** crammed in between the low apartment buildings. Among the noted personalities buried here under grey marble and pink granite are Arthur Honegger, Maurice Utrillo, and Théophile Steinlen.

On leaving, turn left on Rue Saint-Vincent, which skirts the upper part of the cemetery. You will come to the **Montmartre vineyard** and the café **Au Lapin Agile.** The latter has changed little since it was glorified for all time in paintings by impressionists. It is open every evening except Monday from 9 P.M. to 2 A.M. Among the clientele at the turn of the century were Apollinaire, Picasso, Max Jacob, and Vlaminck, as well as a host of small-time crooks.

Take Rue des Saules to the right, past the vineyard. Turn right on Rue de l'Abreuvoir. Just at the corner is a pleasant, inexpensive restaurant with sidewalk tables. Continue down this country lane to Rue Girardon. The manor house here was once a dance hall. Continue up the hill and turn left into Rue Norvins. The sculptured figure advancing from the far wall is writer Marcel Aymé.

At the corner with Rue des Saules is the **Auberge de la Bonne-Franquette.** The garden of this inn served as Van Gogh's model for his famous painting *La Guinguette,* exhibited at the Orsay.

Continue down Rue des Saules to Rue Cortot and turn right. Number 12 was home to Suzanne Valadon and son Utrillo, Raoul Dufy, and Renoir. It is now the entrance to the **Museum of Old Montmartre,** which is located down the garden path and through the arbor. It is the oldest house on the butte and belonged to actor Claude La Roze de Rosimond, an adept Molièrian who followed so closely in the footsteps of his master that he met death, in 1686, on stage, as had Molière. The Museum retraces the history of Montmartre. It is open from 2:30 P.M. until 6 P.M., on Sundays from 11 A.M., and is closed on Mondays.

Continue up Rue Cortot to the water tower and turn right in Rue Mont-Cénis. At the end of the street is **Saint Peter's Church,** all that remains of a Benedictine Abbey that once covered the butte. Dating from 1147, Saint Peter's also can claim to be the oldest church of the city. It is classified as early Gothic, but vestiges of Romanesque capitals have survived as well. The bright stained glass windows date from 1955.

A telegraph pole was affixed to the church tower for many years. Thanks to the new invention, Napoleon's victories were honored in Paris minutes after the battles of Strasbourg and Lille (1792).

To the left on leaving Saint Peter's is the Sacré-Coeur Basilica, which was placed atop Montmartre hill following the Paris Commune of 1871. After Paris's fall to the Prussians, the people of Montmartre rose to save their quarter from the invaders. They amassed 171 cannons at the Place du Tertre and prepared to face the Prussian army. It was, however, Napoleon III's army which advanced on the butte. Two generals were taken prisoner and killed by the crowd. Throughout the city, people then rose against the regime. The result was the Paris Commune, a revolutionary government that remained in power for a mere two months. It was brutally dismantled in house-to-house fighting that left 30,000 dead.

Since the Commune had originated in Montmartre, the succeeding "loyalist" parliament was not about to extend pardon. On the contrary it voted to build the Sacred Heart Basilica as a monument of atonement. Criticism of the project was vociferous. The building was begun in 1876 and completed only in 1910. The style is 12th-century Byzantine. There are souvenir shops on either side of the transept.

On leaving the Basilica, take the first street to the right and then first left to **Place du Tertre**. This was the village square. Today it is covered with restaurant tables and artists' easels.

To return to central Paris, you can take the funicular from up here or you can leave the square through Patachou's pastry shop and cross the small terrace past the Wax Museum until you reach Rue Norvins. Go left at Clement Square and right at Rue Ravignan until you come to Emile-Goudeau Square. On the right is the Bateau Lavoir reconstructed after fire consumed it in 1970. It was here that Picasso painted his celebrated *Demoiselles d'Avignon,* considered to be the beginnings of cubism. At the time he and Max Jacob shared a bed, one occupying it by day and the other by night.

As you go down, take Rue Ravignan to the right. Continue on Rue Durantin. At the corner of Rue Tholozé, you will get a look at the now-sequestered Moulin de la Galette, the windmill-dance hall made famous in paintings by Renoir, Van Gogh and Willette. Go left on Rue Tholozé and left again at Rue des Abbesses to Place des Abbesses. There you will find a fine Guimard turn-of-the-century métro entrance.

Some Useful Words and Phrases

époque (f)	epoch, time, era
selon	according to

Le vin du vignoble de Montmartre n'est pas de la meilleure qualité. (The wine from the Montmartre vineyard is not of the best quality.)

Les artistes et les écrivains ont aimé Montmartre pour sa tranquillité. (Artists and writers liked Montmartre for its tranquility.)

La vie n'était pas chère à Montmartre à l'époque. (Life was not expensive in Montmartre at the time.)

Il reste deux moulins à vent sur la colline de Montmartre. (There remain two windmills on Montmartre hill.)

Selon la légende, il a mis sa tête sous son bras et il est parti à pied à Saint-Denis. (According to legend, he put his head under his arm and he went on foot to Saint-Denis.)

VII   The Eiffel Tower to the Trocadéro

Location: Eiffel Tower, Quai Branly

Métro: Ecole Militaire, Bir Hakeim
Bus: 42, 69, 82, 86

The Eiffel Tower was built for the Universal Exhibition of 1889. It was a temporary structure, the expression of the triumph of the industrial age. Its success was so great, however, that it remained and became the symbol of Paris.

During its construction, Parisians flocked to the site on weekends to measure progress. It was then the tallest man-made building in the world. With its TV, radio transmitter and antennae, it now rises 1,263 feet off the ground. On the top platform is an aircraft meteorological and navigation station fitted with a revolving beacon. Two-and-one-half million rivets hold the steel latticework together. There are three floors. From the third, at 900 feet, you can see forty miles away on a clear day.

The tower was the brainstorm of two engineers, Koechkin and Nouguier, who worked in Eiffel's office. Its success was immediate.

Everyone, from Queen Victoria to Thomas Edison to Mahatma Gandhi, visited the Eiffel Tower.

In 1986 the lighting was modified. Rather than spotlights from the ground to the Tower, it is now lit from within with sodium lamps. The effect is jewel-like, a devastating fairy scepter over the top of the city.

Some Useful Words and Phrases

bas (m)	bottom, sock, stocking
chaque	each
haut(e)	top, high

Il faut des nerfs d'acier pour monter en haut de la tour Eiffel. (One needs nerves of steel to climb to the top of the Eiffel Tower.)

Faites-vous du progrès en français? (Are you making progress in French?)

Il faut travailler votre français un peu chaque jour. (You have to work on your French a little each day.)

La tour Eiffel est ouverte aux visiteurs tous les jours. (The Eiffel Tower is open to visitors every day.)

Trocadéro/Chaillot Palace

Cross the Iéna Bridge over the Seine to the gardens and fountains of **Chaillot Palace.** On this site Catherine de Médicis built a country home in the 16th century. In the 17th, Henrietta of England, wife of Louis XIV's brother, turned the estate into a convent to which many a past favorite of the court retreated.

Napoleon I razed the convent, built the Iéna Bridge, and made plans for a grand palace for his son, King of Rome, but the empire collapsed before construction began. In 1937 the present palace was built in the pre-war style for the Paris exhibition of that year.

There is a magnificent view of the Eiffel Tower and gardens from here. The fountains surge outward with force during afternoons and evenings. On weekends, skateboard and roller skaters play to the crowds. Vendors, dancers, and mimes are in attendance as well.

The number of museums catering to the most varied interests is considerable. There is much to see at Chaillot Palace, next door at Tokyo Palace, and across the street from the latter at the Guimet Museum and Galliera Palace.

The **Naval Museum** in the west wing of Chaillot Palace has displays on French sea power and shipping throughout the centuries. Life-size and scale models of naval and merchant ships and fishing and pleasure boats are featured. Among the models is Columbus's *Santa Maria*.

The **Museum of Man** in the west wing of Chaillot Palace tells the story of the human race through prehistory, anthropology and ethnology.

The **Museum of French Monuments** in Chaillot Palace's east wing contains reproductions of French monumental art, sculpture, and murals. Romanesque and Gothic frescos have been reproduced on life-size architectural replicas of domes and bits of walls of places like Chartres and Notre Dame, placed at eye level!

The **Cinema Museum** in the east wing of Chaillot Palace has posters, authentic costumes, film décors, a French movie set, and displays of some of the industry's predecessors, such as magic lanterns, shadow plays, and Edison's kinetoscope.

The **Aquarium** at the east-end garden entrance of Chaillot Palace contains the principal species of freshwater fish from the rivers of France.

The **Guimet Museum** at Place d'Iéna is devoted to Asian art. Exceptional pieces from Cambodia, Vietnam, India, Tibet, China, and other lands are displayed, including an unequalled collection of ceramics.

The **Museum of Modern Art,** down the hill on the right side of President Wilson Avenue, has 20th-century paintings not removed to the Pompidou Center. Included is Dufy's fabulous mural *Fairy Electricity,* 180 feet long and thirty feet high. Temporary exhibits also are organized here.

The **Children's Museum** in the east wing of Tokyo Palace has very inventive and didactic temporary exhibits.

The **Museum of Fashion and Costume** at Galliera Palace

is just across the way from the Museum of Modern Art. Built in the 1880s in Italian Renaissance style, it possesses a collection of 400 complete costumes that trace the history of male and female dress from 1750 to the present day.

Some Useful Words and Phrases

rivière (f)	river
transport maritime (m)	shipping

L'art des pays asiatiques est presenté au musée Guimet. (The art of Asian countries is presented at the Guimet Museum.)

Le dimanche il y a foule sur l'esplanade du Trocadéro. (On Sunday there are crowds on the esplanade at the Trocadero.)

La France est une des cinq grandes puissances, membres permanents du Conseil de Securité de l'ONU. (France is one of the five great powers, permanent members of the UN Security Council.)

CHAPTER 12

Excursions out of Paris

One of the advantages of Paris is the possibility of leaving the city quickly and finding oneself in a place of choice and wonder. One- or two-day excursions out of Paris can provide a glimpse of a more provincial life style, the pulse of country air and foliage, a taste of regional specialities in food and drink, a look at man-made and earthly marvels. The following trips are within close range, none more than two hours by train from Paris.

I *Giverny*

At Giverny are the home and gardens of Claude Monet. Here the artist lived from 1883 until his death in 1926. With his own hand he transformed the marshes into a fairyland of flower gardens, moist country paths and lily ponds under the famous Japanese bridge.

Monet's home is now as it was at the time of his death. One may wander from room to room and admire his extensive collection of Japanese prints; one may touch his rustic furniture. The sunken living room with the worn couch and armchairs await the arrival of the master after a stroll around the lily pond. The table is set for eight in the bright yellow and green dining room.

Following the Second World War, the property was in a sorry state. The gardens were gone, the pond was overrun with weeds, the house and studios were musty with disuse and in need of renovation. It was thanks to Lila Acheson Wallace of *Reader's Digest* that this estate has regained its past glory.

Train: From St. Lazare Station to Vernon, 2½ miles from Giverny: 45 minutes. Trains at frequent intervals. Sunday schedule differs. For train information call 4582-5050. Buses meet certain trains. Bicycles are for hire at the railway station. Taxis are available at the station.

Tourist buses: Excursions certain afternoons at 2 P.M., operated by: **Paris Vision,** 214 Rue de Rivoli, métro Tuileries or Palais-Royal, tel. 4260-3125. **Cityrama,** 4 place des Pyramides, métro Tuileries or Palais-Royal, tel. 4260-3014.

Car: Take A13, the Autoroute de l'Ouest (Western Parkway) towards Rouen. Get off Parkway at Bonnières and take road to Vernon, then Giverny.

Hours: 10 A.M. to 6 P.M. from April 1st to October 31st. Closed Mondays.

Time: Half to full day.

Restaurants: **Jardins de Giverny,** Chemin Roy, Giverny, tel: 3221-6080. Lovely restaurant, moderately expensive fixed-price menu.

Accommodations: **Relais Normand,** 11 Place Evreux, Vernon, tel: 3221-1612. Pleasant, inexpensive.

Some Useful Words and Phrases

Je vais chercher l'horaire du train. (I'm going to get the train schedule.)

Aller (to go) is an irregular verb and is conjugated as follows in the future tense:

j'irai	nous irons
tu iras	vous irez
elle, il ira	elles, ils iront

II *Versailles*

Versailles is the palace of palaces, envied by kings and would-be monarchs, and copied the world over. It was commissioned by Louis xiv in 1661: Louis Le Vau was the architect, replaced upon his death by Jules Hardouin-Mansart. The painter-decorator was Charles Le Brun and the landscape architect, Le Nôtre.

Construction lasted for fifty years. Thirty-seven thousand acres of marshland were drained. A river was diverted to feed the 1400 fountains. One hundred fifty thousand plants were bedded and 100 statues sculpted for the gardens alone. Thirty-five thousand workers were still employed on the site when the king and his court went into residence in 1682.

The court numbered some 20,000. This figure included 9000 soldiers billeted in the town and 5000 servants in an annex. One thousand noble men and women and their 4000 servants were housed at the palace. Louis xiv overlorded this establishment keeping an eye on all, creating rivalries, indulging in favors, maneuvering on his society chessboard. When he died in 1715, the court returned to Paris.

Louis xv went back to Versailles in 1722. Louis xvi and Marie Antoinette lived there until 1789. As the symbol of monarchial absolutism, Versailles was marked for plundering. Its furniture was auctioned; its works of art transferred to the Louvre; even its destruction was envisaged.

The palace was saved during the rule of Louis-Philippe, who contributed personally to its renovation in order that it become a museum "to the glories of France." A large donation from John D. Rockefeller following the Second World War provided the means for its restoration.

RER train: C-5 line from Left Bank, one-half hour.
Rail: From Montparnasse or Saint-Lazare railway stations.
Bus: 171 from Pont-de-Sèvres métro stop.

Palace: 9:45 A.M. to 5 P.M. Closed Mondays and public holidays.
Grand Trianon: 9:45 A.M. to 12 P.M. and 2 to 5 P.M. Closed Mondays and public holidays.
Petit Trianon: 2 to 5 P.M. Closed Mondays and public holidays.
Gardens: Every day from sunrise to sunset.
Fountains: Shows on Sundays at 3:30 P.M. June through September.
Sound and Light Shows: Certain Saturdays in July, August and September. Time varies. Tel: 3950-3622.
Chapel: Mass first Sunday of month at 5:30 P.M.

Restaurants: **Potager du Roy,** 1 Rue Maréchal-Joffre, tel: 3950-3534. Closed Sundays and Mondays. Excellent fixed price menu by famous chef, moderately priced. **Brasserie du Boeuf à la Mode,** 4 Rue Pain, tel: 3950-319. Another famous chef's pot-au-feu, medium-priced.

Accommodations: **Eden Hôtel,** 2 Rue Philippe-de-Dangeau, tel: 3950-6806. Moderately priced.

Some Useful Words and Phrases

autrefois	in other times, previously
coûteux/coûteuse	costly
diviser	to divide
syndicat (m)	trade union

En France la terre est mesurée en hectares. (In France land is measured in hectares.)

Les syndicats d'ouvriers ne sont pas aussi forts qu'autrefois. (Workers' trade unions are not as strong as in other times.)

La maintenance des grandes propriétés est coûteuse. (The maintenance of large estates is costly.)

III *Fontainebleau*

Like many French monuments and palaces, **Fontainebleau Castle** was redesigned, redecorated, and added onto over the years. In the 13th century it was a hunting lodge for kings. In the 16th century, Francis I assembled some of the most brilliant artists of Italy to enhance the place. Their work and that of their French disciples and colleagues sparked the French Renaissance and what has become known as the Fontainebleau School. Louis xiv would bring his court here in the autumn for the hunt. Napoleon, who called it the "house of centuries", made Fontainebleau his residence.

Inside the castle, in the Louis xv-wing, is the school of American art. Outside there are 84 hectares of gardens designed by Le Nôtre, including sixteen hectares of English gardens. Nature lovers will enjoy the nearby Forest of Fontainebleau.

In town, the **Napoleonic Museum of Art and Military History** possesses a fine collection of uniforms and arms of the 19th century.

The **Hôtel d'Orléans,** an 18th-century mansion, and the **Vieux Logis** are pleasant visits.

If you have come to Fontainebleau by car, you might stop at **Barbizon** (8 kilometers to the north), the 19th-century artists' colony, to visit Millet's studio at Père Ganne's Inn. **Milly-la-Forêt** (19 kilometers to the west) is noted for the Saint Blaise-des-Simples Chapel decorated by Jean Cocteau, and its 15th-century marketplace. **Moret-sur-Loing** (10 kilometers to the southeast) is also a charming village.

Train: From Montparnasse Station, 30 minutes.
Car: Take A6, the Autoroute du Sud (Southern Parkway),

to Barbizon-Fontainebleau exit, then route 5: approximately one hour.

Château: 10 A.M. to 12:30 P.M. and 2 to 5 P.M. Closed on Tuesdays.
Grounds: From sunrise to sunset.
Musée napoléonien d'Art et d'Histoire militaire: 88 Rue Saint-Honoré. 2 to 5:30 P.M. Closed Sundays and Mondays and from end of August to September 20.
Hôtel d'Orléans and Le Vieux Logis: 10 A.M. to noon and 2 to 4 P.M. Closed on Sundays.

Restaurants: ***Route du Beaujolais,** 3 Rue Montebello, tel: 6422-2798. Simple, copious, moderately priced. **Table des Maréchaux,** 9 Rue Grande, tel: 6422-2039. Fine atmosphere and fine food, moderately expensive.

Accommodations: **Napoléon,** 9 Rue Grande, tel: 6422-2039. Peaceful and comfortable. Moderately expensive. **Hostellerie Le Vieux Logis,** 5 rue Sadi-Carnot, 77810 Thomery, tel: 6096-4477 (9 kilometers west of Fontainebleau). Lovely 18th-century home, tastefully decorated. Half pension available. Excellent cuisine, medium priced.

Some Useful Words and Phrases

lever du jour (m) daybreak

En France les enfants vont à l'école le samedi. (In France children go to school Saturdays.)

Ils sont libres le mercredi. (They are free Wednesdays.)

Nous marcherons dans la forêt au lever du jour. (We'll walk in the forest at daybreak.)

Fontainebleau est au sud de Paris. (Fontainebleau is south of Paris.)

IV *Chartres*

In 1194 the cathedral which existed on this spot was destroyed by fire except for the royal portal. Its sacred relics—a statue of the Virgin and her veil—were carried to safety. With tremendous zeal the people set about reconstructing the edifice. Entire villages saddled themselves to the wagons which hauled the heavy limestone blocks from the quarries at Berchères. The builders gave freely of their labor; contributions arrived from all of France. In 1260 Notre-Dame of Chartres was dedicated. Over the centuries chapels were added, the interior was remodeled. Another fire, in the 19th century, reduced the wooden beams to ash.

The sculptures of the royal portal are among the finest in the world. The elongated statues and contemplative heads are indicative of the spirituality of the 13th century, as compared to the terrified, rigid forms of earlier times.

The reputation of Chartres is, of course, because of its stained glass windows, the most exquisite set to be found anywhere in the world. The blues are particularly glorious.

The nave is the widest in France. The chancel is enclosed by sculpted stone dating from the 16th century. In the Saint-Forts chapel of the huge crypt, seashell belts offered by native Americans after their evangelization by missionaries from Chartres are on display.

A walk around the town of Chartres is also delightful. On leaving the cathedral, take Rue du Cardinal-Pie to your right, the Tertre St. Nicolas to **Saint-André**, a 12th-century church recently restored. Then go over the river to Rue de la Tannerie and Rue de la Foulerie for some lovely **views.** The St. Hilary Bridge will bring you back into town and to Place Saint-Pierre where there is another **12th-century church** interesting for its stained glass windows.

To go back to the cathedral, mount the steps to the Town

Hall, then take Rue des Grenets and Rue des Changes to Place de la Poissonnerie.

If you are driving you may want to go to **Illiers-Combray,** 25 kilometers to the southwest of Chartres. Marcel Proust spent his summer vacations here as a child. The house has been turned into a **Proust museum,** open from 2 to 5 P.M., except Sundays and Tuesdays.

Train: From Montparnasse Station: one hour.
Route: Take A6, the Autoroute du Sud. After Rungis follow signs to A10 and Chartres. Approximately one hour.

Hours: 7 A.M. to 7 P.M.

Illuminated: Christmas, Easter and Fridays, Saturdays, Sundays and Mondays from May to October.

Time: All day.

Restaurants: *****Pichet,** 19 Rue Cheval-Blanc, tel: 3721-0835. Inexpensive. *****Taverne,** 8 Rue Porte-Cendreuse, tel: 3734-9957. Fish and seafood restaurant, moderately priced. **Vieille Maison,** 5 Rue Lait, tel: 3734-1067. Excellent restaurant, moderately expensive.

Accommodations: **Grand Monarque,** 22 Place Epars, tel: 3721-0072. Old world charm, moderately expensive. **Mercure,** 6 Avenue Jehan-de-Beauce, tel: 3721-7800. Pleasant garden, moderately expensive.

Some Useful Words and Phrases

brûler	to burn
cendrier (m)	ashtray
indiquer	to indicate

Chartres a une renommée mondiale. (Chartres is renowned worldwide.)

Les poutres ont brûlé au dix-neuvième siècle. (The beams burned in the 19th century.)

Le panneau signale que la route de Chartres est à droite. (The sign indicates that the road to Chartres is to the right.)

A Pâques mon frère partira pour l'Italie. (At Easter my brother will leave for Italy.)

V *Chantilly*

The château at Chantilly contains magnificent paintings and works of art collected by the Duke of Aumale in the last century. Raphaël, Fra Angelico, Watteau, Van Dyck, Ingres, Botticelli, Poussin, Delacroix, and others are well represented.

Chantilly is also well known for its race track and stables. *Les Grandes Ecuries* were built in the 18th century overlooking the track. From April to October, afternoon equestrian shows are organized here. The Horse Museum is interesting and attractively arranged.

Chantilly Forest is a wonderful place for nature walks, and is well marked. Lovely homes line the streets of the town.

The nearby **Royaumont Abbey** (at Lys-Chantilly, 10 kilometers to the southwest) is also superb for its buildings and grounds. It was commissioned by Saint Louis in the 13th century. After the French Revolution it served for a while as a spinning mill. It is now a cultural center.

Train: From Gare du Nord (North Station): 50 minutes.
Car: Take the N1 north to Groslay and the N16 to Chantilly. Less than one hour.

Château: The museum is open from 10:30 A.M. to 6 P.M., except on Tuesdays. From November through February it closes at 5 P.M. and in October and March at 5:30 P.M.

Stables: 10:30 A.M. to 5:30 P.M. from April to October. Equestrian shows at 2:30 and 4 P.M.

Restaurants: **Tipperary,** 6 Avenue du Maréchal-Joffre, tel: 4457-0048. Medium-priced.

Accommodations: **Hostellerie du Lys,** 63 Septième Avenue, *Lamorlaye* (7 kilometers south on the N16) tel: 4421-2619. Comfortable, calm and moderately priced.

Some Useful Words and Phases

autour	around
connaître	to know, to be acquainted with
connu(e)	known
mieux	better, best
plusieurs	several
présentation (f)	show, presentation
saison (f)	season

Il y plusieurs champs de courses situés autour de Paris. (There are several racetracks located around Paris.)

Le mieux connu est Longchamps. (The best known is Longchamps.)

On peut y aller en métro. (One can go there by métro.)

Beaucoup de monde y va le dimanche après-midi en saison. (A lot of people go there on Sunday afternoons in season.)

NOTE: the use of **y,** pronounced **i.** It means **there, in that place** and is used in lieu of **là** when the place to which one is referring has just been stated.

VI *Provins*

Provins is a beautiful medieval city. Known throughout France in the 12th and 13th centuries for its textiles, leather goods and annual fair, Provins declined in the 15th century, becoming the peaceful town you see today. It is a town to walk about in. If you start your visit downtown, off the main street (Rue du Val), take Rue des Capucins, turn right at Rue Saint-Thibault and left at Rue Sainte-Croix. There is a lovely **church** here, begun in the 12th century. Continue on to Boulevard d'Aligre and turn left towards the ramparts.

Another walk takes you down Rue Saint-Thibault (away from the ramparts) to the **Saint-Ayoul Church,** also 12th century, and the **Notre-Dame-du-Val Tower.**

For promenades in the high town, take Rue Saint-Thibault uptown. At number 16 is the entrance to the **underground passages** of the town, open on Sundays. To your left is the **Saint-Quiriace Church** and the **Caesar Tower,** an impressive dungeon built in the 12th century to protect the city from attacks out of the east. It also functioned as a prison. Its tower, well worth the climb, served as belfry for Saint-Quiriace. It now houses the **Provins Historical and Archaeological Society.** In Rue du Palais is the **Provinois Museum.**

Place du Châtel in the heart of the high town is lined with lovely old homes. Above the Place, the Rue Saint-Jean, is another interesting church called the **Dimes Grange** which, back in the 12th century, was a warehouse for peasant produce on which a ten percent tax in kind had to be paid to the governor.

From here, through the Saint-Jean Gate, also a defensive structure, you will come to the **ramparts.** Go left for a lovely view of the city and return to the right for a tour of the area. You will come first to the square **Luxemburg Tower** which housed the executioners of the dungeon until the end of the 18th century. Continue on around the ramparts.

Train: From Gare de l'Est (East Station): one hour.
Car: Take the N19: roughly one hour.

Underground passages: 16 Rue Saint-Thibault. 2 to 6 P.M. Sundays only.

Provinois Museum: 4 Rue du Palais. Sunday afternoons from 2 to 6 P.M., April 1 to November 11.
Caesar Tower Donjon: 10 A.M. until noon and 2 to 5 P.M., from April 1 to September 30, and 2 to 4:30 P.M. the rest of the year.

Restaurants: **Quat'Saisons,** 44 Rue Val, tel: 6408-9944. Pleasant garden, traditional fare, medium-priced.

Accommodations: **Hostellerie aux Vieux Remparts,** 3 Rue Couverte, tel: 6408-9400. New hotel, traditional architecture, medium-priced.

Some Useful Words and Phrases

bourreau (m)	executioner
cuir (m)	leather
entrepôt (m)	warehouse
impôt (m)	tax
loger	to house
paysan(ne)	peasant, farmer
rempart (m)	rampart
rue principale (f)	main street
souterrain(e)	underground

En France on fait sa déclaration d'impôts à la fin février. (In France one files one's income tax return at the end of February.)

Il reste très peu de paysans en France. (There remain very few peasants in France.)

L'agriculture est devenue une industrie. (Agriculture has become an industry.)

Le tourisme et l'armement sont les industries françaises les plus importantes. (Tourism and armaments are the most important French industries.)

VII *Amiens*

This is a lively city. Despite heavy destruction in the First World War, despite massive damage in World War II, despite economic depression, Amiens throbs. It was the manufacturing center for the world's finest velvet for several centuries. Unfortunately, many French clothiers now find it cheaper to buy their fabrics and to manufacture their merchandise elsewhere in the world.

Numerous thriving small cities of France have lost their spark and lapsed, some becoming bedroom communities, others turning solely into tourist sites. Amiens has maintained its verve; it is a university city with a young population. The factories have made it a workers' town. And its proximity to Paris, good transport, housing, educational and cultural facilities for families have enticed small firms to locate here.

City construction projects are everywhere. The old quarter near the river has been entirely and attractively rehabilitated. A modern cultural center is in the works. The downtown stores are well stocked, the bookshops are excellent.

And Amiens is guardian to the most elegant, the most perfect, the most awe-inspiring Gothic cathedral in all of France! If that does not suffice, come and see the house and tower in which Jules Verne traveled in order to write his imaginative stories for children.

Tour

On leaving the railway station turn right. Take Rue Gloriette to the left; it will become Rue de l'Oratoire and lead you to the rear of **Notre-Dame Cathedral.**

The sculpted facade furnishes an example of religious statuary and culture in the 13th century: the central portal with its statue of Christ surrounded by the apostles represents the Last Judgment. Present below are the virtues and vices, the arts and trades of Amiens, the fables of the fox and the stork and of the wolf and the crow. The right portal is devoted to

Mary and the left portal to Saint Firmin, the patron saint of Picardy.

Step inside the cathedral; the impression is powerful. The tallest cathedral in France is airy, almost white, bathed in light. At first glance there is an absence of ornamentation except for the checkerboard marble floor. On closer inspection the base of the loggia of the upper gallery of windows contains a beautifully sculpted frieze of leaves.

Placards are posted on the columns of the transept in memory of those men of Canadian, New Zealand, Australian, British and American units who died in the Battle of the Somme in 1916 and in defense of Amiens in 1918. The sculpted wooden stalls are among the most beautiful in the world. The stained glass windows of the chancel are superb in reds and blues. Even the simple glass elsewhere is gratifying for its purity. Near the entrance to the treasury are the remains of murals from the 16th century, a time when the walls of the entire church were covered with religious scenes.

Construction of the cathedral began in 1220. The main church took fifty years to build; chapels were added in the 14th and 15th centuries. The style of the cathedral is Classic Gothic, superceding Primitive Gothic and preceding Late or Flamboyant Gothic.

Outside the cathedral turn right. On the lower level go right again into Rue du Hocquet. There are a number of interesting shops selling folk art from around the world. Turn left at Les Feuillantines, a charming teashop. In Rue du Don, Jean-Pierre Facquier makes and sells wooden marionettes.

From the little square cross over to the **Saint Leu Quarter**. On examination of the area, the first impression is of a theater backdrop. The old fishermen's neighborhood is in fact very much alive with restaurants and bars. Notice how the new constructions replacing homes bombed out in World War II blend in with the old.

If you leave Saint Leu to the left over the bridge and climb up and cross the high road you can descend again into **Les**

Ortillonnages. This area was marshland until the arrival of the Romans when it was turned into garden plots for fruits, vegetables and flowers. It is still partially cultivated. Go down Chemin du Halage. At the Auberge du Vert Galant, flat-bottomed row boats are rented by the hour, map included; a pleasant interlude may be spent in floating gardens, among flora and fauna, namely ducks, waterfowl, frogs and swans.

From the Ortillonnages take the high road to the left, past the railway station. Boulevard de Belfort leads you into Mail Albert Ier; turn left on Rue Charles-Dubois for the **Jules Verne Documentation Center,** located in the writer's former residence. From his tower he traveled around the world in his imagination. According to the guide, Jules Verne's books are surpassed in readership only by the Bible and Marx.

Outside the Center, go left on Mail Albert Ier and right again on Rue de la République for the **Picardy Museum.** Here the antiquities are beautifully presented; unfortunately the explanations are in French only. Upstairs see the works of Fragonard, Hubert Robert (the architectural painter), the Flemish and Dutch artists, Simon Vouet portraits, and the Puvis de Chavannes frescos.

Train: From Gare du Nord (North Station): 2 hours.
Car: From Paris on the A16: 90 minutes.

Tourist Info: 1 Rue Jean-Catelas, 80000 Amiens, tel: 2291-7928. Railway station, tel: 2292-6504.

Cathedral: 7:30 A.M. to 7 P.M. in season, 7:30 A.M. to 12 noon and 2 to 5 P.M. October through March.
Sound and Light Show: Cathedral. Evenings from April through October except Sundays and Mondays, in English, French or German. See Tourist Office.
Jules Verne Center: 2 Rue Charles-Dubois. 9:30 A.M. to 12 and 2 to 6 P.M. Closed Sundays and Mondays.
Picardy Museum: 48 Rue de la République. 10 A.M. to 12:30 and 2 to 6 P.M. Closed Mondays and holidays.

Bar: **Vents et Marées,** 48 Rue de Don, tel: 2292-3778. Unique location, boat-like bar at water level on canal, doubles as art gallery, warm atmosphere, good drinks.

Restaurants: **Marissons,** 68 Rue Marissons, tel: 2292-9666. Closed Saturdays for lunch, Sunday evenings and Mondays. Surrounded by water, former boathouse become elegant restaurant with yellow tablecloths and royal blue chairs, fine cuisine, moderately priced. **Saladin,** 6 Rue Chaudronniers, tel: 2292-0515. Specialty: salads, moderately priced. ***Soupe à Cailloux,** 16 Rue Bondes, tel: 2291-9270. Closed Mondays. "In" restaurant, good food and ambiance, many vegetable dishes, moderately priced.

Accommodations: **Postillon,** 16 Place Feurre, tel: 2291-4617, fax: 2291-8657. Comfortable, medium-priced. **Prieuré,** 17 Rue Porion, tel: 2292-2767, fax: 2292-4616. Tastefully decorated rooms, period furniture in hotel and annex, close to cathedral, moderately priced. **Victor Hugo,** 2 Rue de l'Oratoire, tel: 2291-5791. Pleasant, old-fashioned hotel in former bordello, near cathedral, inexpensive.

Some Useful Words and Phrases

apôtre (m)	apostle
cygne (m)	swan
esprit (m)	mind, spirit
flotter	to float
logement (m)	housing
malgré	despite
marbre (m)	marble
marchandise (f)	merchandise
mélanger	to blend
mémoire (f)	memory
tissus (m)	fabric, cloth
tour (m)	tour, excursion, turn
tour (f)	tower

université (f)	university
usine (f)	factory
velours (m)	velvet
vif/vive	live
vivant(e)	lively

En France, un collège n'est pas une université. (In France a college is not a university.)

Un collège est une école secondaire. (A college is a secondary school.)

Jules Verne avait une vive imagination. (Jules Verne had a lively imagination.)

Amiens a été le centre de la manufacture du velours. (Amiens was the center for the manufacture of velvet.)

Elle ne l'est plus. (She (it) is no longer.)

Les usines ont fermé. (The factories have closed.)

Les usines sont fermées. (The factories are closed.)

VIII *Other One-day or Overnight Excursions*

A number of pleasant trips just a short distance from Paris by train or car are described in the chapters about each region.

Reims, Epernay and **Troyes** are wonderful cities to visit in Champagne country, between 60 and 90 minutes from Paris by train. You can visit the cellars and taste the magnificent beverage. See Chapter 14.

Le Mans is also closed to Paris, just 50 minutes, and makes a wonderful outing. See Chapter 18.

CHAPTER 13

Alsace

Hemmed in between the Vosges Mountains to the west and the Rhine to the east, Alsace has been pushed and shoved by peoples and potentates through the centuries.

In the year 58 B.C., Caesar drove the Germans back across the great river and instituted a Pax Romana which lasted five centuries. In the fourth and fifth centuries A.D. invasions from the east recommenced. After Charlemagne's reign, and as part of his legacy, Alsace came under Louis the German's jurisdiction. With the institution of the Holy Roman Empire, the province was totally separated from France between 962 and 1648. The Munster Treaty, at the end of the Thirty Years War, which saw Alsace devastated by both battle and plague, then awarded most of the region to France. In 1871, the German Empire's victory over France signified severance from French sovereignty anew. In 1918 Alsace was brought back into France. When the latter went down in 1940, the Germans retrieved the area only to relinquish it again in 1945.

Alsatians speak a German dialect among themselves. It is one of the rare regional languages to have survived the democratization of the French school system. It is also one of the few regions to maintain local customs and traditions in its daily life.

Back in the third century A.D. Alsatians began making wine. Their dry white gewurztraminers, reislings, tokays and sylvaners have attained international standing. Their beers are staples throughout France. Less known are the extraordinary

fruit brandies made from pears, plums and raspberries. And then there is the famous Alsatian cooking: fish, poultry, and pork specialties, like ham and different types of sausage, with or without sauerkraut. And that odorous and unctuous cheese called Munster and the soft-dough pastries, cakes and flaming tarts can not be forgotten.

In short, Alsace is a feast for the palate and for the eyes, as we shall see.

Strasbourg

A trip to Alsace necessarily begins in Strasbourg, a gem of a city. Its center is entirely surrounded by the River Ill which boasts locks and a river port. Its fabulous cathedral is built of rose-red stone and many of its houses are timbered and stain-glassed. Gutenberg experimented with his historic invention here; Goethe attended the university. The *Marseillaise,* despite the title by which it is known, was written here by Rouget de Lisle. A crossroads since Roman times, Strasbourg has a name derived from *Strateburgum,* meaning city of the roads. Today, seat of the European parliament, it is one of the capitals of Europe.

Notre Dame Cathedral dominates the city of Strasbourg. The facade of this Gothic church, begun in the latter half of the 12th century on the foundations of a Romanesque cathedral almost entirely consumed by fire, was designed by Erwin de Steinbach. Some 265 years later the remarkable tower we see today was completed. The work was financed essentially by contributions in money, in kind and in work.

The Reformation had a tremendous impact on the region and the cathedral was at the center of the struggle between Catholics and Protestants. In the early 16th century it accommodated both for a short while. The Reformists finally won out until the end of the 17th century when, under Louis xiv, the cathedral reverted to Catholicism. The city is now roughly half-Protestant and half-Catholic.

The street in front of the cathedral, Rue Mercière, affords

the best view of the facade and its gracefully wrought six-floor steeple. The **pharmacy** at the corner is the oldest in France. Go there at night to see the square and church illuminated. In the summer there is a sound and light show.

During the French Revolution a large number of statues on the facade were damaged or destroyed; many have been replaced. The statuary of the portals recounts significant moments of religious history; the central portal is especially noteworthy. Inside, the stained glass windows, the organ and the astronomical clock count among the treasures of the cathedral. The clock's best "show" is at 12:30 P.M. The view from the tower is lovely.

If you leave the cathedral from the doorway near the clock, you will be in front of three major museums. The middle one is the **Museum of Notre Dame** which keeps watch over an exceptional collection of Alsatian medieval and Renaissance art. The oldest known figurative stained glass window, the Wissembourg head of Christ, is among the masterpieces. The original plans and drawings for the cathedral, the workshops of some of the craftsmen and many of the originals of their work can be seen.

Another very beautiful building containing several major museums is the **Rohan Palace,** on your right as you leave the Museum of Notre Dame. Although the palace faces the river, the entrance is located in the courtyard on the cathedral side. This was originally the archbishop's residence. Among the most interesting visits are the **apartments,** the **Fine Arts Museum** and the **Museum of Decorative Arts** (for its ceramics and porcelain collection). The third museum close at hand, on the other side of the Museum of Notre Dame, is the **Museum of Modern Art.**

On leaving Place de la Cathédrale, take Rue Rohan (between the Museum of Notre-Dame and the Rohan Palace) and turn right on Rue des Cordeliers. At Place de la Boucherie is the **Historical Museum** which houses a very complete collection of weapons and military uniforms. Also on display are cardboard soldiers, a specialty of Strasbourg.

At the next corner, Rue du Vieux-Marché-aux-Poissons, the **Ancienne Douane,** a former customs house, organizes temporary shows and exhibits. Turn left over the bridge and then left for the **Cour du Corbeau,** a charming 14th-century courtyard. Back at the riverside, past the bridge, is the **Alsatian Museum** of costumes and regional traditions, located in a superb old Alsatian house. The exhibits of the interiors of homes and of a chemist's laboratory are authentic.

Further down **Quai Saint-Nicholas,** Number 18 was once the home of Louis Pasteur. The Protestant church near the bridge was the parsonage of Albert Schweitzer from 1899 to 1913.

Cross back over the river and go left on Quai Saint-Thomas. You will arrive at **Saint Thomas' Church.** Built in the 12th century, it became Lutheran in 1529. It is famous for the painting of the *Mausoleum of Marshall Saxe* by Pigalle.

Continue on Quai Saint-Thomas. At Pont Saint-Martin, turn right and then left on **Rue des Dentelles** which will become **Rue des Bains-aux-Plantes.** This very well-preserved old quarter is called **la Petite France** and was originally inhabited by fishermen, tanners and millers. At the tip of this area, to the left, are **covered bridges** and the remains of the city's former ramparts. There is a good panoramic view from the **Vauban Dam.** Take the bridges to Quai de l'Ill and turn right.

Train from Paris: From Gare de l'Est (East Station) 4 hours.

Tourist Info: 10 Place Gutenberg, 67000 Strasbourg, tel: 8832-5707.
Place de la Gare, 8832-5149.
Pont de l'Europe, tel: 8861-3923.

Cathedral: Sound and light shows, inside the church, from beginning of April to mid-October: 8:15 P.M. in German and 9:15 P.M. in French.

Museum of Notre Dame: 3 Place du Château, 10 A.M. to 12 noon and 2 to 6 P.M. Closed Tuesdays and major public holidays.

Rohan Palace: 2 Place du Château. Same as above.

Museum of Modern Art: 5 Place du Château. Same as above.

Historical Museum: 3 Place de la Grande-Boucherie. Same as above.

Alsatian Museum: 23 Quai Saint-Nicholas. Same as above.

Harbor Visits: Boats leave from 25 Rue de la Nuée-Bleue, tel: 8884-1313, mid-February through December.

Flea market: Place du Vieil-Hôpital (near the Cathedral). Wednesdays and Saturdays.

Restaurants: ***A l'Ancienne Douane,** 6 Rue de la Douane, tel: 8832-42190, fax: 8822-4564. Large beer hall restaurant, typically Alsatian, hearty, family-type food, moderately priced. **Buerehiesel,** 4 Parc de l'Orangerie, tel: 8861-6224, fax: 8861-3200. Closed Tuesday evenings and Wednesdays. Superb pavilion in the middle of a lovely park, one of the finest tables of France, expensive. **Chaumière,** 12 Rue de la Fonderie, tel: 8832-3523. Rustic dining room centered around open fireplace on which kettle of soup or lentils slowly simmer as skewered meat or fish broil, medium-priced. **Maison Kammerzell,** 16 Place de la Cathédrale, tel: 8832-4214, fax: 8823-0392. Delicious dining in quaintest of gingerbread houses around the cathedral, medium-priced. Rooms available, moderately expensive.

Other good restaurants with reasonable prices: **L'Ami Schutz,** 1 Rue des Ponts-Couverts. **Chez Yvonne,** 10 Rue du Sanglier. **D'Choucrouterie,** 20 Rue Saint-Louis. **Au Coin des Pucelles,** 12 Rue des Pucelles. **L'Oignon,** 4 Rue des Moulins. **Au Pont Corbeau,** 21 Quai Saint-Nicholas. **Au Rocher du Sapin,** 6 Rue Noyer. **Saint-Sépulcre,** 15 Rue des Orfèvres.

Accommodations: **Gutenberg,** 31 Rue des Serruriers, tel:

8832-1715, fax: 8875-7667. Old-fashioned hotel, comfortable, moderately priced. **Régent Contades,** 8 Avenue de la
Liberté, tel: 8836-2626, fax: 8837-1370. Spacious rooms on
the river, expensive. **des Rohans,** 17 Rue Maroquin, tel:
8832-8511, fax: 8875-6537. Calm, elegance and comfort
close to the cathedral, medium-priced.

Wine Route

Take the airport road, the D392, out of Strasbourg. At
Entzheim just past the airport, pick up the N422 for **Obernai**
on the D426 offshoot. The first stop on the Wine Route is
this typically Alsatian town, birthplace in the 7th century of
the patron saint of Alsace, Saint Odile. Part Gothic and part
Renaissance, it was one of the ten free cities of Alsace at the
time of the Holy Roman Empire. Kronenbourg, the leading
French beer, is made here.

Leave your car in one of the public parking lots and head
for the center of town, the picture postcard **Place du Marché,**
its Saint Odile fountain and old Alsatian homes. The belfry,
called the **Chapel Tower,** dates from the 13th century. The
building at the other end of the square with its bell-shaped
roof was once the **grain marketplace.** Across the way, the
Six-Pail Fountain is ornamented with biblical inscriptions in
German. Behind the town hall, in the narrow **Rue des Juifs,**
the former Jewish ghetto, look for the old houses with
wooden balconies.

Tourist Info: Belfry Chapel, 67210 Obernai, 8895-6413.

Restaurants: *Agneau d'Or, 99 Rue du Général-Gouraud,
tel: 8895-2822. Closed Mondays and January. Alsatian specialties, inexpensive. **A la Cour d'Alsace,** 3 Rue Gail, tel:
8895-0700, fax: 8895-1921. Closed Sunday evenings. Elegant hotel dining, medium-priced.

Accommodations: **A la Cour d'Alsace** (see above). Former
residence of Baron of Gail, comfortable, fashionable, moderately expensive. **Diligence, Résidence Exquisit et Bel Air,**

23 Place de la Mairie, tel: 8895-5569, fax: 8895-4246. Pleasant group of three hotels with garden, moderately priced.

The D426 out of Obernai will take you to **Ottrott** and **Ottrott-le-Haut,** known for red wine which is relatively rare in Alsace. From here you can drive up to **Saint Odile Mountain** for a magnificent panoramic view of the entire region of hills and plains and river.

Pilgrimages are made here several times a year. According to legend, Odile was born in the 7th century, blind and feeble-minded. Her father, Duke Etichon, ordered her to be put to death but her wet-nurse raised her in secret. Cured of blindness on her baptism, a beautiful Odile was presented to her father on becoming of age. The Duke's reaction was to strangle his son, Odile's accomplice, with his bare hands and arrange for her marriage despite her desire to lead a religious life. She went into hiding until her father conceded to her wishes. The convent founded by Odile stood on this spot Ravaged by flames in the 16th century, it has been rebuilt. The Romanesque chapels alone survived the fire.

Hotel-Restaurants: ***A l'Ami Fritz,** Ottrott-le-Haut, tel: 8895-8081, fax: 8895-8485. Closed Wednesdays. Excellent regional cooking in perfect surroundings, moderately priced. Comfortable hotel a five-minute walk from here. **Hostellerie des Châteaux,** 11 Rue des Châteaux, Ottrott-le-Haut, tel: 8895-8154, fax: 8895-9520. Restaurant closed Sunday nights and Mondays off season. Picturesque old Alsatian house, medium-priced.

Take the D854 for **Barr.** In the stretch descending towards this charming village, there is a turn-off for the **Spesbourg and Haut Andlau Châteaux,** magnificent old ruins both, well worth a promenade on foot. Barr is known for its gewurztraminer wine. The **Folie Marco Museum,** installed in a lovely old house, contains a good collection of china, tapestries, furniture and pewter.

Tourist Info: Place de l'Hôtel-de-Ville, 67140 Barr, tel: 8808-6665.

Wine tasting: **Domaine Klipfel,** 6 Avenue de la Gare, 10 A.M. to 6 P.M. **Fred Schoen & Fils,** Avenue des Vosges, 9 A.M. to 7 P.M.

Folie Marco Museum: 10 A.M. to 12 and 2 to 6 P.M., except Tuesdays from July 1 to October 1; weekends only in June and October.

Just down the hill from Barr is **Mittelbergheim,** a pictur-esque village producing fine white wine since Roman times. Do not hesitate to stop and taste the delicious brews.

Wine tasting: **Armand Gilg & Fils,** 2 Rue de la Montagne, 8 A.M. to 12 noon and 1:30 to 6 P.M.; closed Sunday after-noons. **Albert Seltz,** 21 Rue Principale, 8 A.M. to 6 P.M.; closed weekends.

Hotel-Restaurant: **Hôtel Gilg,** 1 Route de Vin, tel: 8808-9137. Restaurant closed Tuesday evenings and Wednesdays; fine cuisine in warm, traditional setting, old-fashioned rooms, moderately priced.

The D62 will take you to **Andlau,** site of an historic **abbey,** partially restored, and a lovely **Romanesque church.**

Hotel-Restaurant: ***Kastelberg,** 10 Rue du Général-Koe-nig, tel: 8808-9783; fax: 8808-4834. Restaurant open eve-nings only, all day Sundays; typical Alsatian home and food, moderately priced.

From Andlau take the D253 for the views, then left on the D203 and right on the D35 to **Dambach-la-Ville,** another pretty fortified town known for its wines. The **Saint Sebas-tian Chapel,** just above the village, is worthy of a visit for itself and for the panorama.

Wine tasting: From July 1 to September 15 free guided tour Tuesdays and Fridays at 5 P.M.; inquire at Tourist Office, Town Hall.

Hotel-Restaurant: *A la Couronne, 13 Place du Marché, tel: 8892-4085. Restaurant closed Thursdays; comfortable family-type establishment, moderately priced.

The D35 will lead you to **Scherwiller,** known for the quality of its riesling.

Wine tasting: **Domaine Guntz-Palmer,** 27 Rue de Dambach, 9 A.M. to 8 P.M.

Continue on the D35 past Châtenois to **Kintzheim.** The village possesses an interesting **Stork and Recreation Park.** Then take the D159 to the right to **Kintzheim Château.** In the former courtyard of the castle an experimental **zoo for birds of prey** is in operation: see eagles, vultures and condors; organized demonstrations are breathtaking. Two kilometers up the road is **monkey mountain,** another experimental zoo.

Stork and Recreation Park: Route de Sélestat, 10 A.M. to 7 P.M. every day from April 1 to September 8; from September 9 to October 15, Wednesdays, Saturdays and Sundays only.
Flying Eagles: Daily afternoon shows from April 1 to September 30; Wednesdays, Saturdays and Sundays only from October 1 to November 11.
Monkey Mountain: 10 A.M. to 12 noon and 1:30 to 6 P.M. every day from April 1 to October 15; Wednesdays, Saturdays and Sundays only from October 16 to November 11.

Continue up the D159 to the **Haut Koenigsbourg Château.** This tremendous fairy-tale castle, begun in the early part of the 12th century, was destroyed during the Thirty Years War. Its ruins remained until 1901 when the city of Sélestat offered the castle to the German Kaiser, William ii, who had it rebuilt.

Haut Koenigsbourg: 9 A.M. to 6:15 P.M. from June 1 to September 30; lunchtime and earlier evening closings rest of the year.

On leaving here, take the GR5 to the right to **Thannenkirch,** another charming village surrounded by forest.

Hotel-Restaurant: *Auberge La Meunière, 30 Rue Sainte-Anne, tel: 8973-1047, fax: 8973-1231; superb old inn, fine cuisine, moderately priced.

From Thannenkirch the D42 will take you down to the pretty village of **Bergheim** which has a reputation for fine gewurztraminer. Above the village is a German military cemetery.

Wine Tasting: **Robert Berger & Fils,** 20 Rue des Vignerons, 9 A.M. to 8 P.M.

Restaurant: **Wistub du Sommelier,** 51 Grand-Rue, tel: 8973-6999; closed Sundays. Typical 18th century home, well-chosen regional wines and good food, moderately priced.

On the D1B is **Ribeauvillé,** one of the riesling capitals. The yearly fife festival on the first Sunday of September is a lively occasion; wine flows freely from the town square fountain. The little **town hall museum** contains a collection of silver and vermeil drinking vases. The **Butchers' Tower** and the little streets around the town hall are worth a visit.

Above Ribeauvillé are the ruins of three châteaux. The most interesting of them is **Saint-Ulrich,** four kilometers out on the D416. From the top of the belvedere, the region is at your feet.

Tourist Info: 1 Grand'Rue, 68150 Ribeauvillé, 8973-6222.

Wine tasting: **Cave Coopérative,** 2 Rue de Colmar, 9 A.M. to 12 noon and 2 to 5 P.M.; closed from January through

March. **Domaine Jean Sipp,** 60 Rue de la Fraternité, 9 A.M. to 12 noon and 2 to 5:30 P.M.
Distillery (tasting): **Gisselbrecht,** 6 Rue Friedrich, 2 to 6 P.M.

Restaurant: **Wistub Züm Pfifferhüs,** 14 Grand'Rue, tel: 8973-6228, closed Wednesdays and Thursdays. Beautiful historic building, Alsatian specialties, moderately priced.

Hotel-Restaurants: **Clos Saint-Vincent,** Route de Bergheim, tel: 8973-6765, fax: 8973-3220; restaurant closed Tuesdays and Wednesdays. Comfortable, tastefully decorated rooms, magnificent view over the vineyards, good food, expensive. **Vosges,** 2 Grand'Rue, tel: 8973-6139, fax: 8973-3421; comfortable, fine cuisine, medium-priced.

The gentle village of **Hunawihr** on the D1B just out of Ribeauvillé lies below an interesting 14th-century **church** serving both Catholics and Protestants in the same building. A **stork center** aimed at sublimating storks' migratory instincts in order to retain them in Alsace is located at the entrance to the village.

Stork Center: Mornings and afternoons from April through September; Wednesdays, Saturdays and Sundays only from October 1 to November 11. Afternoon programs on wading birds.

The D1b and the D3 will take you to one of the most beautiful villages of France: **Riquewihr** as it was in the 16th century. Leave your car at the entrance to the village and proceed on foot under the town hall and down Rue du Général-de-Gaulle. The château to your left is now a **Post and Telecommunications Museum.** The decorative **Dolder** at the top of the street was one of the town's entrance gates; it has been turned into a **museum of local history.**

Behind the Dolder to the right is the old **Jewish ghetto.** A narrow staircase leads to the **Thieves Tower,** former prison. From here wander down the streets from one side of town to the other to see beautiful old homes, courtyards, fountains, and wonderful bits of sculpture and decoration.

Tourist Info: 2 Rue de la Première-Armée, 68340 Riquewihr, tel: 8947-8080.

Post and Telecommunications Museum: 10 A.M. to 12 and 2 to 6 P.M. from end of March to November 11; closed Tuesdays except in July and August.

Dolder Museum: 9:15 A.M. to 12 and 1:30 to 6:15 P.M. from July 8 to September 7; Saturdays and Sundays only from September 7 to November 1.

Thieves Tower: 9:15 A.M. to 12 and 1:30 to 6:15 P.M. from Good Friday to November 11.

Restaurants: *Arbalétrier, 12 Rue du Général-de-Gaulle, tel: 8949-0121; closed Tuesday evenings and Wednesdays. Good Alsatian cooking, moderately priced. **Auberge du Schoenenbourg,** 2 Rue Piscine, tel: 8947-9228. Lovely view, excellent cuisine, fine wines, medium-priced.

Hotel-Restaurants: **Sarment d'Or,** 4 Rue Cerf, tel: 8947-9285, fax: 8947-9923; restaurant closed Sunday evenings and Mondays. Beautiful 17th-century residence along the ramparts, comfortable, typical Alsatian cooking, moderately priced. ***Au Riesling,** 3 Route du Vin, *Zellenberg,* 1 kilometer on the D1B, tel: 8947-8585, fax: 8947-9208; closed Mondays for lunch and, from November through April, Sunday evenings and Mondays. Comfortable establishment in the vineyards, fine wines and food, moderately priced.

Take the D3 out of Riquewihr. At the junction with the D1b is **Beblenheim** which has the reputation of producing some of the finest wines in Alsace: pinot gris, tokay, muscat and gewurztraminer.

Wine tasting: **Au Château,** 14 Rue de Hoen. 8 A.M. to 12 noon and 2 to 6 P.M.; closed weekends from January 1 to March 15. **Maison Bott-Geyl,** 1 Rue du Petit-Château, 8 A.M. to 7 P.M.

The next town down the road, **Mittelwihr,** is noted for its gewurztraminer and reisling wines.

Wine tasting: **François Edel & Fils,** Domaine du Bouxhof. 9 A.M. to 8 P.M. **E. Schaller & Fils,** 1 Rue du Château. 8 A.M. to 7 P.M.

Distillery (tasting): **Théo Preiss,** 8 Rue du Château. 8 A.M. to 5 P.M.; closed weekends.

After Mittelwihr and Bennwihr, stay on the D1B for **Sigolsheim.** The **church** dates from the year 1200. Take Rue de la Première-Armée for two kilometers to the **allied military cemetery** of French, African and American soldiers killed in the Second World War.

Just beyond on the D1B is **Kientzheim,** seat of the Saint-Etienne Brotherhood whose task is the quality control of Alsatian wines. The locality is also interesting for its **Museum of Alsatian Vineyards and Wines.** In the **church** see the tombstones; one is of Schwendi, who is presumed to have been the importer of the first tokay vines from Hungary.

Museum of Alsatian Vineyards: Château: 10 A.M. to 12 and 2 to 6 P.M., from June through October.

Wine tasting: **André Blanck et Fils,** Ancienne Cour des Chevaliers-de-Malte.

Hotel-Restaurants: **Hostellerie de l'Abbaye d'Alspach,** tel: 8947-1600. Dinner only; restaurant closed Wednesdays and Thursdays. Attractive hotel in 13th century convent, comfortable, moderately priced. *****Schwendi,** tel: 8947-3050, fax: 8949-0449. Restaurant closed all-day Tuesdays and Wednesdays for lunch. Quiet, comfortable hotel, moderately priced.

The D28 takes you right into **Kaysersberg,** a particularly pleasant medieval village known for fine tokay wines. Like the other towns of Alsace in the Middle Ages, Kaysersberg was bought and sold by various feudal lords who embellished its château and fortified its ramparts against the cupidity of others. In the 13th century ten such towns, including Kaysersberg, proclaimed their freedom and joined an alliance of "free cities" called the Décapole.

It was here in the 16th century that Lazare de Schwendi brought his Hungarian vines to be planted. Kaysersberg was the birthplace of Albert Schweitzer in 1875; the humanist's home is now a **cultural center** open to visitors. You can leave your car in the parking lot across the street from the center, and walk down Rue du Général-de-Gaulle and cross the impressive **fortified bridge.** You will come to the **Museum of Local History** with its mixture of objects discovered in the township over the years. The **church** possesses a remarkable gilt wooden retable from the 16th century. To the left of the church is a **cemetery** of those fallen in the defense of the town over the centuries.

Back on the main street is the **town hall,** a magnificent Renaissance structure. **Rue de l'Eglise** to the right is lined with wonderful old Alsatian homes. For other treasures take the first right and continue around the little block.

Tourist Info: 37 Rue du Général-de-Gaulle, 68240 Kaysersberg, 8978-2278.

Cultural Center: 9 A.M. to 12 noon and 2 to 6 P.M. during Easter holidays and every day from May 2 to October 31.

Museum of Local History: 10 A.M. to 12 noon and 2 to 6 P.M. during Easter holidays and every day from July 1 to August 31; weekends only in May, June, September and October.

Wine tasting: **Victor Ancel,** 3 Rue du Collège, 8 A.M. to 7 P.M.

Hotel-Restaurants: **Arbre Vert,** tel: 8947-1151; restaurant closed Mondays. Pleasant hotel, Alsatian cooking, moderately priced. **Chambard,** 9-11 Rue du Général-de-Gaulle, tel: 8947-1017, fax: 8947-3503; restaurant closed Mondays and for lunch on Tuesdays. Lovely hotel, beautifully decorated, fine food, moderately expensive.

Take the N415 out of Kaysersberg. At Ingersheim turn right on the D11 for **Niedermorschwihr.** The old houses on the main street warrant a stop.

Restaurant: ***Caveau Morakopf,** 7 Rue Trois-Epis, tel: 8927-0510; closed Sundays. Typical Alsatian fare and excellent house wines, moderately priced.

The D10vii will lead you rapidly into **Turkheim** through the Brand Gateway. Brand is also the name of a wonderful local wine. Along the **Grand'Rue** are a number of fine 16th- and 17th-century homes. Note as especially pretty the **Place Turenne** and the **Hôtel des Deux-Clefs.** A planned walk through the vineyards on the outskirts of town is well laid out with signposts and explanations.

Vineyards Walk: Begins on the D10vii just before the Brand Gateway into town.
Wine tasting: **Marcel Hurst,** 21 Rue du Conseil, 8 A.M. to 12 noon and 2 to 8 P.M. from May through September; 9 A.M. to 12 and 2 to 6 P.M. other months.

Accommodations: **Berceau du Vigneron,** Place Turenne, tel: 8927-2355. Classic Alsatian hotel, moderately priced.

Colmar

From Turkheim, the D417 brings you into Colmar, another of the ten "free cities" of Alsace in the 14th century. In 1648 it became part of France. In the 19th century the textile industry developed and contributed to the city's prosperity. Today the wine trade and tourism are its principal activities. The charming town center, very much intact, and the river district have been renovated.

Any tour of Colmar begins with a "must": the beautiful **Unterlinden Museum** located in a 13th century Dominican convent known of old for its rigid rules and austerity. The visit begins with the red sandstone cloister through which is the entrance to the exhibit rooms. The masterpieces of Rhenish religious art are numerous: the Stauffenberg retable, Gaspard Isenmann's retable from Saint Martin's Collegiate Church, *Melancholy* by Cranach l'Ancien, as well as a 15th-century still life considered to be the first of its kind. In the chapel is the most renowned of the many gems of medieval art this museum possesses: the Issenheim retable by Matthias Grünewald. The twenty-four panels of the Passion by the Schongauer studio are also remarkable.

The second floor exhibits are varied: sculpture, paintings, furniture, porcelain, and toys of different periods. On the lower ground floor some modern art and in the former cellar of the convent some archaeological finds from the Gallo-Roman period have been collected.

From Place Unterlinden, take Rue des Têtes to the right past the **Heads House** at Number 19 and turn left on Rue des Boulangers. The **Dominicans Church**—sedate Gothic architecture from the 13th and 14th centuries—contains some superb stained glass windows and a magnificent Schongauer, *Virgin at the Rosebush*.

Rue des Serruriers to the left will direct you to **Saint Martin's Collegiate Church,** also known as the Cathedral, with its varnished tile roof. Only one of its towers was ever completed and that one carries the inscription *Memento Mori* (think about death!) on its sundial.

From the loggia of the **Old Guardhouse** on Place de la Cathédrale, the city's magistrates were sworn in and sentences were pronounced back in the 16th and 17th centuries. Through the arcades is the **Bartholdi Museum,** birthplace of the sculptor of the Statue of Liberty. On the second floor one can follow the progress of that world famous monument from start to finish.

To the right of the museum are several fine old homes, the most exquisite of them being the **Pfister House** across the street. Continue along Rue des Marchands to Place de l'Ancienne-Douane. The meetings of the *Décapole,* the representatives of the ten "free cities" of Alsace, took place on the second floor of the former **customs house.** The ground floor served as warehouse for storing merchandise on which duty was due.

From here take Rue des Tanneurs, cross the river and turn right. The walk along Quai de la Poissonnerie is picturesque. To the left on Rue de Turenne is the **Museum of Natural History.** Turn back over the river at Pont Saint-Pierre, the third bridge. Right again at Rue du Manège which, after the **Roesselmann Fountain** by Bartholdi, becomes Rue Saint-Jean. This pleasant walk will take you back to the customs house. Continue on the Grand'Rue, past the **Pilgrim's House** and the lovely **Arcade House.** You will arrive at **Saint Mathew's,** originally Franciscan, now a Protestant church. At Place Jeanne-d'Arc turn left in Rue des Clefs which will take you back to Unterlinden.

Tourist Info: 4 Rue Unterlinden, 68000 Colmar, tel: 8941-1229.

Unterlinden Museum: 1 Rue des Unterlinden. 9 A.M. to 12 noon and 2 to 6 P.M. April through October; until 5 P.M. and closed on Tuesdays November through March.
Dominicans Church: Place des Dominicains, 10 A.M. to 6 P.M. from mid-March to mid-November.
Saint Martin's: Place de la Cathédrale, 8 A.M. to 6:30 P.M.; music hour Tuesdays in season at 8:30 P.M.
Bartholdi Museum: 30 Rue des Marchands, 9 A.M. to 12 noon and 2 to 6 P.M. every day from April through October; Saturdays and Sundays only the rest of the year.
Museum of Natural History: 11 Rue de Turenne, 2 to 5

P.M., except Mondays, from April to September; Wednesdays, Saturdays and Sundays only the rest of the year.

Saint Mathew's: Grand'Rue, 10 A.M. to 12 noon and 3 to 5 P.M. from June 15 to October 15 and Easter holidays.

Wine tasting: **Martin Jund,** 12 Rue de l'Ange; closed Sundays. **Domaine Viticole de Colmar,** 2 Rue du Stauffen, 8 A.M. to 12 noon and 2 to 6 P.M.; closed weekends.

Distillery (tasting): **Wolfberger,** Chemin de la Fecht.

Restaurants: ***Caveau Saint Jean,** 47 Grand'Rue, tel: 8941-6802; closed Tuesdays. Heartwarming tavern for grilled meat and Alsatian tarts, inexpensive. **Da Alberto,** 24 Rue des Marchands, tel: 8923-3789; closed Saturdays for lunch and Sundays. Excellent Italian cuisine in pleasant garden setting, moderately expensive. ***Flambée,** 1 Rue des Ecoles, tel: 8924-0812. Alsatian tarts and local wines, inexpensive. **Schillinger,** 16 Rue Stanislas, tel: 8941-4317, fax: 8924-2887; closed Sunday evenings and Mondays. Colmar's most elegant restaurant, fine cuisine, expensive. **S'Parisser Stewwele,** 4 Place Jeanne-d'Arc, tel: 8941-4233; dinner only, closed Tuesdays. Alsatian fare with atmosphere, moderately priced.

Accommodations: **Hostellerie le Maréchal,** 4 Place des Six-Montagnes-Noires, tel: 8941-6032, fax: 8924-5940. Charming residence and restaurant on the river, moderately expensive. ***Rapp,** 1 Rue Weinemer, tel: 8941-6210, fax: 8924-1358. Quiet location, restaurant at 16 Rue Berthe-Molly, moderately priced. **Saint Martin,** 38 Grand'Rue, tel: 8924-1151, fax: 8923-4778. Comfortable hotel in old Colmar, medium-priced.

Some Useful Words and Phrases

archbishop	**archevêque** (m)
bishop	**évêque** (m)
brandy	**cognac** (m)
Caesar	**César**

clock	**horloge** (f)
craftsman	**artisan** (m)
to damage	**endommager**
fish	**poisson** (m)
fruit brandy	**alcool blanc** (m)
German	**allemand(e)**
Germany	**Allemagne** (f)
ham	**jambon** (m)
language	**langue** (f)
locks	**écluse** (f)
masterpiece	**chef-d'oeuvre** (m)
mountain	**montagne** (f)
pear	**poire** (f)
poultry	**volaille** (f)
plum	**prune** (f)
raspberry	**framboise** (f)
Rhine	**Rhin** (m)
sausage	**saucisse** (f)
steeple	**flèche** (f)
treaty	**traité** (m)

Qu'est-ce qu'ils vous ont servi? (What did they serve you?)

Ils nous ont offert des alcools blancs. (They offered us some fruit brandies.)

Il m'a demandé si je les aime. (He asked me whether I like them.)

Je lui ai dit que je ne les ai jamais goûtés. (I told him that I have never tasted them.)

Les saucisses sont faites maison. (The sausages are homemade.)

Le vin blanc alsacien est très fruité. (Alsatian white wine is very fruity.)

Il n'est pas aussi sec que le vin blanc de Touraine. (It isn't as dry as the white wine from Touraine.)

As you will see from the above sentences, personal pronoun direct and indirect objects of verbs are placed in front of the verb, not after, as in English.

Direct object	Indirect object
me	me
te	te
le/la	lui
nous	nous
vous	vous
les	leur

NOTE that the only difference between direct and indirect objects is the third person singular and plural.

To make comparisons in French, use **aussi . . . que** which is the equivalent of **as . . . as** in English. Example: **Je suis aussi grand que lui.** (I am as tall as he.)

CHAPTER 14

Burgundy

Traces of man have been found in Burgundy dating from nearly one million years ago. Remains of industry which can be dated to 500,000 B.C. have been uncovered in the region's alluvial valleys. Near Aze are caves which were more or less continually inhabited from well over 100,000 years ago until the Middle Ages. The first agricultural villages, whose dwellers were Mediterraneans, appeared in the early part of the third millennium.

More recently Burgundy has been Gallic, Roman, Burgundian, Frank. The Gauls were colonized by the Romans in 52 B.C. following Caesar's victory over Vercingetorix at Alesia. By the end of the 4th century A.D., Christianity had spread throughout the area and Rome's hold had been broken by Barbarians from eastern Europe. Of the latter, the Burgundians, from the region around the Baltic, remained, settled and finally gave their name to the land.

In the 6th century the Franks, also from the east, invaded the territory. Their hold was firm; Burgundy did not become a province of France until 1477. In the meantime, it was a powerful dukedom which included Alsace, Luxemburg, Champagne, Picardy, Flanders and Holland. The grand dukes of Burgundy who reigned from 1364 to 1477 were the most powerful personalities of Europe. Spite and rivalry made them the enemies of the rulers of France and they allied themselves with the English against the French during the Hundred Years

War. It was one of theirs, Philip the Good, who delivered Joan of Arc to the British in 1430 for a "goodly" sum.

Burgundy was also the seat of a devastating religious empire, that of Cluny. Answerable only to Rome, which distance kept at bay, Cluny's Benedictine abbots exercised tremendous power over the years; by the 12th century they controlled vast domains and numerous abbeys throughout Europe and, more important, intellectual pursuit and the learning process. The wealth of Cluny was considerable: lands, grains and gold, derived from gifts, taxation, purchase and annexation.

In 1112 and thereafter, a young Burgundian by the name of Bernard, dedicated to the rules of piety, chastity and simplicity, countered Cluny with the foundation of the Cistercian abbeys. Banning taxation of the poor peasant populations, the acceptance of gifts or purchase of lands, Saint Bernard created an order based on work, devotion and charity.

The Burgundy of today has many claims to renown: its beautiful villages and rolling countryside and the vestiges of its prestigious past. To which should be added, its rich-flavored wines, pungent mustards, and well-fed snails, only a few of its gastronomic wonders.

Dijon

It is natural that our trip begin with Dijon for it is yesterday's capital, enhanced and enriched by the dukes of Burgundy, and today's regional hub for trade, tourism, administration and university studies.

There were four famous dukes of Burgundy: Philip the Bold, John the Fearless, Philip the Good and Charles the Bold. The second of them, John the Fearless, a man as Machiavellian as he was unseemly, had his cousin the Duke of Orleans assassinated in Paris in 1407. Civil war resulted. Choosing alignment with the British at first, and an arrangement with the King of France secondly, he met his death while attempting to negotiate with the latter. His son, Philip the Good, as handsome as he was single-minded, took up the cudgel against the French monarchs. He entered into profitable alliance with the British and by the second half of the 15th century had become the most powerful ruler in Europe. His territory encompassed a great portion of France, Flanders, Belgium and Luxemburg. His wealth was fabulous; he endowed the great artists of the time, built tribunals, hospices and palaces.

With the end of the Hundred Years War, Louis xi of France had a freer hand to address himself to the problems at his doorstep. Charles the Bold, who reigned in Burgundy upon Philip's death, had continued his encroachment on French territory. In battle over the city of Nancy, Charles met his death. Burgundy was incorporated into France and Dijon lost its role as an independent capital.

Tour

From the railway station, take Avenue du Maréchal Foch past Darcy Square. Continue on Rue de la Liberté and you will arrive at an elegant square—Place de la Libération—which borders on the **Palace of the Dukes of Burgundy.** It was designed by Jules Hardouin-Mansart at the end of the 17th century. Within the Ducal Palace is City Hall on the left and the **Beaux Arts Museum** to the right. Before visiting that especially interesting museum you might want to survey the Honor Court directly in front of you and the Bar Court to the right. Leave Bar Court through the passage on the right and take the first left for the entrance to the museum.

First go through the temporary exhibition area to the old palace kitchen and imagine the preparation of royal feasts on the six giant hearths. The museum visit begins with religious art on the ground floor. On the second floor in the Statues Room: see Carpeaux's ballerina and François Rude's *Departure of the Volunteers.* The staircase to the upper room, lined with French paintings of the 18th and 19th centuries, will lead you to the Dutch painters and a particularly pleasing Brueghel of Mariemont Château.

The museum's most famous pieces are found in the Guard Room. The recumbent statues are spectacular: Philip the Bold in the hands of angels and surrounded by mourners; John the Fearless and Marguerite of Bavaria, lions at their feet in testimony of their strength and courage. Among other works, the tapistry of Charlemagne visiting a construction site is certainly noteworthy. Works of 16th- and 17th-century Italian painters is also well represented on this floor, some lovely canvases by Veronese, Gennari, Strozzi and Titian.

On the third floor are the Granville and Robin donations. After the interesting sculpted birds and animals, you will come to drawings and studies by Géricault, Delacroix and Millet, as well as some small paintings by Bonington from his Italian trip. It is here that you will discover Henri-Edmond Cross's watercolors and see a lovely haystack by Vuillard.

Leave the museum on the left, then turn left again in Rue Longepierre. Go right on Rue de la Verrerie and left on Rue de la Couette. On the right is the **Hôtel de Vogüé,** 17th-century Renaissance, now completely redone and occupied by the architectural services of Dijon. Continue around to the front of **Notre Dame Church.** Its tympanum statues seem to have been whittled away by the elements and time. Inside, you will see some fine stained glass from the 13th century as well as a magnificent 11th-century black virgin sculpted in wood and cloaked in a white jellaba and veil.

Go left on leaving the church and turn right into **Rue des Forges.** Note, in particular, Number 34, with its Gothic courtyard, and 38. The facade of Number 40, dating from the 13th century, is particularly decorative. It was originally the property of a Dijon banker.

Turn left into Rue Liegeard. At Rue de la Liberté go left back to Place de la Libération, which by the way was called Place Royale before the French Revolution. Across the square take Rue des Bons Enfants to the **Magnin Museum.** This superb 17th-century manor house contains some good pieces of furniture, faience and tapestries. There are little known works by some well-known artists and some good pieces by unfamiliar names.

Leave to the right and go right into Rue Philippe-Pot. You will arrive at the **Justice Palace** or courts. If the door to the Penal Court is open, take a glance at the lovely hall (with its plastic chairs). Past the courts go left into Rue Liegeard and right into **Rue Amiral-Roussin.** At Number 23 is a charming manor house. There is another beyond it, at the corner of Rue Vauban. Across the street is a wonderful timbered house. At the end of Rue Piron, slightly to the right, is Rue Michelet which brings you to **Saint Philibert's Church.** The building is in poor condition and cannot be visited, but the plain Romanesque facade and porch are well worth notice.

Beyond here is a **cathedral,** more interesting for its crypt and especially the rotunda around the crypt, than for the church itself. The architecture of the rotunda was inspired by that of the 4th-century tomb of Christ in Jerusalem. The capitals are rare examples of pre-Romanesque art, the designs being purely geometric, except for one. The human figure first appeared in Romanesque church sculpture around the year 1000.

Just behind the cathedral is a wonderful **Archaeological Museum** situated in what remains of an 11th-century Benedictine abbey. In a beautiful room in the cellar are interesting steles and bronzes from the Gallo-Roman period. In the old monk's dormitory on the ground floor there is medieval sculpture, and on the upper floor early furniture, as well as pottery, some attractive pieces of jewelry, including a heavy gold bracelet dating from the 9th century B.C., and numerous pieces from the bronze age.

Take Rue Mariotte in front of the cathedral to the railway underpass. Go through and cross over to the **Museum of Natural History,** totally reconstructed and opened once again to the public in June 1992. Didactic, attractive, amusing—this place is a delight for both adults and children. Did you know that pigeons contribute to the degradation of buildings and spread disease? Why do some animals have eyes in the front and others on the side of their heads? Why have some become aerian? Did you know that a glutton is an animal? Have you ever seen a calao rhinoceros? (a bird with an amazing beak)

The exhibits are artistically presented, complete with sound effects and explanations. The coleopterans and butterflies, scarabs, beetles, etc., literally run off their boards. Outside the museum are **botanical gardens,** a **vivarium** and a **dinosaur exhibit.**

Train from Paris: From Gare de Lyon, 2 hours (TGV).
Tourist Info: Place Darcy, 21000 Dijon, tel: 8043-4212.
    34 Rue des Forges, tel: 8030-3539.
    4 Rue Montmartre, tel: 8041-6135.

Beaux-Arts Museum: Place de la Sainte-Chapelle. 10 A.M. to 6 P.M.; closed Tuesdays and from 12:30 to 2 P.M. Sundays.
Magnin Museum: 4 Rue des Bons-Enfants, 9 A.M. to 12 P.M. and 2 to 6 P.M.
Archaeological Museum: 5 Rue de Docteur-Maret, 9:30 A.M. to 6 P.M. from June 1 to August 31; 9 A.M. to 12 P.M. and 2 to 6 P.M. rest of year; closed Tuesdays.
Museum of Natural History: 1 Avenue Albert-Ier, 9 A.M. to 12 P.M. and 2 to 6 P.M.; closed Tuesdays.

Restaurants: **Jean-Pierre Billoux,** 14 Place Darcy, tel: 8030-1100, fax: 8049-9489; closed Sunday evenings, Mondays and first half of August. Savory cuisine from Dijon's top chef, moderately expensive. ***Chandelier,** 65 Rue Jeannin, tel: 8066-1582. Pleasant tavern food, inexpensive. **Thibert,** 10 Place Wilson, tel: 8067-7464; closed Mondays for lunch, Sundays and August. Excellent and inventive, medium-priced. ***Petite Flamande,** 9 Rue des Bons-Enfants, tel: 8067-1656. Interesting menus, moderately priced.

Accommodations: **Cloche,** 14 Place Darcy, tel: 8030-1232, fax: 8030-0415. Handome, palatial hotel, moderately expensive. **Jacquemart,** 32 Rue Verrerie, tel: 8073-3974, fax: 8073-2099. Well situated, comfortable, pleasant, moderately priced. **Palais,** 23 Rue du Palais, tel: 8067-1626. Located in quiet, old Dijon, newly renovated, moderately priced.

Wine Route

Leave Dijon on the D122, the wine route. All along this road are wonderful villages to visit and wines to taste. In **Chenôve,** at the Cuverie des Ducs de Bourgogne, are magnificent grape presses from the 13th century. The burnished steeple of the **Fixin** church can be seen from afar. Here you can visit a museum of souvenirs of Napoleon's campaigns created by a certain Noisot, captain of the emperor's Imperial Guard, on his own estate. You will pass **Gevrey-Chambertin,** where Napoleon's favorite wine was produced.

The château at **Vougeot** produces one of the most famous wines of the region. The Clos de Vougeot is now the property of a brotherhood of winetasters whose self-proclaimed task is to make Burgundy wines known around the world. **Chambolle-Musigny** is also a charming village.

At **Nuits-Saint-Georges,** the vineyard has been in existence since the year 1000. Louis XIV was particularly fond of this vintage. Charlemagne owned vineyards in **Aloxe-Corton.**

Fixin
Wine tasting: **Clos Saint-Louis,** Rue Abbé-Chevalier, tel: 8052-4551; 10 A.M. to 7 P.M.; closed November 1 to March 31.
Hotel-Restaurant: ***Chez Jeannette,** 7 Rue Noisot, tel: 8052-4549. Pleasant, inexpensive.

Gevrey-Chambertin
Wine tasting: **Geoffroy Lucien et Fils,** 1 Place des Lois, tel: 8034-1065, 9 A.M. to 12 P.M. and 2 to 6 P.M. Monday to Friday. **Mortet et Fils,** 22 Rue de l'Eglise, tel: 8034-1005, 9 A.M. to 12:30 P.M. and 2 to 6 P.M.; closed Sunday afternoons.
Restaurant: **Rôtisserie du Chambertin,** Rue Chambertin,

tel: 8034-3320, fax: 8034-1230; closed Sunday evenings, Mondays and February. Upgraded regional cuisine, moderately expensive.

Accommodations: **Grands Crus,** Route des Grands-Crus, tel: 8034-3415, fax: 8051-8907. Renovated homestead in the middle of the famous vineyards, quiet, medium-priced.

Vougeot

Wine tasting: **Château de la Tour,** Clos de Vougeot, tel: 8062-8613, 10 A.M. to 7 P.M. except Tuesdays.

Hotel-Restaurant: **Château de Gilly,** Gilly-lès-Citeaux, tel: 8062-8998, fax: 8062-8234, closed February. Remarkable buildings and surroundings of former Cistercian abbey, moderately expensive to expensive.

Chambolle-Musigny

Wine tasting: **Domaine Henri Felettig,** tel: 8062-8509, 2 to 7 P.M. Monday through Saturday, plus Saturday and Sunday mornings.

Nuits-Saint-Georges

Wine tasting: **Philippe Gavignet,** 36 Rue Docteur-Louis-Legrand, tel: 8061-0941, 8 A.M. to 12 P.M. and 2 to 6 P.M. Monday through Saturday. **Henri et Gilles Remoriquet,** 25 Rue des Charmois, tel: 8061-0817, 10 A.M. to 12 P.M. and 2 to 7 P.M.

Hotel-Restaurants: **Côte d'Or,** 37 Rue Thurot, tel: 8061-0610, fax: 8061-3624; closed Wednesdays, Thursdays for lunch and February. Comfortable rooms, excellent wines and young chef, medium-priced. **Gentihommière,** 13 Vallée-Serrée, tel: 8061-1206, fax: 8061-3033, closed Mondays and for lunch on Tuesdays. Country setting for modern rooms and interesting cuisine, medium-priced.

Aloxe-Corton

Wine tasting: **Pierre André,** Château de Corton-André, tel: 8026-4425, 10 A.M. to 6 P.M.

Accommodations: **Clarion,** tel: 8026-4670, fax: 8026-4716.

Charming 17th-century manor house overlooking vineyards, moderately expensive.

Beaune

You will immediately perceive that this small city is not to be bypassed. It contains illustrious monuments. Drive straight through the town to the **Hôtel-Dieu.** Founded in 1443 during Philip the Good's reign, the hospice was designed to assist the poor of a region who had suffered tremendous hardship during the Hundred Years War. The style is Flemish Burgundian; it is greater and grander than the Valenciennes Hospital it was modeled after. One of the rare medieval civilian structures to have survived intact until now, it was a working hospital until 1971. It still serves as a home for the elderly.

From the lovely square the first thing to attract the eye are the tile roofs. Another great vista is possible from the Honor Court. Within the hospice, in the Great Hall or Hall of the Needy with its wood-paneled keep vaults, you count 31 beds in a line-up, like old pullman cars (without an upper tier). During busy periods, patients were put two to a bed.

Saint Hugues' Hall was vacated by its patients just twenty years ago. From the glass tiles in the floor of Saint Nicholas' Hall you can see the waters of the river over which the hospital was built in order to facilitate the evacuation of waste and used waters. Wonderful copper and brass utensils decorate the old kitchen area. The gears and pulleys of the spit were designed by a clockmaker. Through the pharmacy is Saint Louis' Hall lined with tapestries from Aubusson and Brussels, including the Story of Jacob.

A Flemish tapistry of the Last Judgment by Roger Van de Weyden is displayed in the Polyptic Hall; it hung originally in the Great Hall of the Needy. Through a magnifying glass one can see clearly the details of the weaving. Also magnificent is a tapestry in tones of blue, gray and pink called One Thousand Flowers.

On leaving the hospice and the market place, take Avenue

de la République. You will come into view of the **Notre Dame Collegiate Church.** Although it brings together a number of styles spanning several centuries, it remains basically 12th-century Romanesque. The portico is beautifully proportioned. The carved wooden doors with their gothic motifs are delicate. On the inside, light streams in gently through gray and gold 19th-century stained glass and reflects on the rose and ochre stone floor slabs.

The **Museum of Burgundy Wines** is located in a former residence of the dukes of Burgundy. In addition to numerous artifacts concerning wine, the museum recounts the history of the region's vineyards. A sizable collection of presses and vats can be seen in an adjoining hall.

Before continuing your journey, drive around the outside wall of the city for a look at the old **ramparts.**

Tourist Info: Place de la Halle, 21200 Beaune, tel: 8022-2451.

Hôtel-Dieu: 9 A.M. to 6:30 P.M. from May 1 to September 30; 9 to 11:30 A.M. and 2 to 5:30 P.M. from October 1 to April 30.

Museum of Burgundy Wines: 9 A.M. to 12:30 P.M. and 2 to 5:45 P.M.

Restaurants: ***Ciboulette,** 69 Rue Lorraine, tel: 8024-7072; closed Mondays for dinner and Tuesdays. Neighborhood restaurant, inexpensive. **Jardin des Remparts,** 10 Rue Hôtel-Dieu, tel: 8024-7941; closed Sunday evenings, Mondays and January. Wonderful setting for leading, new chef, medium-priced.

Accommodations: **Cep,** 27–29 Rue Maufoux, tel: 8022-3548, fax: 8022-7680. Deluxe hotel, period furniture, moderately expensive. **Le Home,** 138 Route de Dijon, tel: 8022-1643. Charming hotel and garden, well-decorated rooms, medium-priced.

Hotel-Restaurant: **Central,** 2 Rue Victor-Millot, tel: 8024-

7724, fax: 8022-3040. Convenient, comfortable, appetizing, medium-priced.

Autun

Out of Beaune take the D74, which will lead you into the D973. You will skirt vineyards of famous vintages: **Pommard,** then **Volney,** which produces fine red wine appreciated, we are told, by Louis XI. **Nolay** is also an interesting town with a lovely old market hall built in the 14th century from chestnut wood.

In Autun go straight up to **Saint Lazarus' Cathedral.** It is most famous for its tympanum created between 1130 and 1135 by one Gislebertus who left his name just under Christ's feet. *The Last Judgment* is rendered with infinite expressiveness; its elongated figures are both humble and simple, and assure us they are caring. The capitals in the Capitular Room are also moving in their naïveté.

The grand dimensions of the cathedral seem astonishing today for this small, sleepy town. Autun was founded by the Roman emperor Augustus and was a prosperous relay on the road from Lyon to Boulogne. In the third century numerous invasions reduced Augustus' city to ruins. Those of a theater exist on the hillside at the entrance to the town. In the 12th century, the bishops of Autun, anxious to rival Vézelay, set about the construction of the impressive cathedral. In the 14th century, Autun had become a prestigious religious center.

Go left on leaving the cathedral. You will arrive at the **studio of potter** Gaby du Jeu. Her flower-holders are very clever. As you turn back to the cathedral, you will get a good view of the gold, blue and green varnished tiles of its roof. The effect is decidedly modern.

On the left side of the cathedral is **Le Lutrin** which sells antiques and old tools at reasonable prices.

The entrance to the **Rolin Museum** is just below the shop and to the right. In addition to Gallo-Roman vestiges, you will find some wonderful Romanesque statuary as well as French and Flemish primitive paintings.

Pommard

Wine tasting: **Domaines de Pommard,** Place de l'Europe, tel: 8024-1720, 10 A.M. to 12:30 P.M. and 2:30 to 7 P.M. **André Mussy,** Rue Dauphin, tel: 8022-0556, 9 A.M. to 8 P.M.

Volnay

Wine tasting: **Henri Delagrange et Fils,** Rue de la Cure, tel: 8021-6188. 10 A.M. to 12 P.M. and 3 to 7 P.M. closed Sunday afternoons. **Christophe Vaudoisey,** tel: 8021-2014, 10 A.M. to 7 P.M.

Restaurant: ***Auberge des Vognes,** tel: 8022-2448; closed Mondays. Good price-fixed menus, moderately priced.

Autun

Tourist Info: 3 Avenue Charles-de-Gaulle, 71400 Autun, tel: 8552-2034.

Rolin Museum: 9:30 A.M. to 12 P.M. and 2 to 6:30 P.M., from March 16 to September 30; 4 P.M. closing rest of year.

Restaurant: **Chalet Bleu,** 3 Rue Jeannin, tel: 8586-2730; closed Mondays for dinner, Tuesdays and February. Simple, regional fare, moderately priced.

Hotel-Restaurants: **Ursulines,** 14 Rue Rivault, tel: 8552-6800, fax: 8586-2307. Wonderful view of valley, attractive rooms in former convent, interesting cuisine, medium-priced. **Hostellerie du Vieux Moulin,** Porte d'Arroux, tel: 8552-1090, fax: 8586-3215. Old mill on the river surrounded by garden, comfortable, moderately priced.

Tournus

Leave Autun on the N80 which climbs to the mountain tops and forests of Planoise, then dips to pastureland and cattle. After Montchanin and Saint-Laurent-d'Andenay pick up the D977 and go through the vineyards to **Buxy,** a medieval town surrounded by ramparts and known for its white wine. From here take the D18 to Sennecey-le-Grand, then the N6 south.

When you hit Tournus, you will know that Provence is not far off. There is a change of atmosphere and of color here. The brick-red roof tiles of southern France, the narrow streets with buildings flush to the road, speak of the Midi.

Turn left on Rue Albert-Thibaudet for **Saint Philibert's Church.** (Note that parking is easiest along the River Saône.) The flat, austere character of the facade of the abbey church is broken by the irregularity of the large stone bands which cover it and by the varying shades of rose of the 10th- and 11th-century stone.

Enter the church. The narthex is striking: four short and stout round pillars bear the painted vaults. The latter are checkerboard and form the frame for a 14th-century naïve fresco of the Crucifixion. The nave defies description: the tall, round columns, dating from the 11th century, are devoid of decoration. The space is bathed in the rose of the stone and the stained glass. It is magical!

The transcept and chancel were constructed in the beginning of the 12th century from white, neatly cut stone. From here glance back at the organ. In the crypt are frescos from the 12th century representing the Virgin and Child and a majestic Christ.

From the narthex, mount the stairway to the particularly luminous Saint Michael's Chapel. Then, also from the narthex, go through to the old **abbey.** The Alms Room contains some time-worn and very expressive large-headed or long-legged statues. Go out through the cloister to the former abbey's residence. See the ancient wine cellars, the dining hall, and residence.

Before leaving Tournus, take a walk along the **quai** and the Rue du Docteur-Privey which becomes Rue de la République and Rue du Midi. The **Saint Madeleine Church,** now closed, has a wonderfully severe facade in the Romanesque style of Saint Philibert's Church.

Tourist Info: 2 Place Carnot, 71700 Tournus, tel: 8551-1310.

Hotel-Restaurants: **Greuze,** 5-6 Place de l'Abbaye, tel: 8540-7777, fax: 8540-7723. Lovely old residence alongside the abbey, extremely comfortable, fabulous chef, very Burgundian, expensive. *****Aux Terrasses,** 18 Avenue du 23-Janvier, tel: 8551-0174, fax: 8551-0999; closed Sunday evenings except in July and August. Conventional modern rooms, good traditional fare, moderately priced.

Road to Cluny

Leave Tournus on the D14, a pretty country road. In the right season dried corn adorns the facades and balconies of many of the houses along the way. **Ozenay**'s church dates from the 12th and 13th centuries and is considered a precursor of Burgundian Gothic.

Stop at **Brancion.** To the left, after mounting the passageway from the town gate, is the old market hall. Behind a sprawling vine-covered house dripping with geraniums and roses is a wonderful church. It is ochre-colored; its floor is composed of great stone slabs covering tombs of the past. In the bay to the right is a splendid mural from the 13th century and a recumbent figure of a crusader killed in Egypt. Notice the roof of the church which is composed of tiles of flat lava stone. The view from the medieval castle is breathtaking.

Continue on the D14 to **Chapaize** to visit the Romanesque church. Its great Lombardian tower surveys the countryside for miles around. The church is structured on huge round pillars fifteen feet in diameter topped by decorative inverted triangles. The old wooden pews are still in use. Chapaize, you will learn, numbers 135 inhabitants who request a contribution of five francs (about one dollar) per visitor to help defray the costs of repairs and upkeep. The roof of the church is covered with heavy lava tiles.

Continue on the D14 to **Cormatin** and turn left on the D981. The elegant Renaissance château here is worth a visit.

Built in the early 17th century, its role was probably defensive until the end of the century when the rampart walls were dismantled. The interior decoration is lavish: gilt, paintings, statuary overwhelm. The allegoric nature of the paintings, the virtues ascribed to the colors in the decoration of the various chambers are indicative of the sophistication of the times. The monumental staircase of the northern wing is unique. The château was designed to pay homage to sumptuous Parisian royal residences, at a time of intense Protestant revolt!

Take the D14 out of town and turn left on the D414 for **Ameugny.** Its church of reddish hue is peacefully tucked into a hillside and surrounded in part by cemetery, the tombs of which are covered with ceramic, plastic and living flowers. Among the brochures on the table inside is one in excellent English providing an eloquent description of the history of the church.

Continue on the D414 to **Taizé,** the seat of an international ecumenical community founded in 1940. Dedicated to peace and reconciliation, the brotherhood receives young people from all over the world for short stays in its tent village. The town itself displays charm and hollyhocks.

Leave Taizé to the left and go right on the D981 into Cluny.

Ozenay
Restaurant: *****Bonne Auberge.** Simple village restaurant run by knowing cook, inexpensive.

Brancion
Château: 9 A.M. to 6:30 P.M. from Easter to November 11 and on Sundays and holidays rest of year.
Hotel-Restaurant: **Auberge du Vieux Brancion,** tel. and fax: 8551-0383. Comfortable establishment in isolated medieval village, moderately priced.

Cormatin
Château: 10 A.M. to 12 noon and 2 to 6:30 P.M. during Easter, on weekends and holidays in May/June and from June 15 to November 1.

Hotel-Restaurant: **Ecu d'Or,** across from château. Newly opened, moderately priced.

Cluny

Alongside the state *hara* or stud farm you will find a public parking lot. Leave the visit to Napoleon's horsebreeding establishment to last. Instead take Rue de la Porte-des-Prés into the heart of abbatial Cluny, one-time center of Christian thought and influence. From its inception in 910 until the 14th century, the abbey wielded tremendous power, crowning popes and counseling kings. Its decline began gradually in the 14th century, was precipitated in the 16th with the wars of religion and was total after the Revolution when it was systematically dismantled.

The remains you see today are those of the church and abbey begun in 1088 during the reign of Abbot St. Hugh and finished in 1130. They were constructed on the foundations of two smaller Romanesque churches, for Cluny required edifices in keeping with its standing.

The 10th century brought troubled times. Charlemagne's former empire was asunder, feudal lords were claiming land and jostling for power. Disillusioned, without direction, men turned to religion and the monastic life. Cluny, adopting modernized Benedictine rules, became the central authority for some 1500 monasteries across France, Germany, Italy, Catholic Spain and England. The power exercised, both religious and political, was concentrated in the hands of the abbot. The place you are about to visit was often called "the second Rome." Prior to the construction of St. Peter's, it was in fact the largest church in the world.

Tour

From Rue de la Porte-des-Prés you will come to Place du 11-Août. On your left is the entrance to the **abbey** now occupied by the National School of Arts and Trades. The first stop will be the **cloister** with its wide stone staircases set at angles and its sundial.

Take the passageway into **St. Peter and St. Paul's Church.** Of the original narthex, five naves, two transepts, five belfrys and two front towers, only the arms of the right transepts remain surmounted by a lovely belltower. Let your imagination flow, reconstruct that grandiose edifice in your mind. The little which remains is awesome; that which has gone was certainly overwhelming.

Continue through the abbey buildings to the gardens; cut diagonally across to the right of the **former grain mill.** Under a superb roof of oak beams, eight columns and capitals from the church ruins are displayed in the upper room. To the left of the entrance to the upper hall is a plaque to the memory of Kenneth John Conant, member of the Medieval Academy of America "who devoted his life and his work as architect, archaeologist and art historian to the study and monumental resurrection of Cluny" (1894–1984).

Go back to Place du 11-Août from where you will see the base of the narthex of the old church. Climb the stairs to the **Ochier Museum,** former abbatial palace built in the 15th century. Other fragments from the church, including the Roman doorway and the narthex capitals found during the excavations carried out by Mr. Conant, are on exhibit here.

Behind the museum is the **Town Hall,** a former abbey residence.

Above the museum is Rue de la République. Go left and at Rue du Merle turn left. You will quickly come to the **Cheese Tower** which is open to visitors ready to mount the 120 steps for a view of the old abbey.

On your way back to the parking lot stop at the **national stud farm** created by Napoleon in 1806 for the breeding of horses for his military campaigns. Breeding, training and artificial insemination are still practiced here. The last time I passed through Tarzan had just fathered Magie, Impériale and Noémie.

Tourist Info: Rue Mercière, 71250 Cluny, tel: 8559-0534.

Abbey: 9 A.M. to 7 P.M. July through September, 9:30 A.M. to 12 noon and 2 to 6:30 P.M., April, May, June; 10:30 A.M. to 12 and 2 to 4 P.M. rest of year.
Ochier Museum: 9:30 A.M. to 12 P.M. and 2 to 6:30 P.M. April through September; 10 A.M. to 12 and 2 to 4 P.M. rest of year.
Cheese Tower: 9:30 A.M. to 12 and 2:30 to 6:30 P.M. March through October; 2 to 6 P.M. rest of year.
Stud Farm: 9 A.M. to 7 P.M.

Restaurant: ***Potin Gourmand,** Place Champ-de-Foire, tel: 8559-0206. Closed Sunday evenings, Mondays, January and February. Rustic atmosphere, family-type cuisine, moderately priced.
Hotel: **Saint-Odilon,** Route Azé, tel: 8559-2500, fax: 8559-0618. New hotel, view of countryside, moderately priced.
Hotel-Restaurants: **Bourgogne,** Place de l'Abbaye, tel: 8559-0058, fax: 8559-0373. Closed Mondays, Wednesdays for lunch and mid-December to mid-February. Tasteful, quiet and across from abbey, medium-priced to moderately expensive. **Moderne,** Pont de-l'Etang, tel: 8559-0565, fax: 8559-1943; closed Wednesdays for lunch and Thursdays, February and second half of November. Classic restaurant and hotel, moderately priced.

Paray-le-Monial

Leave Cluny on the D980 south. Pick up the N79 to the right for about two miles. The D17 offshoot is a pretty road which will take you to La Fourche. All along the way you will see the famous Charollais cows grazing in green pasture. If you are a meateater, you will certainly want to sample Charollais beef at one of your stops. At La Fourche turn left on the D983, then right on the N79-E62 for Paray-le-Monial.

Leave the car at the parking lot near the weeping willows and cross the river. The harmonious **Sacred Heart Basilica** of local, ochre stone was built between 1090 and 1108 by the monks of Cluny during the reign of Abbot St. Hugh. Before all else, take a long look at the outside, skirt the church to see the interlocking tiers of the chevet surmounted by an elegant steeple. From the steps of the Chamber of Relics of a former cardinal's house of pages, there is an excellent view. Go around to the facade and enter the church either through the narthex or the left side. Again, harmony of tone and structure, sobriety and order. Everywhere there are multiples of three: in the tiers, naves, bays, chapels and windows. The sober, geometric designs in general and those of the left doorway in particular are reminiscent of Arab decorative motifs, introduced most probably by St. Hugh following two trips to Islamic Spain.

Next door to the basilica along the river is the **Faience Museum** located in the former Benedictine abbey dining hall. The turn-of-the-century floral and butterfly designs by Elisabeth Parmentier in rose, green, yellow and Charollais blue are particularly lovely. The explanations concerning the tiered kilns and their functions and timing are clear and contribute to respect for this delicate art.

The street behind the basilica, Rue de la Visitation, takes you past the **Visitation Chapel** in which Saint Marguerite-Marie received her first revelations in 1673. To the right on Rue de la Paix is the **Hiéron Museum** of sacred art.

In the opposite direction on Rue de la Paix is the **Town Hall,** an elegant Renaissance building, originally the private mansion of a wealthy draper. Just beyond is the **Saint Nicholas Tower,** belfry of a former church.

Tourist Info: Avenue Jean-Paul-ii, 71600 Paray-le-Monial, tel: 8551-1092.

Faience Museum: 10 A.M. to 12 P.M. and 2 to 6 P.M. from Easter to November 1; until 7 P.M. July/August; closed Tuesdays.

Hiéron Museum: Rue de la Paix. 9 A.M. to 12 P.M. and 1:30 to 6:30 P.M. May through September; 2 to 4 P.M. in winter.

Hotel-Restaurant: **Trois Pigeons,** 2 Rue Dargaud, tel:
8581-0377, fax: 8581-5859. Classic, old-fashioned establishment, good food, moderately priced.

Nevers

Leave Paray-le-Monial on the N79-E62. At Digoin pick up
the D979 which follows the course of the Loire River. Just
before Decize cross the river and proceed onto the D116 and
the D13 into Nevers.

It was by way of Nevers that the Italian art of faience was
introduced into France in the late 16th century. The Duke of
Nivernais brought a group of Italian artists and potters to his
city, put them to work at their trades as well as training others.
He sold glass, enamel and faience products to other towns of
the Loire Valley. Three factories are still making hand-deco-
rated faience in Nevers.

If you began your walk from the parking lot to the right
of the Loire Bridge after you come over it, go back towards
the bridge to enter the city on your right. From Place Mossé,
take Rue Saint-Genest down to Rue des Jacobins and turn
left. You will come to the **Porte du Croux,** a handsome
square tower originally part of the city's fortifications. Turn
left into the park. After the rose arbor you will come to the
Municipal Museum which contains a good collection of Nevers faience in varying styles. See also the Fernand Chalandre
room of soothing river watercolors and woodcuts. The paintings of country scenes by Hector Hanoteau are very agreeable, as are a number of the small impressionist canvases.

Go back to Rue des Jacobins and up to **Saint Cyr's and
Julitte's Cathedral.** While the exterior of the church represents an imposition of styles of different periods, the interior
is essentially Gothic except for the west transept and one apse
which are Romanesque. The brilliance of the modern stained
glass shocks at first sight, but one adjusts after a few minutes,
especially as colored reflections from the glass shimmer on
the walls. A moving, albeit faded, fresco of Christ adorns the

Romanesque apse. The curious clock in the nave is generally one hour off. The last time I was there someone was scraping the wax of tapers from their holders.

Amble out and around the cathedral for a look at the complicated structure of pinnacles ascending to the square tower. Continue on to the Ducal Palace behind the church. The style is Renaissance. At the far end of the gardens there is a wide vista of the river and countryside. From here go left to Rue du Commerce, past the belfry and then right on Rue du Rempart and left on Rue Saint-Etienne to the Romanesque **Church of Saint Etienne.** The chevet is remarkably well seated creating a wide solid frame for the building. From the outside, the church gives the impression of a patchwork of brick-colored tiles, radiating and harmonious. The inside is particularly sober, the church bathed in soft yellow light.

Tourist Info: 31 Rue de Rempart, 58000 Nevers, tel: 8659-0703, 1 Avenue du Général-de-Gaulle, tel: 8661-2775.

Municipal Museum: 10 A.M. to 12 P.M. and 2 to 6 P.M.; closed Tuesdays.

Restaurants: *Apple Pie, 18 Rue du 14-Juillet; open Wednesdays through Saturdays. Authentic American specialties, inexpensive. *Bonlaï, 29 Rue du 14-Juillet. Very tasty Asian specialties, inexpensive.

Hotel: Molière, 25 Rue Molière, tel: 8657-2996, fax: 8659-5825. Pleasant hotel in peaceful street, moderately priced.

Hotel-Restaurants: Morvan, 28 Rue Mouësse, tel: 8661-1416; closed Tuesday evenings and Wednesdays. Regional specialties, moderately priced. **Château de la Rocherie,** *Varennes-Vauzelles,* 6 kilometers north on N7, tel: 8638-0721, fax: 8638-2301; closed Saturdays for lunch, Sundays and November 1 to 15. Authentic Napoleon III château being progressively overhauled, agreeable meals and grounds, medium-priced.

La Charité-sur-Loire

Leave Nevers on the N7. About five kilometers from La Charité-sur-Loire there is a turn-off which follows the river into the city.

As late as the middle of the 19th century La Charité-sur-Loire's active port was a major stop-off for trade up and down the Loire. Today La Charité is a pleasant, lazy place huddled under a wonderful 11th-century church, annex of Benedictine Cluny.

Try to find a parking space in Grande-Rue alongside the **Priory Church of Notre Dame.** A major fire destroyed much of the building in 1559, which is why the facade and the remaining square tower are separated from the rest of the edifice. The transcept and chancel of the church, made of the Loire's white stone, are intact. The chapels and the deambulatory are particularly elegant. Under the modern stained glass windows the stone motifs are Islamic.

Leave the church through the side door. At Number 45 Grande-Rue go left through the covered passageway to the excavation site. The view of the church's chevet and tower is fine from here. The stairway down will lead you to the old priory and to the ramparts overlooking the river and the **Museum.** In addition to archaeological finds, a collection of art nouveau and art décoratif, as well as an exhibit of files and rasps produced in the region in the 19th century and first half of the 20th, are on display.

Tourist Info: Place Sainte-Croix, 58400 La Charité-sur-Loire, tel: 8670-1506; off season: 8670-1612.

Museum: 10 A.M. to 12 noon and 3 to 7 P.M. from June 25 to September 15; closed Tuesdays and rest of year except for afternoons during school holidays.

Hotel-Restaurant: **Grand Monarque,** 33 Quai Clemenceau, tel: 8670-2173; closed Fridays off season. Pleasant view of river, regional dishes, moderately priced.

Vézelay

The next leg of our journey, along the N151 out of La Charité, is especially satisfying. The villages of **Nannay** and **Varzy** are picturesque. Medieval **Clamecy** is worth a brief stop. From here continue on the D951 through the forest to Vézelay. When, from the distance, you see the village and its church set on the mountain top and framed by the sky, you will know something exceptional is waiting.

Leave your car at the foot of the ramparts and take one of the two recommended walks up. As you climb the one and later descend the other, you will see a myriad of sights to make you rejoice: ramparts, roundhouses and gardens, gray and white stone, brick-colored tiled rooftops, glimpses of mountain, valley and field, medieval houses in the business street, vendors of the region's white wine and syrups. . . .

Briefly, Vézelay's story is the following: an abbey of nuns was founded near here in 855 by a Burgundian count, Girard de Roussillon. When the abbey was destroyed by the Normans a few years later, the count moved the abbey to this adjacent hill, more easily defendable, and housed it with Benedictine monks rather than abbesses and nuns. In the 11th century it came under the aegis of Cluny.

By the middle of the 12th century the abbey was one of the principal relays on the road to Santiago de Compostela. As keeper of the relics of Saint Magdalena, its popularity extended to yearly pilgrimages as well. It was here that Richard the Lion Heart and Philip Augustus, King of France, chose to join forces in a third Christian crusade to the Middle East. It was also here that Saint Francis of Assisi founded his first convent in France. The decline of the abbey was precipitated by the discovery of other supposed relics of Saint Magdalena elsewhere. The pilgrimages and celebrations tapered off. Religious dissension and then strife also played their parts. In 1569 the abbey was stripped by Huguenots and later destroyed during the French Revolution. In the middle of the

19th century Viollet-le-Duc was commissioned to restore the church. The Vézelay **Basilica** is now in the keeping of Franciscans.

Except for the Gothic facade pediment, the exterior of the basilica is pure Romanesque. The left tower was never completed, the right has lost its steeple. The tympanum of the central Roman doorway presents Christ and the apostles in the most direct, simple fashion. Walk slowly around the church and then go in.

First the narthex, a church in itself: in this space are some of the most admirable examples of religious art in the world. The capitals depict scenes from the Old Testament (Joseph beaten and imprisoned, Samson and the lion) and the New (John the Baptist, Saint Benedict). The famous central tympanum presents Christ resurrected with the apostles and surrounded by followers. Over the right-hand doorway scenes from Christ's childhood are portrayed; over the left Christ revived with the apostles and with the disciples of Emmaus.

Through the central doorway, the long nave is inviting. Dusky shades and occasional tints of rose invade the space. The polychromy of the intersecting vaults brings the structure closer. The capitals are superb. This is strong, naive sculpture: most based on the Bible, some pagan. According to certain experts, one can divine the hand of five anonymous sculptors. Note the leaf friezes between the two stories and around the arches. The transept and the chancel are early Gothic. Under the chancel is a crypt built on bedrock.

Clamecy
Tourist Info: Rue du Grand-Marché, 89450 Clamecy, tel: 8627-0251.
Restaurant: *Angélus, 11 Place Saint-Jean, tel: 8627-2325; closed Wednesdays for dinner and Thursdays except in July and August. Pretty restaurant, interesting menus, moderately priced.
Hotel-Restaurant: **Hostellerie de la Poste,** 9 Place Emile-

Zola, tel: 8627-0155, fax: 8627-0599. Old-fashioned hotel, regional dishes, moderately priced.

Vezelay
Tourist Info: Rue Saint-Pierre, tel: 8633-2369, April–October.

Hotels: **Compostelle,** Place Champ-de-Foire, tel: 8633-2863, fax: 8633-3434; closed January. Peaceful views of garden and countryside, half-pension available, moderately priced. **Pontot,** Place Pontot, tel: 8633-2440; closed November to Easter. Historic residence, elegant rooms, moderately expensive.
Hotel-Restaurant: **Espérance,** *Saint-Père-sous-Vézelay,* 3 kilometers southeast on D957, tel: 8633-2045, fax: 8633-2615; closed Tuesdays, for lunch on Wednesdays and January. Marc Meneau is one of France's top-rated chefs (19.5 over 20 from Gault Millau). Dining here is an elegant, memorable experience in luminous dining hall surrounded by greenery. Rooms in main building or in rivermill are glorious. Expensive to luxury prices.

Auxerre

Take the D951 north to where it joins the N6. Stay on the N6 north until you come to Cravant. Follow the riverside. Just before Vincelottes, turn right on the D38 to **Irancy** among the vineyards, then turn left on the D956 for **Saint-Bris-le-Vineux,** two excellent wine villages. Although less well known than Chablis, they are of equal quality. The D956 will take you into Auxerre.

You will come into the city on its right bank. Before crossing the river, note the skyline of church chevets. The Paul Bert Bridge will take you to Quai de la République. Just below **Saint Stephen's Cathedral,** it becomes Quai de la Marine. Leave your car along the quai or up above in front of the church.

This fine Gothic cathedral was built over a period of centuries, from the 13th to the 16th, on the foundations of a Romanesque church. The facade is flamboyant Gothic. The stained glass windows of the chancel are marvelously blue.

The original Romanesque crypt, which dates from the 11th century, is strikingly simple. The murals are wide-eyed and ochre-colored except for that of Christ, framed in blue. The portrayal of Christ on horseback is unique.

Leave Saint Stephen's to the right on Rue Cochois and you will arrive at the former **Saint Germain Abbey** founded in the 6th century at the time of Clovis, the first of the Frank kings. During the Middle Ages, the abbey was frequented by students from all over Europe who came to study philosophy with the masters in residence. The present-day church, started in the 13th century, is Gothic. The pre-Romanesque crypt appears to be a partially underground church. The central nave and sanctuary were built in the 5th century during Saint Germain's lifetime. The lateral naves date from the 6th century, the ambulatory and the chapels from the 9th. The frescoes are also 9th century and represent the life and death of Saint Stephen. The tomb is that of Saint Germain.

Irancy
Wine tasting: **Anita et Jean-Pierre Colinot,** Rue des Chariats, tel: 8642-3325, 9 A.M. to 12 P.M. and 2 to 8 P.M. closed Sunday afternoons. **Domaine Saint-Germain,** Chemin du Tour-de-ville, tel: 8642-3343, 11 A.M. to 1 P.M. and 3 to 7 P.M.; closed Sundays.

Saint-Bris-le-Vineux
Wine tasting: **Domaine Félix,** 17 Rue de Paris, tel: 8653-3387, 9 to 11:30 A.M. and 2 to 6:30 P.M. **La Cave du Maître de Poste,** 12 Rue de Paris, tel: 8653-6076, 8 A.M. to 12 P.M. and 2 to 6 P.M.
Restaurant: *Saint-Bris, 13 Rue de l'Eglise, tel: 8653-8456; closed Monday evenings and Tuesdays. Family-run country bistro, moderately priced.

Auxerre
Tourist Info: 1 and 2 Quai de la République, 89000 Auxerre, tel: 8652-0619.

Cathedral crypt: 9 A.M. to 12 noon and 2 to 6 P.M.
Abbey crypt: 9 A.M. to 12:30 P.M. and 1:30 to 6:30 P.M.; closed Tuesdays.

Restaurants: **Jean-Luc Barnabet,** 14 Quai de la République, tel: 8651-6888, fax: 8651-5085; closed Sunday evenings and Mondays. Fine cuisine in handsome décor, medium-priced. **Jardin Gourmand,** 56 Boulevard Vauban, tel: 8651-5352, fax: 8652-3382; closed Sunday evenings and Mondays off season and December. Very refined table, inventive recipes, moderately expensive. ***Primavera,** 37 Rue du Pont, tel: 8651-4636. Very Greek, very Mediterranean fare, inexpensive.

Accommodations: **Maxime,** 2 Quai de la Marine, tel: 8652-1419, fax: 8652-2170. Comfortable, old establishment with view on river or cathedral, medium-priced. **Normandie,** 41 Boulevard Vauban, tel: 8652-5780, fax: 8651-5433. House and garden plus sauna, moderately priced. **Parc des Maréchaux,** 6 Avenue Foch, tel: 8651-4377, fax: 8651-3172. Pretty rooms in pleasant setting, medium-priced.

Ancy-le-Franc

Leave Auxerre on the N65 which will become D965. Go through **Chablis** where the famous white wine is made. After Tonnerre get on the D905.

There is an exquisite Renaissance **castle** at **Ancy-le-Franc,** one of few still in the hands of descendants of its 16th-century owners. The exterior is severe in aspect; however, the inside decor is sumptuous. In addition to splendid salons, chambers and galleries, there is a small automobile museum of models from the early 1900s. The château is open to visitors.

Five kilometers south of Ancy-le-Franc you will pass the **Nuits château,** another jewel-like Renaissance structure.

Chablis

Wine tasting: **La Chablisienne,** 8 Boulevard Pasteur, tel: 8642-1124, 8 A.M. to 12 noon and 2 to 6 P.M. **Louis Michel § Fils,** 9 Boulevard de Ferrières, tel: 8642-1024, 8 A.M. to 12 noon and 2 to 6 P.M.; closed Saturday afternoons and Sundays.

Restaurant: ***Au Vrai Chablis,** Place du Marché, tel: 8642-1143; closed for dinner on weekdays off season. Neighborhood restaurant, local wines, moderately priced.

Hotel-Restaurants: **Hostellerie des Clos,** Rue Jules-Rathier, tel: 8642-1063, fax: 8642-1711; closed Wednesday evenings and Thursdays for lunch off season and December 10 to January 10. Wonderful house and grounds and radiant dining room are background for fine cuisine, moderately expensive restaurant, medium-priced rooms.

Ancy-le-Franc

Château: 10 A.M. to 12 noon and 2 to 7 P.M. from April 1 to November 11.

Hotel-Restaurant: **Centre,** tel: 8675-1511, fax: 8675-1413; closed Friday evenings and Saturdays for lunch off season. Moderately priced.

Fontenay

Just after Montbard turn off D905 onto D32 to Fontenay Abbey. Fontenay has survived to tell its story, providing an example of a Cistercian abbey, self-contained and self-sufficient. Fontenay was created in 1118 by Bernard, abbot of Clairvaux. His hostility towards the ever-increasing grandeur and luxury of the churches of the time conditioned the design of Fontenay and two other abbeys he founded. In his own words: "why those excessive heights, those disproportionate lengths, the superfluous widths, those sumptuous ornaments, those curious paintings which catch the eye and trouble one's attention and meditation. We monks have left the ranks of the people, we have renounced riches and the brilliance of the world for the love of Christ. Whose devotion do we pretend to awaken with these ornaments?"

The watchwords of Fontenay were sobriety, austerity, self-sufficiency. All Cistercian abbeys followed the same lines. Vows of poverty and humility being central to the Cistercian philosophy, the monks turned from the beaten path, did not actively seek adepts or converts. There was no reason to signal their presence by belltowers or chimes. Ornamentation is also absent. None of which lessens the simple beauty of the abbey.

With some three hundred monks and converts in residence, Fontenay prospered until the 16th century. The system of nominations of abbots by royal favor, as well as the religious conflicts of the times, provoked its decline. The abbey functioned as a paper mill after the Revolution until it was bought in 1906 by its present owners who have restored it and opened the grounds and most of the buildings to the public.

The guided tour begins at the entrance. To the right was the shelter for pilgrims and travelers and to the left their chapel, followed by the monks' bread ovens. These have been turned into a small lapidary museum. Further on is the pigeon-house.

The abbatial church was financed by Ebrard, the bishop of Norwich (England) who joined the brotherhood. Notice the pinkish hue of the stone from which it was built and the slightly tinted stained glass windows as well as the stark simplicity (except for the music). From the right side of the transept a staircase leads to the dormitory, where the monks slept on straw mats, separated one from the other by a low partition. The capitular room which faces the cloister served as meeting room for the order of the day. The scriptorium is just beyond. The small "warming" room off the scriptorium was the only room, except for the kitchens, which was heated. Mortification was an element of Cistercian austerity.

The old forge which the monks operated for toolmaking is as beautiful a building as any other on the grounds. Its construction dates from the 13th century. There is also a prison, an infirmary and a garden of medicinal plants.

Fontenay
Abbey: Guided tours on the hour from 9 A.M. to 12 noon all year, plus on the half-hour from 2:30 to 6:30 P.M. in July and August; tours last 45 minutes.

Montbard
Hotel-Restaurants: **Ecu,** 7 Rue Auguste-Carré, tel: 8092-1166, fax: 8092-1413. Comfortable, welcoming establishment, regional dishes, medium-priced. **Château de Malaisy,** *Fain-lès-Montbard,* 6 kilometers southeast on D905, tel: 8089-4654, fax: 8092-3016. Peaceful château on hillside, sauna, medium-priced to moderately expensive.

The most direct road back to Dijon is the D905 south. It joins the A38 parkway near Sombernon.

Some Useful Words and Phrases

bed	**lit** (m)
Belgium	**Belgique** (f)
to bring	**apporter**
brotherhood	**fraternité** (f)
Burgundian	**bourguignon(ne)**
canvas	**toile** (f)
capital	**chapiteau** (m)
cave	**caverne, grotte** (f)
Christianity	**christianisme** (m)
to climb	**monter**
devotion	**dévouement** (m)
to drive	**conduire**
estate	**propriété** (f)
furniture	**meuble** (m)
Gallic	**gaulois(e)**
kitchen	**cuisine** (f)
to look	**regarder**
millenium	**millénaire** (m)
past	**passé** (m)

roof	toit (m)
seat	siège (m)
to show	montrer
veil	voile (m)
wealth	richesse (f)
wine tasting	dégustation (f)
work	travail (m)

Ils ont visité l'église rapidement. (They visited the church quickly.)

Nous avons dégusté trois vins différents. (We tasted three different wines.)

Je vous montrerai mes achats. (I will show you my purchases.)

Pouvez-vous parler plus lentement? (Can you speak more slowly?)

Il fait vraiment frais dans l'église. (It is really cool in the church.)

Notre chambre est joliment décorée. (Our room is prettily decorated.)

Adverbs are formed by adding **ment** to an adjective.
Example: **triste** (sad) becomes **tristement** (sadly).

CHAPTER 15

Castles on the Loire

The castles along the Loire are lauded afar for their beauty and refinement. They are grandeur *per se*. Less well known is their place in the social history of France. For centuries the fertile valley of the Loire was prey to invaders: from Barbarians to Romans, from Huns to Visigoths and Franks, from Arabs to Normans, and, of course, the English.

The empire of the Frank king Charlemagne extended over much of present-day France, Germany and Italy. After his death in 814, the realm was divided among incompetent and avid heirs who battled each other for the spoils of the defunct empire. The lack of central authority favored the rise of local barons who hastened to occupy the power vacuum. Each would raise an army, coin money and fortify his villa. Neighbor went to war against neighbor. Overlords entered into alliances with knights who were awarded fiefs on becoming vassals.

In addition to the local and area rivalries, this was also a time of Norman incursions. In the Loire Valley every hillock gradually accrued a tower or donjon for the defense of an estate.

The vassal system was shaky at the outset, but by the 11th century it had some rules and by the 12th it had been institutionalized with a very detailed feudal code defining services and obligations. At the apex of the system was the king, at the base were the vassals whose rights had in the meantime become hereditary.

Castles on the Loire

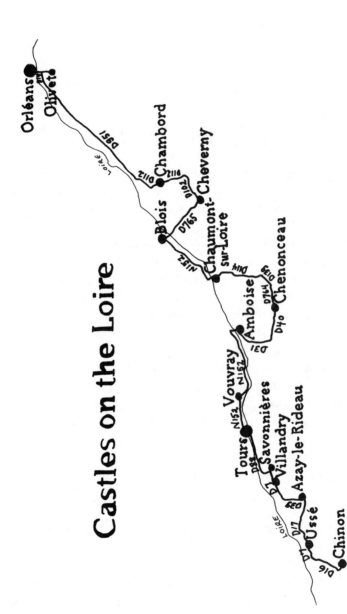

Soon the keep or donjon was surrounded by courts and yards and an outer protective wall of stone. Along this wall, guard posts and small towers were constructed. Within were living quarters for the lord, his family, soldiers and personnel, as well as stables and barns, chapels, kitchens, wine cellars. In the event of attack it was inside this enclosure that serfs and peasants gathered for protection.

With the return of the crusaders in the 13th century, the military aspects of the domains improved: ramparts were thickened, moats were enlarged, new weaponry was introduced and vantage points were strengthened. Architects were employed and living quarters became slightly more than utilitarian. Beds and other furniture made their entry for the first time. Tapestries covered the walls. By the time of the One Hundred Years War between France and England (14th and 15th centuries) the fortresses were turning into castles. The outer walls and the inner towers were linked by roofed structures and passageways creating an overall ensemble.

In the 16th century France was a single, unified country. The castle no longer served as a military establishment. It no longer dominated the countryside but nestled in valleys, alongside rivers. Emphasis was on comfort, elegance and beauty. Italian-style galleries, courtyards, peaked roofs, large windows openings appeared. Interior decoration was stylish, even lavish. It was the Renaissance.

In the 17th and 18th centuries, châteaux were designed as luxurious country estates with no thought to defense. Many of the castles you will visit in the Loire Valley are essentially medieval, feudal structures, redesigned in the 14th or 15th centuries to meet the requirements for opulence of new and old aristocrats. Others, like Chambord and Cheverny, were created as purely pleasurable enterprises.

The bitterness of religious strife in the Loire Valley regions of Touraine and Anjou during the 16th century needs mention. Luther and Calvin's theses spread like wildfire among intellectuals and aristocrats. Calvin lived and studied in Orléans for several years. Beginning in 1540 the Catholic Church set about routing the Reformists and many were burned at the stake. Still the Huguenots gained ground, particularly with crafts and business people. Confrontation between Catholics and Protestants became inevitable and throughout the 1560s armies clashed. Henry IV, a Protestant, became king of France in 1589 and converted to Catholicism. When, in 1598, he promulgated the Edict of Nantes, a bill guaranteeing the rights of Calvinists to practice their religion, calm returned to the Loire Valley.

Louis XIV revoked the Edict of Nantes in 1685 sparking off the persecution of Protestants and the desecration of their temples, as well as large-scale emigration.

Orléans

Orléans was long considered the center of France. Celtic resistance to Rome was initiated here. Gallo-Roman resistance to Attila and the Huns was victorious here. In the 10th century Orléans was second only to Paris. The event which would, however, make Orléans sacred for all time was the liberation of the encircled city by Joan of Arc in 1429. The advance of the English army along the Loire was stopped here. It was the turning point in the struggle against foreign domination.

Today Orléans is an industrial city and market center for produce from the region. During World War II it was heavily bombarded.

From the railway station, take Rue de la République, then go left on Rue de la Bretonnerie which will lead you to the **Holy Cross Cathedral.** Begun in the 13th century, it was damaged considerably by the Huguenots in the 16th. Henry IV had it rebuilt in Gothic style. Note the woodwork of the stalls in the chancel. The archbishop's garden behind the cathedral is pleasantly tranquil.

Next door to the cathedral is the **Fine Arts Museum** which contains a vast and varied collection of painting, sculpture, carved ivory and prints from the primitive to contemporary. Some of the fine, old paintings once adorned the walls of châteaux in the region.

Take Rue Jeanne-d'Arc in front of the cathedral and turn left on Rue Sainte-Catherine to a **Historical Museum** noted for its Gallo-Roman bronze collection. It also houses interesting exhibits of local ceramics, sculpture from the Middle Ages and an impressive German tapestry of Joan of Arc.

Leave the museum to the right and turn right on Rue du Tabour. You will arrive at Place du Général-de-Gaulle and **Joan of Arc House.** The building is a replica of the 15th-century house in which the national heroine was lodged during her stay in Orléans. The square was totally destroyed during World War II. The exhibit, comprising period costumes and weaponry, includes an audiovisual presentation of Joan's arrival in Orléans.

Two pleasant walks from the Joan of Arc House can finish off your day: Rue de Bourgogne to the right, which quickly becomes pedestrian only, and Quai du Châtelet along the river. Rue de la République to the right leads you there.

Train from Paris: From Gare Montparnasse, one hour (TGV).

Tourist Info: Place Albert-Ier, 45000 Orléans, tel: 3853-0595.

Fine Arts Museum: 1 Rue Fernand-Rabier, 10 A.M. to 12 noon and 2 to 6 P.M.; closed Tuesdays.

Historical Museum: Square Abbé-Desnoyers, 10 A.M. to 12 noon and 2 to 6 P.M., closed Tuesdays.

Joan of Arc House: Place du Général-de-Gaulle, 10 to 11:45 A.M. 2 to 5:30 P.M. from May 2 to October 31; afternoons only the rest of the year.

Restaurants: **Antiquaires,** 2 Rue au Lin, tel: 3853-5235; closed Sundays and Mondays, Christmas and Easter weeks and August. Orléans' best restaurant, medium-priced. **Chan-**

cellerie, 27 Place Martroi, tel: 3853-5754; closed Sundays. Good food, excellent wines, historic house, moderately expensive. ***Florian,** 70 Boulevard Alexandre-Martin, tel: 3853-0815; closed Sundays and mid-August. Pleasant restaurant with inside garden, good quality, moderately priced. **Lyonnais,** 82 Rue Turcies, tel: 3853-1524; closed Saturdays for lunch, Sundays and first half of August. Real bistro cooking, moderately priced. **Sainte-Catherine,** 64 Rue Sainte-Catherine, tel: 3853-4087. Charm and terrace, moderately priced.

Accommodations: **Jackotel,** 18 Rue du Cloître-Saint-Aignan, tel: 3854-4848, fax: 3877-1759. Pretty rooms in small hotel with garden on a square, moderately priced. **Marguerite,** 14 Place du Vieux-Marché, tel: 3853-7432. Another small hotel, moderately priced.

Olivet

Five kilometers to the south of Orléans is Olivet, city of flowers. Cross the Loire on the George v Bridge and take Avenue Dauphine to the Loiret River and across. Go left on Rue de la Source, the river road, to the **Floral Park of the Source.** The sea of color varies with the seasons, offering tulips and iris in the springtime, roses in July and September, dahlias and chrysanthemums in the autumn. Cranes, deer and pink flamingos may cross your path in the park.

Tourist Info: 226 Rue Paul-Génain, 45000 Olivet, tel: 3863-4968.

Floral Park: 9 A.M. to 6 P.M. from April 1 to November 11; 2 to 5 P.M. the rest of the year.

Hotel-Restaurants: **Quatre Saisons,** 351 Rue de la Reine-Blanche, tel: 3866-1430. Small, comfortable hotel, terrace for dining on the river, medium-priced. **Rivage,** 635 Rue de la Reine-Blanche, tel: 3866-0293, fax: 3856-3111. Peaceful location on the water, medium-priced.

Chambord

Take Rue de la Source back into Olivet where it will change names and become Rue du Général-de-Gaulle, the D14. This road will run into the D951, from which the off-shoot D112A carries you along to Chambord Castle.

In the mind of Francis I in 1518, Chambord was to be a palace, a symbol of power and artistic excellence and a royal residence for kingly pleasures. It was he who, with the diamond of the ring on his finger, etched these words, still visible, on a pane of glass: "Often woman varies, folly he who trusts." He did not live to see the château terminated. Upon the death of his son, Henry II, some twenty years later, in 1559, it was still not completed. Both, however, spent considerable time at Chambord, organized extravagent hunts, receptions of foreign dignitaries and sumptuous balls. Louis XIV finished the task.

No known architect is associated with the construction of Chambord. It is thought that the original design for the château was elaborated by Leonardo da Vinci whom Francis I brought from Italy as the greatest artist of his time in order to contribute to the splendor of Renaissance France. We are told that the work itself was carried out by illiterate master masons.

Although in no sense a fortress, the basic design is that of a medieval castle with a central donjon and four towers to which have been added two tremendous wings: one for the royal apartments, the other for a chapel. The double spiral staircase is illustrious. From the terraces, the court witnessed the military ceremonies, followed the progress of the hunt and intrigue. One sector of the park surrounding the château is open to the public.

Tourist Info: Château, 41250 Chambord, tel: 5420-3486.

Visiting hours: 9:30 A.M. to 5:45 P.M. from June 16 to November 10; 9:30 to 11:45 A.M. and 2 to 4:45 P.M. the rest of the year.

Sound § Light Show: Every day from April 15 to October 15; for schedule and reservations, see Tourist Office.

Hotel-Restaurant: **Grand Saint-Michel,** at entrance to château, tel: 5420-3131. View of castle, medium-priced hotel, moderately priced restaurant.

In the region: **Bonnheure,** 9 Rue René-Masson, *Bracieux,* 5 kilometers south on the D119, tel: 5446-4157. Comfortable hotel without restaurant, moderately priced. **Bernard Robin,** 1 Avenue Chambord, *Bracieux,* tel: 5446-4122, fax: 5446-0369; closed Tuesday evenings, Wednesdays and Christmas week. Highly rated restaurant, inventive chef, expensive.

Cheverny

From Bracieux (on the D119) take the D102 to Cheverny. This elegant château is from the early 17th century and has the rare distinction of still belonging to the family who built it. The interior decoration is sumptuous. Among the splendid paintings are a Titian and a Raphaël; the tapestries are from Aubusson and the Gobelins.

Visiting Hours: 9:15 A.M. to 6:45 P.M. from June 1 to September 15; 9:30 A.M. to 12 noon and 2:15 to 5 P.M. the rest of the year.

Sound § Light Show: 10:30 P.M. certain evenings in July and August; inquire at Tourist Office in Blois or at château.

Hotel-Restaurants: **Château du Breuil,** Route de Fougères-sur-Bièvre, 4 kilometers southwest on D52, tel: 5444-2020, fax: 5444-3040. Restaurant closed Sunday evenings and Mondays for lunch and December through February. Pretty château set among the trees, expensive. Fine dining, medium-priced. ***Saint-Hubert,** Rue Nationale, Cour-Cheverny, one kilometer north, tel: 5479-9660. Small, comfortable hotel, regional cooking, moderately priced.

Blois

The D765 will lead you to Blois on the right bank of the Loire. Blois and its château are intimately linked to the history of France. It is not clear when building began nor when the counts of Blois became masters of the region. It is known that their domain covered immense territories, including at one time the Champagne region. One of the counts married William the Conqueror's daughter and their son ruled England from 1135 to 1152. It is also known that in 1392 the castle and its lands were sold to a member of the royal family and thereafter served often as the seat of royal authority in lieu of Paris. Succeeding generations transformed and added to the old "homestead."

Louis XII, Francis I and Henry III spent much of their time here. During the reign of the later, religious conflict was paramount. It was at Blois that the Duke of Guise and his partisans, backed by the king of Spain and the States General, demanded the abolition of Protestantism. Henry III, feeling himself boxed in, had Guise murdered practically in front of his eyes in a room adjoining the Stateroom on the third floor. It seems the king cried out: "Now I am king!"

In the 17th century Blois became a center of intrigue for Cardinal Richelieu and Marie de Médicis. Louis XIII "gave" the counties and dukedoms of Blois, Orléans and Chartres to his brother Gaston in order to keep him at a distance, both from himself and from Richelieu. On the death of Gaston, Blois' role was essentially played out. In 1940 the château and the town were damaged by aerial bombings which preceded the arrival of the German army.

Tour

The tour of Blois begins naturally with the castle and its square, from which the view is magnificent. Inside the château are two museums: the **Archaeological Museum** and the **Museum of Fine Arts** containing a number of portraits of some of the leading actors in the château's history. The room dedicated to **Robert Houdin,** the conjurer, displays a number of his inventions including the electric clock. The Francis I staircase is considered a masterpiece of architecture. In Catherine de Médicis' apartment are 237 carved wood panels which served to conceal her closets. A pedal hidden in the plinth opened them.

From the château a staircase on the town side leads to the remains of the **king's gardens** and **Anne de Bretagne's house,** now the Tourist Office. From the gardens, turn back on the town and skirt the château until you come to the Benedictine **Saint Nicholas Church,** which combines Gothic and Romanesque architecture harmoniously. In back of the church is the former **Jacobin Convent** with its **Museum of Religious Art** on the second floor and **Museum of Natural History** on the third.

Leave to the right and take Rue Saint-Lubin to the right. Turn left on Rue Saint-Martin and again on Rue du Commerce. Take the passage to the right and then Rue Porte-Côté to the left. At Rue du Bourg-Neuf go right and take the first right, Rue Saint-Honoré. The **Hôtel d'Alluye** is a lovely Renaissance mansion built by a financier and admirer of Italian art. Past here to the left is a stairway leading to the **Beauvoir Tower,** as 12th century donjon. Take Rue du Palais. The **statue** here is of Denis Papin, the Blois-born inventor of steam propulsion. This street will take you past the **Denis Papin House** to **Saint Louis' Cathedral.** Behind the cathedral is the former episcopal palace, now the **town hall.** From the **gardens** is another fine view of the surrounding countryside. In the little streets between the cathedral and the river lies some of old Blois.

The **Chocolateries Poulain,** started by the son of a peasant in the 19th century, produces 33,000 tons of chocolate annually. The factory is located to the west of the château at the end of Rue des Lices and is open for visits.

Tourist Info: Pavillon Anne-de-Bretagne, 3 Avenue du Dr-Jean-Laigret, 41000 Blois, tel: 5474-0649.

Château: 9 A.M. to 6 P.M. from March 15 to November 1; 9 A.M. to 12 and 2 to 5 P.M. the rest of the year.
Sound & Light Show: In French at 10:30 P.M. and in English at 11:30 P.M. from June 5 to September 13.
Pavillon Anne-de-Bretagne: 9 A.M. to 12 noon and 2 to 6 P.M. weekdays.
Jacobin Convent: Rue Anne-de-Bretagne. 9 A.M. to 12 noon and 2 to 6 P.M. from June 1 to August 31, afternoons only the rest of the year; closed Mondays.
Hôtel d'Alluye: 8 Rue Saint-Honoré. 2 to 6 P.M. Tuesdays to Fridays.
Chocolateries Poulain: 6 Avenue Gambetta; tours at 8:45, 10 and 11:45 A.M. and 1:30 and 2:45 P.M. on weekdays, except Friday afternoons.

Restaurants: **Orangerie du Château,** 1 Avenue Jean-Laigret, tel: 5478-0536, fax: 5478-2278; closed Sunday evenings and Mondays. Lovely, historic building situated in the queen's gardens, very inventive cuisine, medium-priced. **Rendez-Vous des Pêcheurs,** 27 Rue Foix, tel: 5474-6748, fax: 5474-4767; closed Sundays and Monday evenings. Excellent cuisine by chef trained by one of France's best, medium-priced. ***Via Vietnam,** 2 Boulevard Vauban, tel: 5478-8699; closed Wednesdays. Family-run restaurant, Asian cooking, inexpensive.

Accommodations: **Urbis,** 3 Rue Porte-Côte, tel: 5474-0117, fax: 5474-8569. Pleasant hotel, centrally located, moderately priced.

In the region: **Hostellerie La Malouinière,** 1 Rue Bernard-Lorjou, *Saint-Denis-sur-Loire,* 6 kilometers northeast on the N152, tel: 5474-7681. Elegant, comfortable, peaceful 18th-century residence surrounded by gardens, fine, classic cuisine, expensive.

Chaumont-sur-Loire

The ride from Blois on the N152 is pleasant. Some fifteen kilometers out, take the first bridge across the Loire for Chaumont-sur-Loire, another landmark of royal retaliation. The castle was erected in the 15th century on the remains of a medieval fortress dismantled by Louis XI in order to chastise the reigning family of the region, the House of Amboise. Catherine de Médicis, widow of Henry II, acquired the château in the 16th century in order to force her dead husband's mistress, Diane de Poitiers, to exchange Chenonceau, which she coveted, for Chaumont. While you may visit Diane's chambers and see her emblems on the facade, she never lived here. Catherine de Médicis, however, did consult the stars from the tower in the company of her astrologer Ruggieri.

Benjamin Franklin visited the castle on several occasions. The celebrated Italian artist and ceramist Nini, who had a studio on the grounds for a time, did Franklin's portrait on a medallion.

Visiting hours: 9:15 A.M. to 5:35 P.M. from July 1 to August 31; 9:15 to 11:35 A.M. and 1:45 to 5:35 P.M. the rest of the year; 3:50 P.M. closing from November 1 to March 31. The stables open at 9:30 A.M. and close 40 minutes after the château.

Hotel-Restaurant: **Hostellerie du Château,** 2 Rue du Maréchal-de-Lattre-de-Tassigny, tel: 5420-9804, fax: 5420-9798; closed December 1 to March 1. Pleasant residence with gardens, pool and restaurant, medium-priced.

In the region: **Hôtel Château des Tertres,** Route de Monteaux, *Onzain,* across the river from Chaumont: take the D58 one kilometer from village, tel: 5420-8388, fax: 5420-8921. Charming 19th-century château, beautifully decorated rooms, warm atmosphere, no restaurant, medium-priced. ***Pont d'Ouchet,** 50 Grande-Rue, *Onzain,* tel: 5420-7033. Good food, moderately priced.

Chenonceau

From Chaumont take the D114 to the D139 which joins the D764 just before Montrichard. Stay on the right bank of the Cher (N76) until you reach Chenonceau. For many Chenonceau is the queen of queens. Majestically spanning the river Cher, it is much as it was at its apogee in the 17th century.

The original structure was a fortified mill on the river. In the 15th century a donjon was added on *terra firma*. In the 16th the estate was acquired by Thomas Bohier, tax collector to three kings of France, who began new construction on the mill's foundations. Upon Bohier's death, his own finances were such that the château became part of the royal estate in payment of debts. Francis I turned it into a hunting pavillion. Diane de Poitiers received the château from the hands of Henry II, her royal lover, and created the gardens and the bridge which straddles the Cher. The queen, Catherine de Médicis, upon the death of the monarch, forced Diane to relinquish Chenonceau in exchange for the château at Chaumont. Catherine designed another park and commissioned the two-story gallery on the bridge.

The festivities organized at Chenonceau are legendary. At one of Henry III's country outings at the castle, the ladies of the court half-dressed or undressed assisted the personnel in serving the royal guests. In the 18th century the château again served as backdrop for a very stylish salon of celebrities. It is now privately owned.

Visiting hours: 9 A.M. to 7 P.M. from March 16 to September 15; earlier closings at other times of year.
Sound & Light Show: From June 14 to September 6 at 10:15 P.M.
Château Rotisserie: 9:30 A.M. to 6 P.M. from March 16 to November 30; tel: 4723-9197.

Wine tasting: **Caves Monmousseau,** 71 Route de Vierzon,

Montrichard. **Distillerie Fraise-Or,** 62 Route de Tours, *Chissay-en-Touraine.*

Hotel-Restaurant: **Bon Laboureur et du Château,** 6 Rue du Dr-Bretonneau, tel: 4723-9002, fax 4723-8201. Traditional, comfortable hotel, interesting menus, medium-priced.

In the region: **Château de la Menaudière,** Route d'Amboise, *Chissay-en-Touraine,* on N76 between Chenonceau and Montrichard, tel: 5432-0244, fax: 5471-3458. Authentic 16th-century château, tastefully decorated, elegant dining, medium-priced.

Amboise

Leave Chenonceau on the D40 and turn right on the D31 for Amboise. The original château here dates from the 5th century. In the 15th century Charles VII confiscated Amboise and added it to the royal domains. Charles VIII decided to enlarge it and, in 1492, began its reconstruction. During a trip to Italy he discovered the Renaissance and developed a passion for Italian art and objects. A taste for luxury he had already acquired. He returned to Amboise with a caravan of purchases, as well as intellectuals, architects, artists, gardeners, tailors and inventors. Louis XII and Francis I continued the extension and embellishment of the castle. The latter brought Leonardo da Vinci here in 1516.

Amboise also played an important role in the religious wars of the 16th century. In 1560 the so-called Amboise Conspiracy saw the brutal murder of a large number of Huguenots, hung, beheaded, quartered, thrown from the château into the river in bags. They had come hoping to gain the favor of Francis II in order to worship freely and, at the same time, to get their hands on the Duke de Guise and his brother the cardinal, their arch enemies. Or so it is assumed. In 1563 the first war of religion came to an end with the signing of an edict of tolerance, fittingly at Amboise.

The outer fortifications of the castle were dismantled in the

17th century. Napoleon made a gift of the place to a political personality but the latter lacked the funds for its upkeep. To resolve the problem, he dismantled large portions of the château. What you see today represents much less than half the 16th-century structure. In the gardens, which cover the area occupied by the old buildings, there is a bust of Leonardo da Vinci. It is presumed that he was buried in **Saint Hubert's Chapel,** the lovely church in flamboyant Gothic at the edge of the gardens, decorated by Flemish sculptors. The Minimes Tower on the Loire side of the château was paved to permit horses and riders direct access to the upper floors.

From the château take Rue Victor-Hugo, the street below the gardens, to the **Clos Lucé Manor.** It was in this 15th-century residence that Leonardo passed the last three years of his life at the invitation of Francis I. He had crossed the Alps on a donkey, bringing with him the Mona Lisa which the French king purchased. IBM has executed maquettes of Leonardo's fabulous inventions. They are on display in the basement near the tunnel which Francis I used when he came calling on his ingenious guest.

Tourist Info: Quai Général-de-Gaulle, 37400 Amboise, tel: 4757-0137.

Château: 9 A.M. to 6:30 P.M. from July 1 to August 31; closed from 12 to 2 P.M. the rest of the year; 5 P.M. closing from September 26 to April 10.

Sound & Light Show: Wednesdays and Saturdays in July and August, at 10:30 P.M. in July and 10 P.M. in August. Additional performances occasionally; check with Tourist Office.

Clos Lucé Manor: 9 A.M. to 7 P.M. from March 23 to November 11, until 6 P.M. the rest of the year.

Wine tasting: **Caveau Touraine-Amboise,** Rue Victor-Hugo (under château). **Cave Girault-Artois,** 7 Quai des Violettes.

Restaurant: **Manoir Saint-Thomas,** Place Richelieu, tel:

4757-2252, fax: 4730-4471; closed Sunday evenings off season and Mondays and January 15 to March 15. Very elegant Renaissance manor house, fine cuisine, medium-priced.

Hotel-Restaurants: **Choiseul,** 36 Quai Charles-Guinot, tel: 4730-4545, fax: 4730-4610; closed November 30 to January 18. Beautiful 18th-century manor houses, comfortable, personalized rooms, "panoramic" restaurant, fine chef, moderately expensive to expensive. *Parc, 8 Avenue Léonard-de-Vinci, tel: 4757-0693, fax: 4730-5206; restaurant closed Sunday evenings off season and Mondays and from December 1 to February 28. Comfortable house surrounded by gardens, medium-priced rooms, moderately priced restaurant.

In the region: **Château de Noizay,** *Noizay,* 9 kilometers west on N152 and D78 turn-off, tel: 4752-1101, fax: 4752-0464; closed November 1 to March 15. Lovely 16th-century château, personalized rooms, good food, luxury prices for rooms, restaurant medium-priced. **Château de Pray,** *Charge,* 3 kilometers on the D751, tel: 4757-2367, fax: 4757-3250; closed January 2 to February 15. Small, tranquil château and park overlooking the river, rooms moderately expensive to expensive, restaurant, medium-priced. **Petit Lussault,** *Négron,* 3 kilometers on N152, tel: 4757-3030. Charming hotel along the river, moderately priced.

Vouvray

Along the N152 to Tours is a small town called Vouvray. It is set among vineyards and its white wine is known throughout France as one of the finest of Touraine. Some wine tasting is certainly in order. Vouvray has also conserved some old cave dwellings.

Wine tasting: **Cave des Grands Vins de Vouvray,** 38 Rue de la Vallée-Coquette. **Cave Daniel Jarry,** 99 Rue de la Vallée-Coquette.

Restaurant: **Virage Gastronomique,** 25 Avenue Brûlé, tel:

4752-7002; closed Wednesdays and from July 15 to 25. Regional dishes, moderately priced.

Hotel-Restaurant: **Grand Vatel, 8** Rue Brûlé, tel: 4752-7032, fax: 4752-7452; closed Sunday evenings except in season, Mondays and March 8 to 23 and December 1 to 15. Nice country inn, regional cooking, fine wines, half-pension only, moderately priced.

In the region: **Hautes Roches,** 86 Quai de la Loire, *Rochecorbon,* on N152 between Vouvray and Tours, tel: 4752-8888, fax, 4752-8130; closed Sunday evenings and Mondays off season and from mid-January to mid-March. Unique 18th-century hotel along the tufa cliff wall, large, comfortable troglodyte rooms in the wall itself, all overlooking the Loire, very fine chef, rooms expensive to luxury, restaurant medium-priced.

Tours

Tours is the capital of Touraine, *n'est-ce pas?* It was a Roman city at the beginning of our era, as vestiges still visibly attest. Saint Martin became bishop of Tours in 372. Destroying the symbols of pagan cults, he Christianized the region and built Marmoutiers Abbey. A century later Tours raised a basilica in the Châteauneuf quarter dedicated to him. Another hundred years later, Grégoire de Tours was named bishop. His *History of the Franks* provides the most precise knowledge available of life in those times. He founded the abbey adjoining the basilica. Little by little Tours became a place of pilgrimages. People came from near and far, high and low, to seek succor at Saint Martin's door.

At the end of the 8th century Charlemagne offered Saint Martin's Abbey to Alcuin in his waning years. The Englishman, one of the emperor's leading aides, had organized the training of the religious predicators and educators who would in turn set up schools for the priesthood throughout the empire. In Tours, Alcuin received students from all over

Europe for his two teaching cycles: one elementary and one called the "seven liberal arts." He created a scriptorium for the study of calligraphy and the decoration of manuscripts.

The Norman invasions of the 9th century spelled the end of Tours as an intellectual and artistic center. The churches and abbey were destroyed only to be rehabilitated in the 10th century by the Robertians, lay monks. In 1205 King Philip Augustus captured Tours from the English. The black plague of 1351 and the One Hundred Years War struck Tours with force. The population erected walls around the city for its protection. In 1444 Charles VII signed the Truce of Tours with Henry VI of England.

Louis XI, who sojourned often at Tours, introduced the silk industry in the 15th century. In the 17th, 11,000 looms were in operation. Competition with Lyon, however, led to the industry's decline though not its demise. Even today looms are manufactured and exported around the world and a certain number function for the upkeep of the tapestries and upholstery of the grand residences and châteaux of France.

The Reform had many adepts in Tours among intellectuals and crafts people generally. In 1562 the city was witness to the murder of hundreds of Protestants thrown into the Loire.

By 1800 Tours had considerably declined, numbering no more than 20,000 inhabitants. The arrival of the railroad brought about a renewal of economic energy. Today the capital of Touraine and its outlying districts is home to 250,000 people. The city's universities, including a center for Renaissance studies, a conservatory of music and a school of fine arts, have attracted some 18,000 students. Tours was heavily bombarded during the Second World War.

There are three different quarters to be visited in Tours. We shall begin with the most easterly, around **Saint Gatien's Cathedral,** located between the Mirabeau and Saint Symphorien bridges. It represents the epitome of Gothic styles, from primitive to flamboyant. Its stained glass windows are superb. Leaning against the north wall of the cathedral is **La Psalette,** former cloister in which psalms were sung. From **Place Gré-goire-de-Tours,** in back of the church, there is a good view of the flying buttresses and the other buildings on the square.

On the other side of the cathedral, in the old episcopal palace, is the **Beaux-Arts Museum.** The giant cedar in the courtyard was planted in 1804. The round tower to the left is a vestige of the Roman wall which surrounded the city in the 4th century. Many of the fine works of art here were retrieved from monasteries and châteaux in the region. Silks made in Tours line the walls. Among the masterpieces on display are a Rembrandt, a Rubens, sculpture by Houdon, Greek and Etruscan pottery. The third floor is devoted to 19th- and 20th-century painters.

Rue Jacques Simon to the right will take you to the **château** near the river. All that is left of the castle built by Henry II of England in 1160 is the **Guise Tower,** so called because the son of the Duke of Guise, head of the Catholic League, was imprisoned here at the end of the 16th century. In the **March Pavilion,** next door, is a wax museum, the **Historial de Tour-aine,** which recaptures some of the grand events of the re-gion's history. There is also an **aquarium** of tropical fish.

Leave here on Rue des Maures and turn right on Rue Albert-Thomas which will become Rue Colbert with its an-tique dealers. (For other antique shops, take Rue du Cygne to the left and Rue de la Scellerie.) You will arrive at **Saint Julian's Church.** The plain 13th-century structure is adorned with modern stained glass windows. Among the remains of the 11th century cloister surrounding it is the Saint Julian cellar, a large vaulted room which houses the **Museum of Touraine Wines** (on rue Nationale towards the river).

The most interesting visit at the old cloister is the **Trades Guild Museum** (Musée du Compagnonnage). Assembled here are the tools used by the "companions," as well as prod-ucts of their trades whose perfect execution enabled them to be accepted as master craftsmen.

To the left on Rue Nationale is the **Beaune-Semblançay Garden** with its lovely old arcaded gallery and fountain.

Rue Colbert on the other side of Rue Nationale will become Rue du Commerce and will take you on foot into **old Tours** around **Place Plumereau.** Through the arched passageway is **Place Saint-Pierre-le-Puellier** and gardens. On the left is **Rue Briçonnet,** a street of lovely old houses from different periods. Turn left on Rue des Cerisiers and left on Rue Bretonneau. In Rue du Mûrier is the **Gemmail Museum.** Invented in the 19th century, the *gemmail* process consists of an assemblage of small particles of glass illuminated from behind. The colors are permanent.

Take Rue Bretonneau back to Rue des Cerisiers and turn left. At the end of the street turn right and then left and left again to **Place Robert-Picou** with its crafts shops. Leave here on Rue du Petit-Saint-Martin, go left on Rue de la Monnaie, right on Rue Bretonneau and left at the end of Place du Grand-Marché. You will come into Place de Châteauneuf and see the remains of Saint Martin's Basilica: **Charlemagne's Tower** and the **Clock Tower.** Annual pilgrimages to the new basilica take place on November 11 and the following Sunday.

Three kilometers to the west, along the river on Rue des Tanneurs, is **Saint Cosme's Priory** where the French poet Ronsard is buried. He lived in the lovely 15th-century house which has become a **lapidary museum** containing drawings, photos and prints evocative of the poet's life.

A footnote to a visit of Tours is that it contains one of the highest ratios of top-star restaurants per capita outside of Paris.

Tourist Info: Boulevard Heurteloup, 37000 Tours, tel: 4705-5808.

La Psalette: Guided tour from 9 A.M. to 12 and 2 to 6 P.M.; until 5 P.M from October 1 to May 31. No visits during services.

Beaux Arts Museum: 18 Place François-Sicard. 9 A.M. to 12:45 and 2 to 6 P.M.; closed Tuesdays.

Historial de Touraine: Château, Quai d'Orléans. 9 A.M. to 6:30 P.M. from June 16 to September 15; closed from 11:30 A.M. to 2 P.M. from March 16 to June 15 and from September 16 to November 15; 2 to 5:30 P.M. from November 16 to March 15.

Aquarium: Château, 25 Quai d'Orléans, 9:30 A.M. to 7:30 P.M. in July and August; closed from 12 to 2 P.M. and at 6 P.M. from April through June and September 1 to November 15; 2 to 6 P.M. only from November 16 to March 31; closed Saturday mornings throughout the year.

Saint Julian's Church: 12 Rue Colbert, afternoons only.

Museum of Touraine Wines: 16 Rue Nationale, 9 to 11:30 A.M. and 2 to 4:30 P.M.; to 6:30 P.M. from April through September; closed Tuesdays.

Trades Guild Museum: 8 Rue Nationale, 9 to 11:30 A.M. and 2 to 4:30 P.M.; to 6:30 P.M. from April through September; closed Tuesdays.

Gemmail Museum: 7 Rue du Mûrier, 10 to 11:30 A.M. and 2 to 6 P.M.; closed Mondays.

Saint Cosme Priory: Quartier La Riche, 9 A.M. to 6 P.M. in July and August, 9 A.M. to 12 and 2 to 6 P.M. the rest of the year; to 5 P.M. in February, March, October and November; closed Wednesdays in off-season.

Restaurants: **Jean Bardet,** 57 Rue Groison, tel: 4741-4111, fax: 4751-6872; closed Mondays for lunch in season plus Sunday and Monday evenings off season. One of the twelve best restaurants of France, according to Gault Millau, who named Jean Bardet and Gérard Boyer of the Crayères in Reims chefs of the year 1992. Fabulous décor and cuisine, an experience, luxury prices. ***Corneille,** 49 Rue Colbert, tel: 4766-7255. Wine bar serving daily special and dessert (luncheon only), inexpensive. ***Odéon,** 10 Place du Maréchal-Leclerc, tel: 4720-1265. Country cooking in an elegant brasserie, moder-

ately priced. **Roche Le Roy,** 55 Route de Saint-Avertin, tel:
4727-2200, fax: 4728-0839; closed Saturdays for lunch and
Sundays and from August 1 to 25. Fine, inventive cuisine
served in the garden of the manor, fish specialties, medium-
priced. *** Singe Vert,** 5 Rue Marceau, tel: 4761-5010. Art
Nouveau bistro décor, wide variety, moderately priced. **Tuf-
feaux,** 19 Rue Lavoisier, tel: 4747-1989; closed Sundays and
Mondays for lunch and July 12 to 27. Interesting and inventive regional dishes in pleasant old tufa home, moderately
priced.

Accommodations: **Alliance,** 292 Avenue Grammont, tel:
4728-0080, fax: 4727-7761. Professional, modern, comfortable establishment, medium-priced. **Jean Bardet,** see above.
Magnificent mansion in the middle of a park, perfectly charming rooms, luxury prices. **Mirabeau,** 89 bis Boulevard Heurteloup, tel: 4705-2460, fax: 4705-3109. Centrally located,
completely renovated, moderately priced.

In the region: **Château de l'Aubrière,** Route de Fondette,
La Membrolle-sur-Choisille, 6 kilometers north on the N138,
tel: 4751-5035, fax: 4751-3469. Nineteenth-century château,
spacious rooms, medium-priced to expensive. Restaurant
closed Mondays, medium-priced. **Château de Beaulieu,**
Route de Villandry, *Joué-lès-Tours,* 4 kilometers southwest on
D86 and D207, tel: 4753-2026, fax: 4753-8420. Comfortable, peaceful, 18th-century mansion, tastefully decorated
rooms, restaurant, medium-priced to moderately expensive.

Savonnières

The D88 will lead you out of Tours to Savonnières and the
D7 will take you to Villandry. On the outskirts of Savonnières
are some petrified grottos. Very ancient formations, they were
exploited in the 12th century as quarries. Some are still active.
The **Petrification Museum** contains displays of prehistoric
animals. There is also wine tasting in the caves.

Petrification Museum: 61 Rue des Grottes-Petrifiantes. 9

A.M. to 6:30 P.M. April through September; 9 to 11:45 A.M. and 2 to 5:30 P.M. the rest of the year; closed Thursdays in winter.

Hotel: **Cèdres,** Route de Villandry, tel: 4753-0028, fax: 4780-0384. Pleasant, quiet hotel in old residence, medium-priced.

Restaurant: **Cèdres,** nearby, tel: 4753-3758, fax: 4767-2620. Fabulous selection of wines and whiskeys, moderately priced.

Villandry

Villandry is strictly Renaissance, rare for a Loire château. Its gardens *à la française* are also Renaissance and renowned. The highest of the three terraces is a pool which serves as mirror and also as reservoir for the lower gardens. On the second level are two series of gardens, one symbolizing love and the other music. The lower level is called the vegetable garden: vegetables, boxwood, yew and fruit trees.

The château was built in the 16th century on the foundations of an old fortress of which the keep or donjon is the only remaining part: note the square tower inset. The château was purchased by the Spaniard Joachim de Carvallo in 1906, which explains the presence of Spanish furniture and Spanish and Moorish paintings.

Château: 9 A.M. to 6 P.M. from May 1 to September 15; to 5 P.M. from March 15 to April 30 and September 16 to November 11; closed the rest of the year.
Gardens: 9 A.M. to 7 P.M. or sundown; 8:45 A.M. to 8 P.M. from June 1 to September 15; open all year.

Hotel-Restaurant: ***Cheval Rouge,** tel: 4750-0207, fax: 4750-0877. Classic tourist hotel and restaurant, moderately priced.

Azay-le-Rideau

From Villandry take the D7 to the D39 to Azay-le-Rideau. This is another 16th-century Renaissance castle built on the foundations of a much earlier fortified edifice. Here too royal retribution dealt a death blow: Charles VII, considering he had been insulted by the local garrison, had the château burned and the 350 soldiers stationed there killed. This event took place in 1418 and for several hundred years afterward the town was called Azay-le-Brulé (Azay the Burnt).

The château was rebuilt in the early part of the 16th century by the financier Berthelot. But as others before him, his fortunes turned and he quit the country in some haste. Francis I took over the estate and presented it to the captain of his guard. It passed through many hands until purchased by the State in 1905.

The lines of the castle are particularly graceful and one is reminded of Chenonceau. It has become a Renaissance museum. The sound and light show, consisting of a walk around the château, is especially recommended. The 11th century village church of **Saint Symphorian,** enlarged in the 16th century, is worthy of a visit.

Visiting hours: 9 A.M. to 6:30 P.M. in July and August; 9:30 A.M. to 5:30 P.M. in April, May, June, September, October, November; 10 A.M. to 12 noon and 2 to 4:30 P.M. from October 1 to March 31.
Sound & Light Show: From May 24 to September 20; 10:30 P.M. in May, June and July and 10 P.M. in August and September.

Restaurants: **Aigle d'Or,** 10 Rue Adélaide-Riché, tel: 4745-2458; closed Sunday evenings, Wednesdays, February and December 10 to 20. Pleasant restaurant with garden dining, inventive dishes, medium-priced. *****Automate Gourmand,** 1 Rue du Pard, *La Chapelle-Saint-Blaise,* 1 kilometer from village, tel: 4745-3907; closed Tuesdays and March 12 to 28.

Country inn specializing in regional cuisine, moderately priced.

Accommodations: **Biencourt,** 7 Rue Balzac, tel: 4745-2075; closed from November 15 to March 1. Small hotel with garden, medium-priced. **Château du Gerfaut,** tel: 4745-4016, fax: 4745-2015; open April 1 to October 31. Private château offering small number of guest rooms, magnificent surroundings, medium-priced. **Manoir de la Remonière,** tel: 4745-2488. Fifteenth-century manor with natural bird sanctuary offering small number of guest rooms, lovely house and grounds, moderately expensive.

Ussé

From the D751, take the D17 back to the Loire and then left on the D7 to Ussé. There is a wonderful view of the château from the bridge over the Indre River. Charles Perrault wrote *Sleeping Beauty* with this fairy tale castle in mind.

The old fortress here changed hands many times and each succeeding owner added on, remodeled, embellished. One can see signs of different architectural and decorative styles, from feudal to Gothic to Renaissance.

The castle maintains a permanent show of period costumes. The chapel also is interesting.

Visiting hours: 9 A.M. to 6:30 P.M. from July 14 to August 31; 9 A.M. to 12 noon and 2 to 7 P.M. from April 19 to July 13 and in September; 10 A.M. to 12 and 2 to 5:30 P.M. the rest of the year.

Chinon

From the D7 take the D16 left to Chinon on the Vienne River. The ruins of its castle dominate the medieval village in the heart of a fantastic winegrowing region.

Chinon also played an important role in Joan of Arc's heroic crusade. It was here that the young woman from Lorraine came in order to plead with Charles VII to take heart and strike out against the English. At the time Charles' realm had its seat in Chinon and barely covered Touraine. Henry VI of England occupied Paris and most of France.

Joan's first interview with the king took place at the château. After weeks of questioning in Poitiers during which the court finally recognized her as "God's emissary," she returned to Chinon to be outfitted. On April 20, 1429, she set out with a small army for Orléans under siege.

The château was divided into three parts separated by moats. To the east, was the Saint George Fort, which was dismantled after the Revolution. In the center is the Middle Château, where one can visit the Joan of Arc exhibit and hear the clock strike as it has since 1399. The third part, the Coudray Fort, includes the donjon which served to imprison the Templars in the 14th century. Their graffiti is still visible. On the second floor of the donjon is the reception hall in which Joan of Arc was received by Charles VII.

To visit the old town of Chinon, descend the stairs to the parking lot in Rue Voltaire, below the castle on the river side. Walk along this street underneath the château and you will come to the **Animated Museum of Wine and Cooperage** located in cliff caves which were once wine cellars. At the **Grand Carroi** intersection are a number of beautiful old timbered houses. Here too is the **States General Museum.** It was in this building that Richard the Lion Heart died in 1199. Traditional arts are well represented. On the second floor is a portrait of Rabelais, who was from the region, by Delacroix. Many interesting objects and models are related to navigation on the river. Further along this street is **Saint Maurice's Church.**

On taking Rue Voltaire in the other direction from the parking lot, you will pass a number of quaint medieval houses and you will arrive at **Saint Etienne's Church** and, further on, the impressive ruins of **Saint Mexme's Church** which dates from the 10th century. From there one can climb to the cliffside **Saint Radegone's Chapel** with its Roman portal.

There is also a **Museum of Popular Arts and Traditions** here.

A fun **excursion** will take you from Chinon to Richelieu, fifteen kilometers away, in a turn-of-the-century train powered by an old steam engine. It makes a stop for some wine tasting along the way.

Tourist Info: 12 Rue Voltaire, 37500 Chinon, tel: 4793-1785.

Château: 9 A.M. to 7 P.M. in July and August; until 6 P.M. in April, May, June and September; until 5 P.M. from October to December; closed from 12 to 2 P.M. in February and March.

Animated Wine Museum: 12 Rue Voltaire, 10 A.M. to 12 and 2 to 6 P.M. from April through September; closed Thursdays; 10:30 A.M. to 12 noon and closed Sundays the rest of the year.

States General Museum: 44 Rue Haute-Saint-Maurice, 10:30 A.M. to 12:30 and 2:30 to 6 P.M.; closed Tuesdays.

Saint Etienne's Church: 2:30 to 5 P.M. Tuesdays, Thursdays and Fridays from Easter until November 1.

Saint Radegonde's Chapel: 9 A.M. to 6 P.M. from July 15 to August 31.

Steam train: Departures at 2:30 and 6:15 P.M. from May 24 to August 30; 2:30 departure only on Saturdays and Sundays; one hour round trip.

Wine tasting: **Cave Montplaisir,** Quai Pasteur.

Restaurants: **Plaisir Gourmand,** 2 Rue Parmentier, tel: 4793-2048; closed Sundays for dinner and Mondays, February and November 16 to 30. Charming restaurant and garden, excellent cuisine, medium-priced. **Orangerie,* 79 bis Rue Haute-Saint-Maurice, tel: 4798-4200; closed Sunday evenings in winter and from December 15 to February 1, inexpensive.

Accommodations: **Chris' Hotel,** 12 Place Jeanne-d'Arc, tel:

4793-3692, fax: 4798-4892. View of the château and the river, moderately to medium-priced. **Diderot,** 4 Rue Buffon, tel: 4793-1887, fax: 4793-3710. Charming 18th-century home in quiet street, moderately priced.

In the region: **Château de Marçay,** *Marçay,* 6 kilometers south on D749 and D116, tel: 4793-0347, fax: 4793-4533; closed Sunday evenings and Mondays off season and from January 10 to March 21. Superb château hospitality and elegance, fine creative cuisine, moderately expensive to luxury prices. ***La Giraudière,** *Beaumont-en-Véron,* 5 kilometers on D749, tel: 4758-4036, fax: 4758-4606; closed January and Tuesdays and Wednesdays from September 15 to May 15. Welcoming 17th-century mansion, quiet and comfortable, moderate to medium-priced.

Some Useful Words and Phrases

cliff	**falaise** (f)
cotton	**coton** (m)
crusader	**croisé** (m)
feudal	**féodal** (e)
finger	**doigt** (m)
foreign, foreigner	**étranger/étrangère**
guest	**invité**(e)
to hide, to conceal	**cacher**
honey	**miel** (m)
jam	**confiture** (f)
land	**terre** (f)
level	**niveau** (m)
linen	**lin** (m)
neighbor	**voisin**(e)
pedestrian	**piéton**(ne)
rule	**règle** (f)
sacred	**sacré**(e)
silk	**soie** (f)
staircase	**escalier** (m)

state	**état** (m)
to study	**étudier**
sugar	**sucre** (m)
taste	**goût** (m)
wax	**cire** (f)

Le pullover de ma mère est en laine pure. (My mother's pullover is of pure wool.)

Le tissu de la jupe est un mélange de lin et de soie. (The skirt fabric is a mixture of linen and silk.)

Mon fils préfère le miel pour le petit déjeuner. (My son prefers honey for breakfast.)

La patronne de l'hôtel a bon goût. (The hotel owner has good taste.)

Combien de sucres prenez-vous dans votre café? Deux morceaux, s'il vous plaît. (How many sugars do you take in your coffee? Two lumps, please.)

Combien coûte un billet de métro? (How much does a subway ticket cost?)

Remember that in French possessive adjectives are expressed in descriptive phrases. Examples: **la chambre de mon frère** (my brother's room); **le propriétaire du restaurant** (the restaurant owner)

CHAPTER 16

Champagne

The names of few regions ring as many bells as Champagne: on the one hand, there are the chimes of bubbly and, on the other, the death knolls of war. This region has in fact been overrun by people coming from the east as far back as prehistoric times and as recently as the Second World War. Luckily many vestiges of the past have survived battles and bombings. And there is also the bubbly brew to entice one to Champagne country.

Let it be known that champagne comes only from the Champagne region of France. Anywhere else in the world it should be labeled "sparkling" wine. Let it also be known that the bubbles on champagne are a natural phenomenon and not injected. The process is unique, requiring two fermentations of the grape juice, personalized handling, and time. A bottle of champagne may not be put on the market until three years after the grape harvest.

Two varieties of red grapes and one of white are used to make champagne. They are selected and picked by hand and are specially pressed to avoid prolonged contact between the pulp and its skin. The growers are experienced; wine has been made in this region since well before our era. Sparkling wine has evolved essentially since the 17th century, particularly aided by Dom Perignon and the Benedictine monks of Hautvillers Abbey who discovered the double fermentation process. Most champagne houses organize visits of their cellars and samplings of their products.

Champagne is just to the east of Paris. The cities of Reims [pronounced **rance** like **dance**] and Troyes [pronounced **trwa**], which can be reached by direct train in a little over an hour from Paris, have much to offer the visitor: each is well worth a trip on its own. For those wishing to travel around the region, the following itinerary is suggested. The city promenades start at the railway station, which also works for those traveling by car.

Reims

In 496 A.D. Clovis, leader of the Franks, adopted the Christian religion and was baptized in this city. In 816 Louis the Pious was coronated here in remembrance of Clovis' act, and from then until 1825 the kings of France, with few exceptions, received their sacred crown in Reims. After the construction of the present cathedral in the Middle Ages, the ceremonies took place there. During the First World War the city was heavily bombarded by the Germans and suffered massive destruction. On May 7, 1945, unconditional surrender terms were signed by the German military authorities at General Eisenhower's headquarters in Reims.

From the railroad station, go left on Boulevard Joffre to Place de la République and the **Mars Gateway,** the largest commemorative archway of the Roman Empire (2nd century A.D.).

Go left on Avenue de Laon and left on Rue Franklin-Roosevelt. At number 10 is the **War Room** of the technical school in which the Germans signed their capitulation in 1945.

Back at Place de la République, take Rue du Champ-de-Mars to **Our Lady of Peace Chapel** for frescos by Foujita. Just across the street is the entrance to the **Mumm Champagne cellars.** A guided tour in English is available.

At Place de la République once again, go left on Rue de Mars past **City Hall,** a lovely 17th century building. Take either Rue Colbert or Rue de Tambour to **Place du Forum,**

site of an ancient Roman forum. Continue straight on to
Place Royale, a handsome 18th-century square. The statue
in the center is of Louis xv.

Leave the square to your right on Rue Carnot. You will
come to Place Myron T. Herrick. Across from the Justice
Palace at number 14 is a wonderful café, **Le Palais,** decorated
with memorabilia and excellent black and white photos by
Gérard Rondeau. Go past the café and to your left; you will
see the statue of Joan of Arc and then the cathedral.

Notre Dame Cathedral is one of the most beautiful Gothic
churches in France. Begun in 1211, it took one hundred years
to build. Severely damaged during World War I, it has been
restored thanks to a generous donation from the Rockefellers.
Fortunately, a number of stained glass windows were saved
from destruction. The sculpture of the portals, in particular
the central portal dedicated to the Virgin Mary, is splendidly
expressive. The sound and light shows, organized during the
tourist season, have the power of bringing the cathedral to
life. Check with the tourist office for days and times.

Go left on leaving the cathedral and you will come immediately to the **Tau Museum** and **Carnegie Library,** reconstructed after the First World War with a grant from Dale
Carnegie. This was the archbishop's palace in the 17th century, built by Mansart and de Cotte.

From the Tau Palace, go left on Rue Hincmar and right
on Rue Chanzy to the **Beaux Arts Museum** which contains
a varied collection of Renaissance, impressionist and contemporary art. It possesses the largest number of landscapes by
Corot anywhere in the world.

On leaving the museum, go right on Rue Chanzy which
will become Rue Gambetta. At Rue des Moulins turn right
and then left on Rue Simon to the **Saint-Rémi Basilica** (and
Museum). Parts of this old Romanesque abbey date from the
11th century. Early Gothic was added with a new facade and
chancel at the end of the 12th century.

Leave Saint-Rémi to your left on Rue Saint-Julien. You will

arrive at Place Saint-Timothée and beyond there Place Nicaise. Skirt to your left until you come to Boulevard Victor-Hugo. On your right are the **Taittinger Champagne cellars.** Tours (fee) are organized throughout the year.

Two other champagne houses in the neighborhood organize tours through their cellars on a regular basis. To reach them, take Rue Saint-Nicaise alongside Taittinger to Boulevard Henry-Vasnier. To your left, at number 51, **Piper-Heidsieck** takes visitors on an underground ride in an especially constructed area. Commentary is in the language of your choice. There is an entry fee. To your right when leaving Rue Saint-Nicaise, you will come to Place du Général-Gouraud. At number 5 are the eleven miles of **Pommery Champagne's** underground cellars. The guided visit, in English or French, is free-of-charge.

If you are interested in antique cars, you will want to visit the **Philippe Charbonneau Collection** at the **Historical Center of French Automobiles,** the only museum displaying the total range of French automobiles from the 1869 Cugnot "self-moving" vehicle to present-day models. To go there from the champagne cellars, return towards the city center on Boulevard Pasteur and turn right on Avenue Georges-Clémenceau to number 84.

Train from Paris: From Gare de l'Est (East Station) one hour.
Road from Paris: A4 Autoroute de l'Est (Eastern Parkway) ninety minutes.

Tourist info: 2 Rue Guillaume-de-Machault, 51100 Reims (next to the cathedral); open daily.

War Room: 10 Rue Franklin-Roosevelt, 10 A.M. until noon and 2 to 6 P.M.; closed Tuesdays and public holidays.
Our Lady of Peace Chapel: Rue du Champ-de-Mars. 2 to 6 P.M.; closed Wednesdays, national holidays, and in very cold weather.

Mumm: 34 Rue du Champ-de-Mars, 9 to 11 A.M. and 2 to 5 P.M.; closed on weekends and public holidays from November 1 to Easter. Free tours and tasting.

Cathedral: 7:30 A.M. to 7:30 P.M.

Tau Palace: Place du Cardinal-Luçon, 10 A.M. until noon and 2 to 5 P.M.; 9:30 A.M. to 6:30 P.M. in July and August.

Beaux Arts Museum (also called Saint-Denis Museum) 8 Rue Chanzy, 10 A.M. until noon and 2 to 6 P.M.; closed Tuesdays and public holidays.

Saint Rémi Basilica: Rue Simon, 8 A.M. until sunset, at the latest 7 P.M.; 9 A.M. on Thursdays and Saturdays. The adjacent museum is open from 2 to 6:30 P.M.

Taittinger: 9 Place Saint-Nicaise, 9:30 A.M. to 1 P.M. and 2 to 5:30 P.M.; closed weekends December 1 to February 28. Guided tour with interpreter; entry fee.

Piper Heidsieck: 51 Boulevard Henry-Vasnier, weekdays from 9:30 to 11 A.M. and 2 to 5 P.M.; open weekdays from 9:30 to 11 A.M. and 2 to 5 P.M.; open weekends from Easter to November 11. Underground ride with recorded English commentary in especially constructed area. Entry fee.

Pommery: 5 Place du Général-Gouraud; tours with English-speaking guide every day from 2 to 5 P.M.; Saturdays, Sundays and holidays, from mid-March through November also open from 9:20 to 11:20 A.M.; open both mornings and afternoons every day in July and August, free-of-charge.

Historical Center of French Automobiles: 84 Avenue Georges-Clémenceau, 10 A.M. to noon and 2 to 7 P.M. from March to November; in winter open weekends and holidays only.

Restaurants: **Boyer,** Les Crayères, 64 Boulevard Henry-Vasnier, tel: 2682-8080, fax: 2682-6552; closed Mondays, for lunch on Tuesdays, and from December 21 to January 13. One of the ten best restaurants in France: 19.5 (out of 20) rating from Gault Millau. What more is there to say! Expensive. **Florence,** 43 Boulevard Foch, tel: 2647-1270; closed

Sundays and from August 1 to 20. Excellent food in lovely setting, expensive. *Paysan, 16 Rue Fismes, tel: 2640-2551; closed Saturdays for lunch and Sundays. Plain and good, inexpensive. **Vigneron,** Place Paul-Jamot, tel: 2647-0071. Regional dishes, wonderful décor of old objects and posters, hearty, regional dishes, medium-priced.

Accommodations: **Boyer,** Les Crayères (see above). Château-restaurant at its best. Large, comfortable and tastefully decorated rooms, expensive. **Consuls,** 9 Rue du Général-Sarrail, tel: 2688-4610, fax: 2688-6633. Newly opened, attractive hotel in quiet, centrally located street, medium-priced. **Crystal,** 86 Place Drouet-d'Erlon, tel: 2688-4444, fax; 2647-4928. Quiet location, pleasant, moderately priced.

Outside of town: **Assiette Champenoise,** 40 Avenue Paul-Vaillant-Couturier, *Tinqueux,* 5 kilometers on N31, tel: 2604-1556, fax: 2604-1569. Comfortable, attractive, four-star hotel, excellent cuisine, pool, moderately expensive.

Champagne Route

The Champagne region is, for the major part, one of wide plains and large, industrial farms. It is noted for the high quality and abundance of its wheat, sugar beets and cabbage. Trees and woods are few, giant silos for stocking grain are many. The exception to the rule are the vineyards covering the hillocks above the plains, in which blossom the red and white grapevines that produce the fruit for champagne.

There are three wine-growing regions of hills and valleys between Reims and Epernay, the other champagne capital, and just beyond Epernay: Reims Mountain, the Côte des Blancs and Marne Valley. All along these routes, stops for tours and tasting in the champagne and wine cellars are definitely in order. Things may seem quiet as you trundle along. Actually the activity of the region is taking place underground, in the chalky wine cellars. If you are in the market for purchasing champagne, it can be considerably cheaper than in the cities . . . and just as delicious.

Leave Reims on route N51 which exits just beyond the Saint-Rémi Basilica. This road will take you to Montchenot, the first village on Reims Mountain. From there take the D26 through Rilly-la-Montagne, Mailly Champagne, **Verzenay** with its windmill, and **Verzy** surrounded by a forest of curiously twisted trees. At Ambonnay, take the D34 to **Bouzy.** If you enjoy wine tasting, the Bouzy red wine has a rich fruity taste. At Louvois take the D9 to Avenay and Mareuil-sur-Ay, then the D1 to **Ay,** where several champagne cellars are located among the gingerbread houses. Then, on to **Hautvillers,** the prettiest village on this route. It was here that Dom Perignon discovered the double fermentation process. The abbey, which still exists, belongs to Moët et Chandon.

From Hautvillers backtrack to Epernay (turn right on the N51).

Montchenot
Restaurant: **Auberge du Grand Cerf,** tel: 2697-6007, fax: 2697-6424. Closed Sunday evenings, Wednesdays and August. Decorative dining room and inventive haute cuisine, moderately expensive.

Ambonnay
Hotel-Restaurant: **Auberge Saint Vincent,** Rue Saint-Vincent, tel: 2657-0198. Closed Sunday evenings and Mondays. Quiet, modern rooms, interesting regional dishes, half-pension required for hotel guests, medium-priced.

Epernay

Coming into Epernay, take the bridge over the Marne River to Rue de Reims, Rue Pierre-Semart, across Place Mendes-France to Rue Gambetta and Place de la République. Go three-quarters of the way around the Place and take **Avenue de Champagne,** which the local population refers to as the Champs-Elysées of the majors.

There to the right and to the left are many of the great names in champagne: Moët et Chandon, Perrier Jouet, de Venoge, Charbaut, Pol Roger, de Castellane, Mercier . . . in approximately sixty miles of cellars in the chalk foundations under Epernay. Some of the tunnels are 100 or more feet below the city streets. Moët et Chandon, de Venoge, de Castellane and Mercier are open at regular hours for guided tours.

Tourist Info: 7 Avenue de Champagne, 51200 Epernay, open every day from Easter to October 15; Closed on Sundays and public holidays from October 16 to Easter.

Moët & Chandon: 18 Avenue de Champagne; 9:30 to 11:30 A.M. and 2 to 4:30 P.M.; closing time Sundays and holidays: 3:30 P.M.; closed weekends and public holidays from November 1 to March 31. No charge.

de Venoge: 30 Avenue de Champagne, 10 A.M. to 12 noon and 2 to 4 P.M.; weekdays only; closed on public holidays.

de Castellane: 57 Rue de Verdun. 10 A.M. to 12 noon and 2 to 6 P.M. from April 27 to November 3; from November 4 to December 15 and from Easter weekend to April 26, 2 to 5 P.M. only. No charge.

Mercier: 70 Avenue de Champagne, 9:30 to 11:30 A.M. and 2 to 5 P.M. December, January and February weekends only. Ride through the cellars with English-speaking guide. No charge.

Restaurants: **Hermite,** 3-5 Place Mendès-France, tel: 2655-2605. Inexpensive. **Terrasse,** 7 Quai de la Marne, tel: 2655-2605; fax: 2655-3379. Closed Sunday evenings, Mondays and February. Regional dishes, medium-priced.

Hotel-Restaurants: **Berceaux,** 13 Rue des Berceaux, tel: 2655-2884, fax: 2655-1036. Restaurant closed Sunday evenings. Comfortable hotel, centrally located, highly rated classic cuisine, medium-priced. **Chapon Fin,** 2 Place Mendès-France, tel: 2655-4003, fax: 2655-9417. Restaurant closed

Wednesdays. Inexpensive rooms, moderately priced restaurant.

Outside of town: **Royal Champagne,** Bellevue, 51160 *Champillon,* 5 kilometers north on route 2051, tel: 2652-8711, Fax: 2652-9070. Four-star hotel with magnificent view over vineyards from delightfully beautiful rooms with terrace. Fabulous young chef, perfect champagnes, expensive.

Avenue du Maréchal Foch will take you out of Epernay to the N51 road to Pierry. At Pierry take the D210 to **Chavot** with its charming Romanesque church on a promontory. At Mancy, go left on the D40, then right on the D10 towards Cuis, **Cramant** and its bottle, and Avize. Go through Le Mesnil-sur-Oger to **Vertus** to see the lovely old homes near the 12th-century church. Take the D9 south to Bergères-les-Vertus, then right on the D33 to **Etoges** and its splendid château-hotel.

On leaving Etoges, go left on the D43 to Fère-Champenoise and Salon. Take the D71 from here to **Arcis-sur-Aube,** the birthplace of Danton. The château, designed by Mansart, is now the town hall. Cross the river out of Arcis for Le-Chêne. Turn left in the village and then right to **L'Huitre** where there is a very lovely church with fine stained glass windows. Leave here on the D9 to **Vinets** with its old mill, then take a left on the D56 to **Ramerupt** where there is a fantastic 15th-century market place. Go over the Aube River on the D960 to **Pont-Sainte-Marie** on the outskirts of Troyes. The church is worth a stop.

Mesnil
Restaurant: Mesnil, 2 Rue Pasteur, tel: 2657-9557, fax: 2657-7857; closed Monday evenings, Wednesdays and last two weeks August. Conventional cuisine, moderately expensive.

Vertus
Hotel-Restaurants: **Reine Blanche,** 18 Avenue Louis-Len-oir, tel: 2652-2076, fax: 2652-1659. Comfortable, rustic, tra-ditional fare, medium-priced. **Thibault** IV, 2 Place de la République, tel: 2652-0124, fax: 2652-1659. Renovated rooms, moderately priced.

Bergères-les-Vertus
Hotel-Restaurant: *Mont Aimé, Rue Vertus, tel: 2652-2131; fax: 2652-2139. Pleasant country inn, rooms on gar-den, good regional cooking, moderately priced.

Etoges
Hotel-Restaurant: **Château d'Etoges,** tel: 2659-3008, fax: 2659-3557. A 17th-century castle completely surrounded by water. Superb rooms, majestic staircase, pretty dining room, moderately expensive.

Arcis-sur-Aube
Restaurant: *Saint-Hubert, 2 Rue de la Marine, tel: 2537-8693; fax: 2537-0150. Closed Friday evenings and Saturdays off season. Hearty, conventional food, moderately priced.

Troyes

Troyes, like Reims, was a major trading center in the 12th and 13th centuries. Its markets and fairs attracted buyers from all over Europe. Occupied by the British in the early 15th century, Troyes regained its freedom in 1429 when Joan of Arc entered the city. In the 16th and 17th centuries it was known as a European art capital. In the 20th century it be-came a center for the knitwear industry. While many of the textile mills have closed because of recession, a number of leading brands of ready-to-wear are still manufactured here, such as Lacoste, Kookaï, Yves St. Laurent, Pierre Cardin, Adidas, and Absorba. The tourist office distributes a brochure listing factory outlet stores and their addresses.

Troyes has suffered many injuries in its history. The Nor-mans burned the city in 889. A fire in 1524 greatly damaged it. During World War II, it was heavily bombarded by the Germans. Considerable renovation has now taken place and it is once again a very pleasant city to roam about. Within its perimeters are a multitude of fine art treasures.

Tour

There are so many things to see in Troyes that I suggest beginning with the outstanding and going back to the other goodies. Rather than start the visit from the railway station, cross town quickly on Avenue du Maréchal-Joffre, which becomes Général-de-Gaulle. If you are traveling by car, take instead Rue Argence which is to the left of Joffre and parallel to it. Turn right on Quai de Dampierre and left on Rue de la Cité or at Place de la Libération to the **Saint Peter and Paul Cathedral.**

Here again is a magnificent Gothic cathedral pushing skyward. Its simple lines are constructed in the white chalk stone of the Champagne country. Begun in 1208, it was not actually completed until the 17th century when a tower was added. Among the stained glass windows, that of the wine press in the fourth bay on the left side is particularly well known.

On leaving the cathedral, go left into the adjacent episcopal palace, now the **Troyes Museum of Modern Art.** You will encounter total enchantment: rooms impeccably restored and prepared to receive one of the most admirable collections of painting and sculpture outside Paris. The museum was begun with the bequest of two thousand works of art from the private collection of Pierre and Denise Levy, local residents whose fortune derives from the hosiery and knitwear industry. Although new pieces have been purchased, the Levy collection, which includes an amazing African arts exhibit, is the heart of the museum. You will see little-known work of renowned painters: moving portraits by Millet, the interior of an arms factory by Vuillard, the use of pinks by Marquet, oranges and mauves by Braque. The fauvist era is particularly well represented. Numerous are the paintings by Derain: an unforgettable London in blue, landscapes in dark greens and deep blues. Not to be overlooked are Balthus, Dunoyer de Segonzac, and an impressive recent acquisition of sculpture by Ousmane Sow.

On leaving the Museum, take Rue de la Cité. Just before the bridge is the **Pharmacy Museum of the Hôtel-Dieu-le-Comte;** its interesting collection of boxes and jars for pharmaceuticals is displayed in an elegant home containing a private chapel and a small Hospital Museum.

When you cross the bridge outside the museum, you will be in Rue Georges-Clémenceau. At your second left is **Saint Urbain's Basilica,** another Gothic masterpiece.

Continue on Rue Georges-Clémenceau until it becomes Rue Champeaux. Turn right in the picturesque **Rue des Chats** until you arrive at **Saint Madeleine's Church.** The 16th-century rood screen in flamboyant Gothic is superb against the austere primitive Gothic of the rest of the church.

Take Rue des Chats back to Rue des Champeaux. Turn left and almost immediately right for **Saint John's Church** and its lovely *grisaille* (yellow and brown) stained glass windows. It was here that Catherine of France and Henry v of England were wed in 1420.

Leave the church through Place du Marché-au-Pain, turn right on Rue Emile-Zola and take your second left on Rue de la Trinité. At Number 7 is the **House of Tools and Craftsman's Library.** This Renaissance mansion houses journeymen's tools from all over France. For those interested in the history of man's handwork, this visit is totally satisfying. The old house is lovely; the unlabeled displays speak for themselves. A brochure in English relates the Hôtel's history.

Saint Pantaleon's Church, just behind the House of Tools is also interesting. Mass is in Polish on certain Sundays. In the same street, Rue Vauluisant, is the amusing **Hosiery and Knitwear Museum:** many items of clothing and looms made in Troyes several centuries ago are displayed here.

On leaving here, cross Rue Emile-Zola and take Rue Juvénal which, after Rue Roger-Salengro, becomes Rue Bruneval. At number 5 is a unique 16th-century **synagogue,** center of the Rachi community founded in Troyes in 1070.

Train from Paris: From Gare de l'Est (East Station) one hour and ten minutes.
Road from Paris: N19, about two hours.

Tourist Info: 16 Boulevard Carnot, 10000 Troyes (near the railway station); open every day from July 1 to September 15; closed Sundays the rest of the year.

Cathedral: 8 A.M. to 6 P.M. in season, 9 A.M. to 12 and 2 to 5 P.M. off season. Sound and light shows Friday and Saturday evenings from June to mid-September, information and tickets at the Tourist Office.
Museum of Modern Art: Place Saint-Pierre, 11 A.M. to 6 P.M. except Tuesdays and public holidays.
Pharmacy Museum: Quai des Comtes-de-Champagne, 10 A.M. to 12 and 2 to 6 P.M. except Tuesdays and public holidays.
Saint Urbain Basilica: Place Vernier, 3 to 4:15 P.M. weekdays, 8:30 to 10:15 A.M. Sundays.
Saint Madeleine's: Rue de la Madeleine, 2 to 4 P.M.
Saint John's: Place du Marché-au-Pain, see Tourist Office for times.
House of Tools: 7 Rue de la Trinité, 9 A.M. to 12 and 2 to 6 P.M.
Saint Panteleon's: Rue de Vauluisant, see Tourist Office for times.
Hoseiry § Knitwear Museum: 10 A.M. to 12 and 2 to 6 P.M. except Tuesdays and public holidays.
Synagogue: 5 Rue Bruneval, services Fridays at 7:15 P.M. and Saturdays at 9:30 A.M.

Restaurants: ***Coin de la Pierre,** corner of Rue de la Pierre and Rue Viardin. Very pleasant, moderately priced. **Table Gourmande,** 1 Rue Raymond-Poincaré, tel: 2573-0505;

closed Sunday evenings and Mondays. Elegant restaurant, good food, expensive. **Valentino,** 11 Cour Rencontre, tel: 2573-1414; closed Sunday evenings and Mondays and from August 15 to September 8. Very creative dishes, expensive.

Accommodations: **Champenois,** 15 Rue Pierre-Gauthier, tel: 2576-1605. Quiet, pleasant, inexpensive. **Relais Saint Jean,** 45 Rue Paillot-de-Montabert, tel: 2573-8990, fax: 2573-8860. Exquisite, pleasurable modern decoration in the heart of old Troyes, moderately expensive. **Royal,** 22 Boulevard Carnot, tel: 2573-1999, fax: 2573-4785. Very comfortable, classic hotel, medium-priced.

Outside town: **Auberge de la Scierie,** La Vove, 10160 *Aix-en-Othe,* 33 kilometers west of Troy on N60 to N374, tel: 2546-7126, fax: 2546-6569. Charming hotel and restaurant in old sawmill on river, lovely grounds, pool, medium-priced.

To the east of Troyes and to the south are two areas of special interest. The first is the region around the Orient Forest National Park, the heart of which are three artificial lakes which supply the Seine River. The second is Langres.

Take route 960 out of Troyes to the northeast. Stop at **Brienne-le-Château,** a forty-kilometer drive. Napoleon studied at the military school here, which is now a museum dedicated to him. The church and market place are worth noting.

Take the D443 to **Brienne-le-Vieille** to see the mill on the river and the 12th-century church. Pick up the D960 again out of Brienne-le-Château to **Soulaines-Dhuys,** a charming village of stone bridges and timbered houses. Then get on the D24 to Mazières and the D2 to **Lentilles** where there is a splendid timbered church.

Continue on to **Bailly-le-Franc** to see the church and then cut westward to **Chavanges,** a very typical village. Go on to **Rosnay-l'Hôpital** for the church and its crypt. Take the road through Lassicourt to **Lesmont** for a walk under the market hall. **Piney** on the D20 also has a fine market hall. Then go on to **Brevonnes.** From here you can visit the lakes. At Orient Lake are beaches, at Temple Lake nature walks and at Amance Lake boating.

If you leave the lakes at the southernmost point, after Mesnil-St.-Père, go left on the N19 to **Dolancourt.** This tiny town on the Aube River boasts a delightful amusement park, miniature Disneyland, both ingenious and inexpensive.

From here you can either return to Troyes or continue on to Langres on the N19.

Brevonnes

Hotel-Restaurant: ***Vieux Logis,** tel: 2546-3017; closed Sunday evenings and Mondays from November to May. Traditional country inn, completely renovated by owner, regional cuisine, moderately priced.

Dolancourt

Hotel-Restaurant: **Moulin du Landion,** Dolancourt, tel: 2527-9217, fax: 2527-9444. Excellent food, dining room overlooking the old mill and river, pool, adequate rooms, moderately priced.

Langres

Take the D19 to this striking old village perched at the edge of a plateau from which the entire countryside can be surveyed and admired. Langres was a military and religious stronghold from the third century and is surrounded by **ramparts and towers.** Visit **Saint Mammès Cathedral,** part Romanesque, part early Gothic. The **Saint Didier Museum,** opposite the cathedral, presents a collection of Gallo-Roman antiquities and sculpture from the Middle Ages. The interesting **du Breuil Museum** is dedicated essentially to Dénis Diderot, 18th-century French encyclopedist. You can walk all the way around the city on the ramparts. Langres produces a pleasant-tasting cheese.

Tourist Info: Square Olivier Lahalle, 52200 Langres, tel: 2587-6767.

du Breuil Museum: 2 Rue Chambrûlard, 10 A.M. to 12 noon and 2 to 5 P.M. except Tuesdays.

Hotel-Restaurant: *Grand Hôtel de l'Europe, 23 Rue Diderot, tel: 2587-1088, fax: 2587-6065. Restaurant closed Sunday evenings and Mondays for lunch. Old-fashioned hotel, moderately priced.

Some Useful Words and Phrases

beet	**betterave** (f)
bombing	**bombardement** (m)
bottle	**bouteille** (f)
box	**boîte** (f)
bubble	**bulle** (f)
cabbage	**chou** (m)
cheap	**bon marché**
cheaper	**meilleur marché**
to check	**vérifier**
to cross	**traverser**
crown	**couronne** (f)
exit	**sortie** (f)
harvest	**récolte** (f)
headquarters	**quartier général, siège** (m)
knitwear	**tricot** (m)
lake	**lac** (m)
neighborhood	**quartier** (m)
skin	**peau** (f)
sparkling	**mousseux/mousseuse = pétillant(e)**
to stop	**arrêter**
surrender	**reddition** (f)
tool	**outil** (m)
tree	**arbre** (m)
wheat	**blé** (m)
window	**fenêtre** (f)

Arrête la voiture près du lac. (Stop the car near the lake.)

Nous aimerions douze bouteilles, s'il vous plaît. (We would like twelve bottles, please.)

Traversez la ville et tournez à gauche. (Cross the town and turn left.)

Vérifiez les prix et prenez le meilleur marché. (Check the prices and take the cheapest.)

Partons maintenant. (Let's leave now.)

Allons-y. (Let's go.)

The imperative tense in French simply drops the personal pronoun. For the **tu** form of verbs ending in **er,** the imperative also drops the final **s.**

Examples: **Ne parle pas trop.** Don't talk too much. (**er** verb)
           Bois ton lait.   Drink your milk.   (**re** verb)
           Finis ton thé.   Finish your tea.   (**ir** verb)

CHAPTER 17

Provence

From the window of the overnight train from Paris, there are few sensations more heartwarming than to open one's eyes in early morning on Orange or Aix or Arles. Step down from a plane originating in northern climes, or leave your car and the gray monotony of a parkway. When you put your foot on the brick-red earth of Provence you will be overcome by nature's way and humanity's treatment of it.

Nothing can compare with the sunlit dust in the streets of a southern town, tiled roofs and pastel-tinted stucco, olive trees and citrus boughs that bend languidly with the musky breeze. The colors are moss-green, burnt sienna, ochre, and lavendar, with a dash of orange. The sounds soothe in Provence. A few kilometers beyond are cactus and palms against Mediterranean azure.

This is an old country, settled at least since the beginning of the first millennium, occupied at different times by Africans, Celts, Greeks, Romans, Wisigoths, Arabs, and Franks. Each has left its mark on the architecture, the language, the morés.

The first recognizable civilization was called Ligurian, the second Celto-Ligurian. Then, the Phocaeans, arriving by sea, occupied what is now Marseilles. Six centuries later the Romans displaced the Greeks and took over Provence.

From the end of the 5th century until the 10th and 11th centuries, the region was subjected to numerous invasions. The villages of the interior and the coastal ports gradually

217

forged a union based on language and customs and became part of the Languedoc nation of the south.

Constituting the link between Catholic Catalonia and Italy at the time of the crusades, the region developed grandly. It was during this period that it became a center for Romanesque art and architecture. In the 13th century Provence succumbed to the expansionism of northern dynasties. Marriage between the royal family of Anjou and that of Catalonia constituted the political means to seal the region's destiny.

In the early years of the 14th century, first Clement v, then Pope John xxii, elected to take residence near or in Avignon. For the next hundred years the popes resided there, contributing to its wealth and renown. In the 15th century, Aix wore the mantle of leading city of art and culture.

In 1482, Provence was forcibly and integrally incorporated into the French kingdom. Early in the 16th century the region was rent by religious strife. The Reformation had numerous adepts in the towns and villages. The authorities at Aix, determined to rout the "heretics," launched attacks of such violence that entire villages were razed. The wars of religion separated Provence from Languedoc, the former adopting Catholicism, the latter remaining firmly reformist and Protestant. Finally, in the 17th century, Louis xiv withdrew whatever remained of the region's "special" status.

In the 19th century, Frédéric Mistral led a powerful renaissance movement in Provence to revive the old language, its literature and customs. Also in the 19th century the first tourists arrived in Provence; for these English the region represented a gentle, sunny haven from the dank north. And so it still is.

There are scores of attractive itineraries across Provence. With great pain, I have limited myself to three. Each itinerary begins in a major city: Nîmes, Avignon, Marseille. Should you not be traveling by car, these towns are valid on their own. They, and others, are linked by both train and bus.

I *Nîmes to Saint-Rémy-de-Provence*

At the base of an arid, aromatic scrubland, Nîmes displays monuments attesting to its Roman past. The Emperor Augustus favored the city and spent a fortune embellishing it with forum, amphitheater, circus, baths, an aqueduct. A key link in the chain of towns dotting the road from Spain to Italy, Nîmes upheld its prosperity until the 8th century. Between 736 and 740 A.D. the Frank leader Charles Martel struck the area with full force and violence. Nîmes submitted and was thrown from its pedestal. It was annexed by the Kingdom of France in 1229.

In the 15th century the plague decimated the city. In the 16th it became a Protestant stronghold. As such, Nîmes was persecuted and its faithful were refused the right to hold office or exercise official responsibilities. Fervent supporters of the Revolution in 1789, the Huguenots considered the overthrow of the Catholic monarchy to be their revenge.

The fortunes of the Protestant bourgeoisie took a turn for the better in the 15th century with textile manufacturing: their silk, wool, and serge products found favor in Spain and Portugal, and later as far afield as India and America. Serge, also called denim (in other words **de Nîmes**), was the original fabric used by Levi Strauss of California for his jeans! Nîmes is no longer an economic and commercial hub. That role is performed now by Montpellier to the west.

From the railway station take Avenue Feuchères, cross Charles-de-Gaulle Esplanade and go directly to the **Arena** on the left. The best conserved of the Roman circuses in France, it can acccommodate 24,000 spectators. Imagine the scene at the time of the Roman games: gladiators, prisoners of war, convicts, adventurers engaged in bloody combat to the death. No slipshod affair: the rules were rigid. The winner was expected to cut the throat of the loser, unless overruled by the raising of the chairman's thumb. Wild beasts and animals

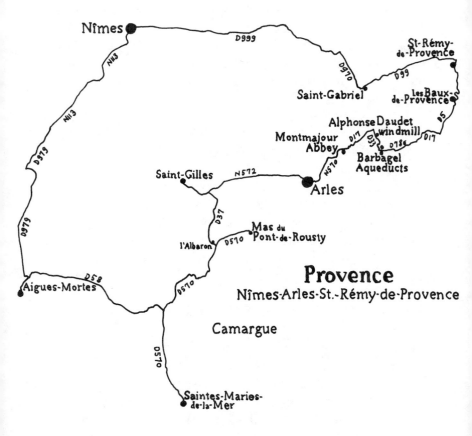

Nîmes

St-Rémy-
de-Provence

D999

D970

D99

Saint-Gabriel

Les Baux-
de-Provence

NII3

NII3

Alphonse Daudet
windmill

D5

Montmajour
Abbey

D17

D33

D979

D79s

D17

Barbagel
Aqueducts

N572

N570

Saint-Gilles

Arles

D37

Mas du
Pont-de-Rousty

D979

l'Albaron

D570

Aigues-Mortes

D58

D570

Provence
Nîmes-Arles-St.-Rémy-de-Provence

Camargue

D570

Saintes-Maries-
de-la-Mer

amused the galleries too in fights to the finish. Gladiator tournaments were outlawed in 404 A.D. Bullfighting was introduced in the arena in 1853 and remains a favorite sport.

On leaving the Arena take **Rue de l'Aspic,** then turn left on **Rue Bernis.** Go to Rue Fresque, then right on **Rue de la Madeleine** which will lead you to the **Museum of Old Nîmes** with its collection of regional handicrafts, furniture, and porcelain. Through the streets of old Nîmes, do not hesitate to enter the courtyards and passageways for a glance at the harmonious superimposition of styles and periods.

Grande Rue behind the cathedral and museum will conduct you to the instructive **Archaeological Museum** located in a former Jesuit school and chapel.

Back at the cathedral take Rue de l'Horloge to the **Square House,** the most impressive vestige of Augustus' reign. This temple, probably part of the forum of Nîmes, was dedicated to the emperor's grandson killed in battle. From here take Rue Auguste to **la Fontaine Garden.** Along **Quai de la Fontaine** are homes built by the Protestant gentry of yore. The garden itself is typically 18th century. **Diane's Temple,** across the bridge to the left, is the remains of a Greek-style temple. Concerts and shows are held here during the summer season.

Walkers among you may wish to climb **Mount Cavalier.** From the top of the 140 steps of the **Magne Tower** a vista of scrubland and hills fills the eyes.

Nîmes organizes a jazz festival during the 14th of July (Bastille Day) week.

Train from Paris: Gare de Lyon, 6 hours (TGV).

Tourist Info: 6 Rue Auguste, 30000 Nîmes, tel: 6667-2911.

Arena: 9 A.M. to 7 P.M. from mid-June to mid-September; 9 A.M. to 12 and 2 to 5 P.M. the rest of the year. No visits during bullfights or shows. Closed on public holidays.

Museum of Old Nîmes: Place de la Cathédrale. 9 A.M. to 6 P.M. except Sunday mornings and public holidays.

Archaeological Museum: 13 Boulevard de l'Amiral-Courbet, 9 A.M. to 6 P.M. except Sunday mornings and public holidays. *Square House:* 9 A.M. to 7 P.M. from mid-June to mid-September, 9 A.M. to 12 and 2 to 5 P.M. the rest of the year; closed on public holidays.

Secondhand market: Avenue Jean-Jaurès, Mondays; Lots Littré, Saturdays.

Restaurants: ***Caramel Mou,** 5 Rue Jean-Reboul, tel: 6621-2708; open evenings only, closed Mondays and August. Good atmosphere and food, moderately priced. **Enclos de la Fontaine,** Quai de la Fontaine, tel: 6667-7025. Elegant garden dining room, very good food. Moderately expensive. **Magister,** 5 Rue Nationale, tel: 6676-1100; closed Saturdays for lunch and Sundays. Excellent value, moderately priced. ***Royal Hotel,** 3 Boulevard Alphonse-Daudet, tel: 6667-2836. Pleasant restaurant, moderately priced. Jazz certain evenings.

Accommodations: **Impérator Concorde,** Quai de la Fontaine, tel: 6667-7025, fax: 6667-7025. Nîmes's best hotel, moderately expensive. **Royal Hotel** (see above). Creative décor, moderately priced.

Outside of town: **Hacienda,** Mas de Brignon, 30320 *Marguerittes,* 6 kilometers east of Nîmes on the A9, tel: 6675-0225, fax: 6675-4558. Charming provençal ranch-type house, home-cooked meals, medium-priced.

Camargue

The region to the south of Nîmes is a delta of marshland, ponds, sea, and free-roaming horses. Much of the area belongs to the National Reserve and the Regional Natural Park and, as such, is protected from the speculators and promoters who have soiled many stretches of France's coastline. The northern part of the Rhône delta is devoted to agriculture (fruits, vegetables, wheat, vineyards, and some rice). To the east and to the west are salt marshes and saltworks, some of which have been exploited since antiquity. The southernmost part of Camargue is nature's finest: prairies, dunes, and the sea. Walk on the dunes, around the lagoons, watch the occasional herd of bulls, sheep or horses. A number of local herdsmen rent horses for riding in the marches and on the beaches.

Take the N113 out of Nîmes toward the south. Get off at the junction with the D979 which will take you to **Aigues-Mortes** (Dead Waters). This port was built from scratch on orders from Louis IX (Saint Louis). Some 35,000 crusaders and the king and queen embarked here in 1248 in 1500 boats bound for the eastern Mediterranean. The city declined in the middle of the 15th century as the sand bar grew filling in the harbor and pushing back the sea.

Leave your car at the municipal parking lot and visit Aigues-Mortes' **ramparts** and the **Constance Tower** on foot. The latter, a cyclindrical donjon, was built to defend the port from attack. Its walls are twenty feet thick. For five centuries religious and political prisoners were incarcerated here. Three kilometers to the south are the **Salins du Midi** or saltworks which are open to visitors in season.

Tourist Info: Porte de la Gardette, 30220 Aigues-Mortes, tel: 6653-7300.

Constance Tower: 9 A.M. to 6 P.M. from April to September, 9 A.M. to 12 and 2 to 5 P.M. the rest of the year.
Salins du Midi: Open from Tuesday to Friday in July and August; see Tourist Office.

Restaurant: **Camargue,** 19 Rue de la République, tel: 6653-8688; evenings only, except Mondays; open all day Sundays. Regional food and gypsy guitar, moderately priced.

Hotel-Restaurants: **Arcades,** 23 Boulevard Gambetta, tel: 6653-8113; closed Mondays, except in the evening in July and August. Lovely 16th-century residence, good food, restaurant moderately priced, hotel moderately expensive. **Saint-Louis,**

10 Rue de l'Amiral-Courbet, tel: 6653-7268, fax: 6623-6864. Comfortable hotel in medieval edifice, fine chef, medium-priced.

Hotel: **Hostellerie des Remparts,** 6 Place des Armes, tel: 6653-8277, fax: 6653-7377. Lovely rooms in old residence, medium-priced.

Saintes-Maries-de-la-Mer

Take the D979 out of Aigues-Mortes and pick up the D58 a few kilometers out-of-town. Leave the D58 for the D38c. (Just beyond this junction are the ruins of the **Montcalm château,** home of the French general who died defending Quebec from the English.) This road will take you to the D570 and **Saintes-Maries-de-la-Mer,** city of blue shutters and rose tamarisks.

This town is known all over France for its **gypsy celebrations** which take place on May 24 and 25 and on the closest Sunday to October 22 for the patron saint Sara. The festivities, many of which involve walking on stilts, are fascinating. Legend has it that three men and three women, all named Mary (Marie in French), fled Palestine after Christ's death. They landed here after a lengthy voyage at sea in a small barque and Sara succored them. The Tziganes liken that eventful journey to their own wandering existence.

Visit the **church** and the **Baroncelli Museum** devoted to the Camargue.

Tourist Info: Avenue Van Gogh, 13460 Saintes-Maries-de-la-Mer, tel: 9047-8255.

Baroncelli Museum: Rue Victor-Hugo, 9 A.M. to 12 noon and 2 to 5 P.M.

Restaurants: **Impérial,** tel: 9097-8184. Agreeable, outdoor dining, moderately priced.

Accommodations: **Lou Maquès,** tel: 9097-8289, fax: 9097-7224. Pleasant, simple hotel, moderately priced.

Outside of town: **Hostellerie de Cacharel,** Route de Cacharel, 4 kilometers north on D85A, tel: 9097-9544, fax: 9097-8797. Charming, typical ranch house in the marshland. No restaurant. Moderately expensive. **Lou Mas doù Juge,** Route du Bac du Sauvage, D85, tel: 6673-5145, fax: 6673-5142. Another typical ranch-type inn, lovely rooms and view, good food, atmosphere, half-pension only, moderately expensive. **Mas du Clarousset,** Route de Cacharel, 7 kilometers north on D85A, tel: 9097-8166, fax: 9097-8859. Beautiful home and view of Camargue, pool, good regional cooking, half-pension only, expensive.

Saint-Gilles

The D570 will take you into the Camargue and to the **Mas du Pont de Rousty,** a Camargue museum which relates the history of the region.

After the museum, double back three kilometers to Albaron, take the D37 turn-off to the right and then the N572 to the left for **Saint-Gilles,** another town which gained its prosperity and notoriety in the Middle Ages as a stepping stone on the crusaders' route. The famous **Benedictine abbey** begun in the 8th century is but a shadow of its former self, which can be judged by the monumental facade. The church behind it has been reduced by half and the dependencies have all disappeared. The **Saint-Gilles spiral staircase** is considered a masterpiece of stonework.

Tourist Info: Maison Romane, Place Frédéric Mistral, 30800 Saint-Gilles, tel: 6687-3375.

Mas du Pont de Rousty: 9 A.M. to 7 P.M. every day in summer, 9 A.M. to 12 and 2 to 6 P.M., except Tuesdays, the rest of the year.
Saint Gilles church: Closed on Wednesdays and Sunday afternoons.
Spiral staircase: Mornings and afternoons, except Sunday afternoons.

Restaurants: ***Rascasse,** 16 Avenue François-Griffeuille, tel: 6687-4296. Closed Tuesday evenings off season and Wednesdays. Inexpensive. **Saint-Gillois,** 1 Rue Neuve, tel: 6687-3369; closed Mondays. Pleasant patio for dining, medium-priced. Rooms available.

Arles

Take the N572 out of Saint-Gilles to Arles, one of the most captivating cities of Provence. Colonized by the Greeks in the 6th century B.C., then by the Romans in 42 B.C., Arles was the dominant city of the entire southern coast. It owed this early prosperity to its position as river and seaport and to its industries: shipping, shipbuilding, textiles, jewelry, and arms. Subjected to invasions from the north, the city declined in the 6th century, rising again only some 700 years later as a provincial capital. Arles, the port, was dealt a final blow with the arrival of the railroad in the 19th century.

The **Arles Festival** of music, dance and theater, which holds sway during July and the beginning of August, includes an annual, international photography event in the second week of July.

Tour

From the railway station, take Rue de la Cavalerie to the **Arena** or amphitheater, built probably at the end of the first century A.D. The building has lost its third or attic floor and its exterior decoration but is nevertheless in good enough condition for bullfights in season. The **Ancient Theater** just beyond dates from Augustus' reign in the first century B.C. Starting in the 5th century it served as a quarry for stone for church buildings. Little by little it disappeared under other buildings, only to be uncovered in the middle of the 19th century.

In front of the Ancient Theater, the peaceful **Saint Trophime church** and **cloister** are magnificent examples of Romanesque art and architecture. They were begun in the 10th century in dedication to a saint about whom many legends have been woven: Saint Trophime, bishop of Arles in the 3rd century.

Leave Saint Trophime to the right and take your first left, Plan de la Cour, and you will come to the **Museum of Christian Art,** located in a 17th century Jesuit chapel. It contains one of the largest collections of paleo-Christian sarcophagi in the world. From the museum one can proceed to underground **Roman crypts** under the forum for some 100 yards.

Exit to your left, take your first left and left again on Rue de la République. The **Museon Arlaten** is an exceptional ethnographic museum founded by Frédéric Mistral, the Nobelprize winning poet of Provence. The "live" exhibits capture the spirit of the region at the turn of the century.

Just across the street is the **Espace Van Gogh** located in the hospital which the artist captured on canvas when he was treated there in 1889.

Return to Saint Trophime and turn left to go across town to the **Réattu Museum.** The building, which dates from the Middle Ages, was once the property of the painter Réattu. The Museum contains numerous drawings by Picasso, a fine collection of major photographers, and contemporary artists, as well as some from the 16th, 17th and 18th centuries. The remains of **Roman baths** are just across the street.

Tourist Info: Esplanade des Lices, 13200 Arles, tel: 9096-4208.

Arena, Ancient Theater and Saint Trophime Church: 8:30 A.M. to 12:30 and 2 to 7 P.M. from June to October; 9 A.M. to 12 noon and 2 to 4:30 P.M. from January to March. Other months: slight changes in schedule.
Museum of Christian Art: Rue Balze; same schedule as above.
Museon Arlaten: Place de la République; open mornings and afternoons; closed on Mondays from October through June.

Réattu Museum: 10 Rue du Grand-Prieuré, open every day, same schedule as other monuments.

Secondhand market: Boulevard des Lices, first Wednesday of the month.

Flea market: Boulevard des Lices, Saturday mornings.

Restaurants: *Hostellerie des Arènes, 62 Rue Refuge, tel: 9096-1305; closed Tuesday evenings and Wednesdays. Outdoor dining, inexpensive. Lou Marquès, 7 Boulevard Lices, tel: 9093-4320, fax: 9093-3347. Very elegant restaurant in 17th century Carmelite convent. Excellent food, moderately expensive. Olivier, 1 bis Rue Réattu, tel: 9049-6488; closed Sundays and for lunch on Mondays, except in July; closed February and November 1 to 15. Superb cuisine in refined setting, medium-priced.

Accommodations: Arlatan, 26 Rue du Sauvage, tel: 9093-5666, fax: 9049-6845. Lovely hotel within historic old walls, beautifully furnished, moderately expensive. Hôtel du Musée, 11 Rue du Grand-Prieuré, tel: 9093-8888. Pleasant, 17th-century residence, moderately priced. Jules-César, same address and numbers as Lou Marquès above. Exquisite château-hotel, expensive.

Outside of town: Auberge La Fenière, *Raphèle-lès-Arles,* 8 kilometers to the southeast on N453, tel: 9098-4744, fax 9098-4839. Peaceful, country inn, good food, medium-priced. Mas de la Chapelle, on the D570 or Petite Route de Tarascon, 5 kilometers from Arles, tel: 9093-2315, fax: 9096-5374. Hotel and restaurant in 16th century chapel surrounded by lovely garden. Half-pension required, moderately expensive.

Take the N570 out of Arles to the north and just outside of town the D17 right to the **Montmajour Abbey.** Benedictine monk-hermits founded the abbey in the 10th century and cleared the surrounding marshlands. Partially destroyed in the

17th century, rebuilt in grand style in the 18th, it was finally closed by Louis XVI in 1786. Parts of the abbey were sold by bits; the remains, in the Romanesque Provençal style, are worth the stop.

Montmajour Abbey: 6 kilometers from Arles on the D17. 9 A.M. to 12 and 2 to 6 P.M.

At Fontvieille, go right on the D33 past the **Alphonse Daudet windmill** where a small museum is devoted to that Provençal author. Take the D78E to the amazing **Barbegel Aqueducts.** One supplies Arles, the other fed a watermill dating from the 4th century, which was so productive it could grind over 650 pounds of flour in an hour. This road will lead you through Paradou and Moussane-les Alpilles to Les Baux-de-Provence.

Les Baux-de-Provence

The **Alpilles** are low, abrupt mountains. Dried by the sun most of the year, skirted by olive and almond trees, they are capped with snow in winter. At their center is Les Baux-de-Provence, at one time ruled by a powerful, feudal family. In the 13th century "love courts" were organized here, and troubadours sang the virtues of courtly love.

Bauxite, discovered in the Alpilles in 1822, took its name from Les Baux. A stone quarry used mainly for statuary still operates. The locality is a classified historic monument: no electric wires or TV antennas are permitted.

Les Baux is in fact two places: the old "dead" town and the village. Wander about. Admire the vistas from either side or end of the promontory. Among the visits possible are the **Contemporary Art Museum** in the village, the **Lapidary and Archaeological Museum** in the "dead" town and the **Cathedral of Images** for audiovisual shows in the stone quarry on the D27, about one mile out of town to the north.

Tourist Info: Impasse du Château, 13520 Les Baux-de-Provence, tel: 9054-3439.

Contemporary Art Museum: Rue de l'Eglise, 9:30 A.M. to 12 and 2 to 6:30 P.M. from Easter through October.
Lapidary and Archaeological Museum: Rue du Trencat, 8 A.M. to 8 P.M. in summer; 9 A.M. to 7 P.M. in winter.
Cathedral of Images: All day from mid-March to mid-November; closed on Tuesdays after October 1.

Restaurants: **Bérengère,** Rue du Trencat, tel: 9054-3563, fax: 9054-4277; closed Tuesday evenings and Wednesdays. Pleasant provençal décor, original fare, medium-priced. **Riboto de Taven,** Val d'Enfer, tel: 9054-3423, fax: 9054-3888. Closed Tuesday evenings and Wednesdays in winter and from February 1 to March 15. Lovely setting under mulberry trees, wonderful cuisine, moderately expensive.

Hotel-Restaurants: **Mas d'Aigret,** Route D78F, tel: 9054-3354, fax: 9054-4137. An 18th-century farmhouse with charm, restaurant under vaulted roof, moderately expensive. **Oustaù de Baumanière,** Val d'Enfer, tel: 9054-3307, fax: 9054-4046; closed Wednesdays and for lunch on Thursdays from November to March; closed January 15 to end of February. *Grande cuisine* and international reputation, luxury prices. Except for manor house, rooms not up to standing of restaurant, expensive to luxury prices.

Hotel: **Bautezar,** Grande-Rue, tel: 9054-3209. Closed January 5 to March 1. Pleasant hotel, medium-priced.

Saint-Rémy-de Provence

Leave Les Baux on the D5 north to Saint-Rémy-de-Provence. You will arrive in what might be considered the "new" city, born in the Middle Ages after its ancient predecessor died from invasion and slow burial under alluvian deposits. That was **Glanum,** one kilometer to the south, where you may visit the exceptional Greco-Roman ruins, some dating from the 3rd century B.C.

The town of Saint-Rémy is pure Provençal: streets lined with plane trees, charming squares, **annual festivals** and bullfighting. The **Hôtel de Sade** and the **Alpilles Museum** are worth the visit. The astrologer Nostradamus was born in Saint-Rémy. Van Gogh spent the last year of his life in the asylum of the **Saint Paul de Mausole Monastery** between Saint-Rémy and Glanum.

Tourist Info: Place Jean-Jaurès, 13210 Saint-Rémy-de-Provence, tel: 9092-0522.

Glanum: One kilometer south on D5; open mornings and afternoons; closed on major public holidays.

Annual festivals: August 15; Carreto Ramado Procession and parade; fourth Sunday in September; saint's day and bull-fights.

Hôtel de Sade: Place Favier, summer months from 10 A.M. to 12 noon and 3 to 6 P.M.

Alpilles Museum: Place Favier, 10 A.M. to 12 and 2 to 6 P.M., except Tuesdays, from April 1 to October 31; Saturdays, Sundays and Mondays only the rest of the year.

Saint-Paul de Mausole Monastery: Church and cloister open every day.

Restaurants: ***Bistro des Alpilles,** 15 Boulevard Mirabeau, tel: 9092-0917; closed Sundays. Good, traditional fare, moderately priced. ***Café des Arts,** 30 Boulevard Victor-Hugo, tel: 9092-0850; closed Wednesdays, February and from November 1 to 12. Pleasant atmosphere and food, moderately priced. **Jardin de Frédéric,** 8 Boulevard Gambetta, tel: 9092-2776; closed Wednesdays. Pleasant outside dining area, moderately priced. **Vallon de Valrugues,** Chemin Canto-Cigalo, tel: 9092-0440, fax: 9092-4401. Spectacularly decorative dining room, excellent cuisine, expensive.

Accommodations: **Canto Cigalo,** Chemin Canto-Cigalo, tel: 9092-1428, fax: 9092-1856. Perfect tranquility, attractive, moderately priced. **Château des Alpilles,** Old Route des Baux, 2 kilometers from town on D31, tel: 9092-0333, fax: 9092-4517. Château decorated with taste, period furniture, extremely comfortable, expensive. **Mas des Carassins,** 1 Chemin Gaulois, tel: 9092-1548. Agreeable family hotel in good taste, medium-priced.

Leave Saint-Rémy on the D99 west to **Saint-Gabriel** with its simple, naive 12th-century chapel. To return to Nîmes, take the D970 to the left on the D999.

Some Useful Words and Phrases

arena	**arène** (f)
bird	**oiseau** (m)
bullfight	**course de taureaux, corrida** (f)
circus	**cirque** (m)
citrus fruit	**agrumes** (m)
custom	**coutume** (f)
dust	**poussière** (f)
engagement	**fiançailles** (f)
humanity	**humanité** (f)
Italian	**italien(ne)**
Italy	**Italie** (f)
kingdom	**royaume** (m)
palm tree	**palmier** (m)
pope	**pape** (m)
spectator	**spectateur/spectatrice**

Nous sommes allés à la corrida hier. (We went to the bullfights yesterday.)

Je n'ai jamais gouté d'aussi bons agrumes. (I never tasted such good citrus fruit.)

Il était devant le musée à 10 heures. (He was in front of the museum at 10 o'clock.)

Beaucoup de spectateurs avaient des fleurs à la main. (A great many spectators had flowers in their hands.)

In the last two sentences above, a different past tense is employed. It is not as useful as the one we have used until now, except for the verbs **être** and **avoir**. They are conjugated below, as is the regular verb **danser**.

This tense is called the imperfect. It is most often translated by the simple past tense of the infinitive plus **ed**. However, it can also signify **used to** plus the infinitive or the past tense of **to be** plus the present participle. See examples below:

être

j'étais	I was, used to be
tu étais	you were, used to be
elle/il était	she, he was, used to be
nous étions	we were, used to be
vous étiez	you were, used to be
elles/ils étaient	they were, used to be

avoir

j'avais	I had, used to have
tu avais	you had, used to have
elle/il avait	she, he had, used to have
nous avions	we had, used to have
vous aviez	you had, used to have
elles/ils avaient	they had, used to have

danser (to dance)

je dansais	I danced, used to dance, was dancing
tu dansais	you danced, used to dance, were dancing
elle/il dansait	she, he danced, used to dance, was dancing
nous dansions	we danced, used to dance, were dancing
vous dansiez	you danced, used to dance, were dancing
elles/ils dansaient	they danced, used to dance, were dancing

Nous regardions la télévision quand le téléphone a sonné.
(We were watching television when the telephone rang.)

Avant son accident il jouait au tennis le dimanche matin.
(Before his accident he used to play tennis Sunday mornings.)

II *Marseilles to Aix*

Marseilles is the second largest city of France and its leading port. It is a colorful, exuberant place, and the source of many legends. The Marseillais are known for their "tall stories."

Massalia, as it was named by the Greeks who colonized the port around 600 B.C., became a prosperous trading center. In order to resist defeat by Celtic tribes in the 2nd century B.C., the city called on Rome for assistance, thus opening the door to the Roman conquest of Provence.

The Dark Ages saw the decline of trade and the plague made its first entry into the region. With the crusades Marseilles became once again an active and prosperous port. Because of greed and lack of respect for quarantine regulations, it was struck by another devastating plague in the 18th century, which it transmitted to all Provence.

During the Second World War the city was subjected to bombing both by the Axis and the Allies; the Germans evacuated and razed the old quarter around the harbor.

The French national anthem is called *La Marseillaise* because, although written in Alsace, it was first popularized here during an army banquet in 1792 and then carried to Paris where it became known as the song from Marseilles.

Marseilles has always been a port of entry and stop-off point for newcomers, be they the Greeks and Romans of old or the Italians, Iberians and North Africans of the 20th century.

Tour

On arriving in Marseilles, head for the **old harbor**. A tourist walk around this quarter is mapped out and easy to follow. The heart of the quarter is the **Quai des Belges;** excursions by boat or ferry leave from here. A colorful fish market is held mornings.

Silvacane Abbey

D543

Provence
Marseilles to Aix-en-Provence

N 7

Aix-en-Provence

N 7

St-Maximin-
la-Sainte-Baume

N560

D80

Espigoulier
Pass

D80   Saint Pilon

D2

Marseilles

D2

St. Pons Park

DS99

D559

Cassis

D141

La Ciotat

Along the marked itinerary are several interesting museums. The **Museum of Old Marseilles** recreates life in the 18th and 19th centuries. The **Museum of Roman Docks** is located on the site of the former Roman port, discovered during construction work in the 1970s. The **Center of Old Charity,** a lovely 17th-century hospice, organizes temporary exhibits. The **Museum of Mediterranean Archaeology** contains a fine exhibit of Egyptian antiquities.

The **Old Major Cathedral** is a good example of 11th-century Romanesque architecture. The new cathedral was built in the 19th century.

From the old port go up the Canebière, Marseilles' main drag. To the right on Rue Ferréol you will come to the **Cantini Museum** of contemporary art. If you climb all the way up the Canebière and then continue on Cours Thierry and Boulevard Longchamp you will arrive at the excellent **Grobet-Labadié Museum** of primitive and Renaissance painting, furniture and *objets d'art.* Just beyond is the **Longchamp Palace** which houses two other noteworthy museums: the **Museum of Fine Arts** and the **Museum of Natural History.**

Before leaving Marseilles you should visit the **new port** to the west of the old port. It has been considerably extended and modernized since World War II.

You may also wish to take a boatride from Quai des Belges to the **Chateau d'If,** made famous by Alexandre Dumas who enclosed his legendary hero, the Count of Monte-Cristo, here. Originally designed, in the 16th century, to protect the harbor from attack, it later became a prison where Huguenots, the man in the iron mask and political rebels generally were incarcerated.

Last but not least, on leaving Marseilles from Quai des Belges, skirt the old port on Quai de Rive-Neuve. At the end of the quay, to your left, is the **Saint Victor Basilica,** all that remains of a famous abbey founded in the 5th century. The most interesting part of the abbey is the crypt containing the original church built on this spot. The **Catacombs** and **Saint Victor Grotto,** as well as numerous ancient sarcophagi, can be seen.

From here, head towards the sea. Go left along Corniche J.F. Kennedy and the Promenade de la Plage for panoramic vistas and the public beaches.

Train from Paris: Gare de Lyon, 7 hours (TGV).

Tourist Info: 4 Rue de la Canebière, 13000 Marseilles, tel: 9154-9111; St. Charles railway station, tel: 9150-5918.

Museum of Old Marseilles: 2 Rue de la Prison. 10 A.M. to 6:30 P.M.
Museum of Roman Docks: 28 Place Vivaux at Rue de la Loge. 10 A.M. to 6:30 P.M.
Center of Old Charity: Rue du Petit-Puits. In summer, from noon to end of afternoon, all day long the rest of the year.
Major and Old Major Cathedrals: Esplanade de la Tourette.
Cantini Museum: 19 Rue de Grignan. 10 A.M. to 6:30 P.M., from 12 noon on weekdays in summer.
Grobet-Labadié Museum: 140 Boulevard Longchamp, 10 A.M. to 12 and 2 to 6:30 P.M. except Tuesdays and Wednesday mornings.
Museum of Fine Arts: Palais Longchamp, 142 Boulevard Longchamp, 10 A.M. to 6:30 P.M.
Museum of Natural History: Palais Longchamp, 142 Boulevard Longchamp, 10 A.M. to 12 and 2 to 6 P.M. except Tuesdays and Wednesday mornings.
New Port: Digue du Large (harbor dyke) is open to the public on Sundays and holidays from 7 A.M. to 9 P.M. from April through September; until 6 P.M. the rest of the year.
Chateau d'If: By boat from Quai des Belges: 90 minutes round trip including visit.
Saint Victor Basilica: 10 A.M to 12 noon and 3 to 6 P.M.

Secondhand Markets: Cours Julien, second Sunday of the month; Espace Madrague, second Saturday of the month.

Specialties: **Breads,** traditional and varied: Boulangerie Michel, 33 Rue Vacon and Four des Navettes, 136 Rue Sainte.

Restaurants: ***Buvette du Pharo,** Jardin du Pharo. Snack bar in the park, magnificent view of the harbor, inexpensive. ***Carré d'Honoré,** 37 Cours d'Estienne-d'Orves, tel: 9133-1680; closed Saturdays for lunch and Sundays. Former garage become traditional Provençal country home, fresh produce and changing menu, moderately priced. **Chez Loury,** Le Mistral, 3 Rue Fortia, tel: 9133-0973; closed Sundays. Fresh fish, good bouillabaisse, nice décor, moderately priced. **Dar Djerba,** 15 Cours Julien, tel: 9148-5536; closed Tuesdays. North African specialties: couscous, pastilla and tajines, moderately priced. **Passédat/Petit Nice,** Corniche J-F-Kennedy, anse Maldormé, tel: 9159-2592, fax: 9159-2808; closed Sundays off season. Most illustrious restaurant of Marseilles, three hats from Gault-Millau, two stars from Michelin, expensive.

Accommodations: **Hotel Beauvau,** 4 Rue Beauvau, tel: 9154-9100, fax: 9154-1576. Lovely rooms overlooking old port, moderately expensive. **Sud,** 18 Rue Beauvau, tel: 9154-3850, fax: 9154-7562, centrally located near old port, moderately priced. **New Hotel Astoria,** 10 Boulevard Garibaldi, tel: 9133-3350, fax: 9154-8075. Well situated, airy and comfortable rooms, medium-priced. **New Hotel Bompare,** 2 Rue des Flots-Bleus, tel: 9152-1093, fax: 9131-0214. In a pleasant garden on edge of town, medium-priced.

Cassis

Continue on, through the Massif de Marseilleveyre, route D599, for a magnificent twenty kilometers. You will arrive in Cassis, a charming fishing port. The **municipal museum of archaeology** is housed in a pleasant 18th-century home. From Quai Saint-Pierre you can take a boat to the **calanques,** inlets or fjords in the mountains. The En-Van and the Port-Pin calanques are wonderful nature reserves with small beaches. Walks in the hills are clearly marked.

The white wine called Cassis has a rich, fruity taste.

Tourist Info: Place Baragnon, 13260 Cassis, tel: 4201-7117.

Municipal Museum: Place Baragnon, Wednesday, Thursday and Saturday afternoons.

Restaurants: **Gilbert,** Quai Baux, tel: 4201-7136; closed Tuesdays for lunch in season, all day Tuesdays and Wednesdays off season. Right on the harbor, moderately priced. **Presqu'île,** Quartier Port-Miou, tel: 4201-0377, fax: 4201-9449; closed Sunday evenings and Mondays, except Monday evenings in July and August. Wonderful outside terrace, lovely food, medium-priced.

Hotel-Restaurant: ***Clos des Arômes,** 10 Rue Paul-Mouton-Rue Agostini, tel: 4201-7184. Provençal-decorated rooms, fabulous garden and regional culinary pleasures. moderately priced.

Saint-Maximin-la-Sainte-Baume

Take the D141, **Chemin des Crêtes,** from Cassis to La Ciotat. Pick up the D599 to the left (or west) from La Ciotat, then the C599A north. At Aubagne, the D2 to the east, through Gémenos, will provide you with breathtaking mountain views of **Saint Pons Park** and **Espigoulier Pass.** At La Couronne turn right on the D80. At the Hôtellerie go right on the GR9 to the Carrefour de l'Oratoire where you can leave your car and walk to **Saint Pilon,** past the Parisians' Chapel. According to legend it was here that Mary Magdalena was carried by angels, seven times a day, to listen to the concerts of Paradise.

Go back to the D80 and continue on to the D560 and Saint-Maximin-la-Sainte-Baume.

At the heart of Saint-Maximin is its **basilica.** According to legend both Saint Mary Magdelena and Saint Maximin were buried on this spot. Tombs found in the 13th century by Charles of Anjou, King of Sicily and Provence, were declared to be theirs. It was the king who started the construction of the magnificient basilica and convent. The buildings were saved from destruction during the Revolution by Lucien Bonaparte, Napoleon's younger brother, who had the *Marseillaise* played on the church organ. This is probably the most noteworthy example of Gothic architecture in Provence. Summer concerts are held in the enchanting cloister garden.

Tourist Info: Hôtel de Ville, 83470 Saint-Maximin-la-Sainte-Baume, tel: 9478-0009.

Basilica: 9 to 11:30 A.M. and 2:30 to 6 P.M.
Convent: Weekdays from 9 to 11:30 A.M. and 2:30 to 6 P.M., afternoons only on Sundays and holidays and from April through October.

Restaurants: **Chez Nous,** Boulevard Jean-Jaurès, tel: 9478-0257; closed Wednesdays except in July and August. Medium-priced.

Accommodations: **Plaisance,** 20 Place Malherbe, tel: 9478-1674. Old residence, spacious rooms, medium-priced.

Aix-en-Provence

The A8 parkway or the N7 will take you from Saint-Maximin to Aix-en-Provence, a very urbane town. Its university was founded at the beginning of the 15th century. During the early part of the 16th the sovereign court of justice was installed in Aix and magistrates and jurists abounded. The large number of private mansions are witness to its 17th- and 18th-century prosperity.

Tour

Visits to Aix must begin from Place du Général-de-Gaulle in order for one to imbibe fully the special atmosphere of **Cours Mirabeau** shaded by its large-leafed plane trees. Start out on the right side for a look at the fountains and the sedate mansions adorned with wrought-iron balconies. At the end of Mirabeau, cross Place Forbin and take Rue d'Italie to the right until you arrive at the Gothic **Church of Saint John of Malta** built in honor of the crusaders at the end of the 13th century. Next door is the **Granet Museum of Fine Arts and Archaeology.** Among the paintings, from primitive to contemporary, are a number by Paul Cézanne, a native of Aix. The archaeological exhibit is comprised essentially of objects from the early settlements at Aix destroyed by the Romans during their conquest of Provence.

Leave the museum on Rue Cardinale. At the lovely Four Dolphins Fountain turn right on Rue du Quatre-Septembre which will take you back to Cours Mirabeau. Directly across Mirabeau is Rue Clémenceau. Turn left at Place d'Albertas and right on Rue Aude. This street, which changes names, will lead you to the **Tapestry Museum** installed in a 17th-century episcopal palace.

Next door is the **Saint Savior Cloister and Cathedral.** The cloister is Romanesque, the cathedral a mixture of various styles.

Among the many worthwhile sites in Aix is **Cezanne's last home and studio,** about one-half mile beyond the cathedral. And, of course, wander about old Aix in the little streets between the cathedral and Cours Mirabeau. Other interesting tours include the **Roman baths,** the **Museum of Old Aix,** the **Hôtel de Panisse-Passis** and the **Pavillon de Vendôme.**

Aix organizes several music festivals in July and August.

Tourist Info: 2 Place du Général-de-Gaulle, 13100 Aix-en-Provence, tel: 4226-0293.
Saint John of Malta Church: Rue Cardinale.
Granet Museum: Place Saint-Jean-de-Malte. 10 A.M. to 12 and 2 to 6 P.M. Closed Tuesdays except in July and August.
Tapestry Museum: 28 Place des Martyrs-de-la-Résistance. 10 A.M. to 12 and 2 to 5 P.M., in summer until 6 P.M. Closed Tuesdays.
Saint Savior Cathedral: Rue de la Roque.

Cézanne's studio: 9 Avenue Paul-Cézanne, 10 A.M. to 12 and 2:30 to 6 P.M.; closed Tuesdays.

Roman baths: Rue Célony.

Museum of Old Aix: 17 Rue de Saporta. 10 A.M. to 12 and 2 to 6 P.M.; closed Mondays and from September 15 to October 15.

Hôtel Panisse-Passis: 16 Rue Eméric-David.

Pavillon de Vendôme: 13 Rue de la Molle. 10 A.M. to 12 and 2 to 6 P.M.; closed Tuesdays.

Secondhand market: Place des Prêcheurs, across from Law Courts, Tuesday, Thursday and Saturday mornings.

Specialties: **Calissons,** almond paste soft candies: Calissons du Roy René, 7 Rue Papassaudi; **Chocolates,** made locally: Chocolaterie Puyricard, 7 Rue Rifle-Rafle; **Fabrics,** traditional provençal patterns: Carcassonne Textiles, 13 Rue Chabrier.

Tearoom: **A la cour Rohan,** 10 Rue de Vauvenargues, Place de l'Hôtel-de-Ville, 4296-1815. Exquisite décor, wonderful snacks, pianist Saturday nights.

Restaurants: ***Bistro Latin,** 18 Rue Couronne, tel: 4238-2288; closed Sundays for dinner and Mondays. Constantly changing and ever-creative menu, moderately priced. **Clos de la Violette,** 10 Avenue Violette, tel: 4223-3071; fax: 4221-9303; closed Mondays for lunch and Sundays. Fashionable manor house restaurant with high ratings from food connoisseurs, moderately expensive. ***Kéops,** 28 Rue Verrerie, tel: 4296-5905; closed Mondays and November. Egyptian specialties, pleasant and original, moderately priced.

Accommodations: **Augustins,** 3 Rue de la Masse, tel: 4227-2859, fax: 4226-7487. A 12th-century convent, classified historic monument, garden, moderately expensive. **Manoir,** 8 Rue Entrecasteaux, tel: 4226-2720, fax: 4227-1797. Spacious rooms in 14th-century cloister, medium-priced. **Mercure Paul Cézanne,** 40 Avenue Victor-Hugo, tel: 4226-3473, fax:

4227-2095. Good location, period furniture, moderately expensive. **Renaissance,** 4 Boulevard République, tel: 4226-0422, fax: 4227-2876. Former home of composer Darius Milhaud completely renovated, medium-priced.

About twenty kilometers out of Aix is the **Silvacane Abbey.** Take the N7 northwest, the D543 turn-off, and left on the D561 for an agreeable excursion to this 11th-century Cistercian abbey set down in the middle of reed marshes. Monks turned the swampland into vineyards and olive orchards. In the 15th century the abbey went into decline. By the time of the French Revolution it was in such a state of ruin and disrepair that it was sold off as farmland. The French Government purchased the abbey in 1949 and is gradually returning it to its former state. **Visits** both morning and afternoons. Closed on Tuesdays.

Some Useful Words and Phrases

angel	**ange** (m)
conquest	**conquête** (f)
green	**vert(e)**
iron	**fer**(m)
long	**long(ue)**
marsh, marshland	**marais** (m)
orchard	**verger** (m)
paradise	**paradis** (m)
people	**peuple** (m)
raincoat	**imperméable** (m)
rain	**pluie** (f)
read	**lire**
tapistry	**tapisserie** (f)
tribe	**tribu** (f)
while	**pendant que**

Il a plu et je n'avais pas un imperméable. (It rained and I didn't have a raincoat.)

Il pleuvait quand je suis sortie. (It was raining when I went out.)

La Provence est un vrai paradis. (Provence is a real paradise.)

Tout était vert à la campagne. (Everything was green in the country.)

Nous avons trouvé des oiseaux de paradis.
(We found some birds of paradise.)

Il a bu un café pendant que je téléphonais. (He drank a coffee while I was phoning.)

III *Avignon and Back*

Avignon owes its celebrity to the popes who made the city theirs. The first to reside in the region was the French pope Clement v who, in 1309, wished to retreat from Italian intrigues and rivalries. His successor Pope John XXII settled in Avignon. Benedict XII, named pope in 1334, undertook the building of a new papal palace. Clement VI not only completed the palace, but bought the city from the reigning queen of Provence.

The French popes remained in Avignon until 1376 when Gregory XI was finally pressured into returning to Rome. Their reign had been decorative, luxurious and relatively liberal. Their critics called it licentious. When Gregory XI died in 1378, a schism occurred; two papal houses reigned: one in Rome, the other in Avignon until 1417.

In the 16th and 17th centuries brotherhoods of penitents were extremely active in Avignon. Designated by the color of their robes—gray, blue, purple or aristocratic white—they pledged mutual aid and service to the community. Their rites were strict. Several orders survived until well into the 19th century.

Vaison-la-Romaine

D975

Orange

D68

D17

Chateauneuf-
du-Pape

Roquemaure

D980

D976

Carpentras

D938

Provence

Avignon and back

Villeneuve-
lès-Avignon

Avignon

N7

Sénanque
Abbey

Fontaine-de-
Vaucluse

D938

Gordes

D171

D2

Roussillon

D102

D25

D100

D110

D2

D100

D973

D149

Cavaillon

D2

D19

Ménerbes

Oppède-
le-Vieux

D188

Bonnieux

D109

At the time of the French Revolution the city was divided between partisans of incorporation into the Republic and those wishing to remain a papal vassal state. In 1791 Avignon voted to join France.

Tour

From the railway station take Cours Jean-Jaurès, which becomes Rue de la République and leads you to the other side of town and the **Papal Palace or Palaces.** For there are actually two, both Gothic: the Old Palace, commissioned by Benedict XII, an austere fortress for prayer and defense of the State; and the New Palace begun under Clement VI. From the outside there is seemingly little difference. The interior decoration of the latter, however, clearly reflected Clement's keen desire for art and refinement.

On leaving the palace turn right for **Notre-Dame-des-Doms,** a Romanesque cathedral of the 12th century to which bays were added in the 14th and 17th centuries. Beyond here is the **Rocher des Doms,** a garden from whose heights vast vistas of the surrounding landscape can be admired.

The **Petit Palais,** former residence of bishops and archbishops, contains a fine collection of Italian primitives and Renaissance artists.

Behind the Petit Palais is the famous **Avignon bridge,** celebrated in a song known to all French schoolchildren: *Sur le Pont d'Avignon.* From here, a promenade on the ramparts (to the left when facing the river) as far as Place Crillon, is in order.

Then take Rue Joseph-Vernet to the right and Rue Saint-Agricol to the left past Saint Agricol's Church. Turn right on Rue Bouquerie behind the church. At Rue Horace-Vernet a right turn will take you to the **Calvet Museum** which possesses a rich collection of paintings, antiquities, and relics displayed in an elegant setting.

If you continue on Rue Joseph-Vernet to the left, and then left on Rue de la Republique, you will arrive in short order at the **Lapidary Museum,** a 17th-century Jesuit chapel. Then retrace your steps and turn left on Rue Henri-Fabre which becomes Rue des Lices. At **Rue des Teinturiers** turn right for a pleasant walk along the River Sorgue.

Two fine manufacturers of colorful handblocked fabrics for clothes and interior decoration have their mills in Avignon: **Souleiado** and **Les Olivades.** They are known far and wide. Souleiado is located at 1, 3 and 5 Rue Joseph-Vernet and Les Olivades at 28 Rue des Marchands.

The **Annual Festival of Dramatic Art,** which attracts theatrical groups from many countries, takes place from mid-July to mid-August.

Train from Paris: Gare de Lyon, 6 hours (TGV).
Tourist Info: 41 Cours Jean-Jaurès, 84000 Avignon, tel: 9082-6511; Châtelet, Pont d'Avignon, tel: 9085-6016.

Palais des Papes: 8:30 to 11:30 A.M. and 2 to 6:30 P.M. in July, August and September; reduced schedules the rest of the year.
Petit Palais: 9:15 A.M. to 12 noon and 2 to 6 P.M.; closed Tuesdays and major public holidays.
Calvet Museum: 65 Rue Joseph-Vernet, 8:30 A.M. to 12 noon and 2 to 6 P.M.; closed Tuesdays.
Lapidary Museum: Rue de la République, 8:30 A.M. to 12 noon and 2 to 6 P.M.; closed Tuesdays.
Secondhand Market: Place Crillon, Saturday mornings.
Flea Market: Place des Carmes, Sunday mornings.

Restaurants: **Bain Marie,** 5 Rue Pétramale, tel: 9085-2137; closed Saturdays and for lunch on Sundays. Charming residence and terrace, interesting menu, moderately priced. **Chistian Etienne,** 10–12 Rue Mons, tel: 9086-1650, fax: 9086-6709; closed Sundays. Delicious, inventive cuisine in former cardinal's residence, expensive. ***Domaines,** 28 Place de l'Horloge, tel: 9082-5886. Good wine bar and regional specialties, moderately priced. ***Entrée des Artistes,** 1 Place

Carmes, tel: 9082-4690; closed Saturdays for lunch and Sundays. One fixed menu each day, inexpensive. **Isle Sonnante,** 7 Rue Racine, tel: 9082-5601; closed Sundays and Mondays and first two weeks of August. Good food, one-price menu, moderately priced. *****Philippe Parc,** 11 Rue de la Balance, tel: 9082-3210; closed Sundays and Mondays. Desserts only, nothing else, moderately priced.

Hotel-Restaurants: **Europe,** 12 Place Crillon, tel: 9082-6692, fax: 9085-4366. Beautiful 18th-century manor. Excellent restaurant (**Vieille Fontaine**) closed Saturdays for lunch and Sundays, lovely rooms, period furniture and décor, expensive. **Mirande,** 4 Place Amirande, tel: 9085-9393, fax: 9086-2685. Former cardinal's palace, beautifully renovated, excellent restaurant, luxury prices.

Hotel: **Ferme Jamet,** Ile de la Barthelasse, tel: 9086-1674. a 16th-century farm and centenary plane trees, medium-priced. **Garlande,** 20 Rue Galante, tel: 9085-0885, fax: 9027-1658. Charming hotel, centrally located, moderately priced.

Villeneuve-lès-Avignon

Just over the Edouard-Daladier Bridge is Villeneuve-lès-Avignon, the city of cardinals across from that of the popes. The **Chartreuse du Val-de-Bénédiction**, a Carthusian monastery founded by Pope Innocent VI in 1356, receives personalities from the world of the arts and culture every summer for an international conclave. Also worth the visit is the medieval **Fort Saint-André** built in the 14th century to protect the city on the other side of the river.

Last but not least, the **Municipal Museum Pierre-de-Luxembourg** exhibits many admirable works of art, among which are an ivory sculpted virgin from the 14th century and Enguerrand Quarton's *Crowning of the Virgin* (15th century).

Tourist Info: 1 Place Charles-David, 30400 Villeneuve-lès-Avignon, tel: 9025-6133.

Chartreuse du Val-de-Bénédiction: 10 A.M. to 12:30 and 3

to 7:30 P.M. from April to September; 10 A.M. to 12 noon and 2 to 5 P.M. the rest of the year.

Fort Saint-André: Same schedule as the Chartreuse.

Municipal Museum Pierre-de-Luxembourg: Rue de la République; same schedule as the Chartreuse.

Secondhand Market: Place du Marché, Saturdays.

Restaurants: **Aubertin,** 1 Rue de l'Hôpital, tel: 9025-9484; closed Wednesdays off season. Wonderful regional dishes, medium-priced. **Pichet,** 17 Boulevard de Laval, tel: 9975-2409; closed Sunday evenings and Mondays and three weeks in August. Moderately priced.

Hotel-Restaurant: **Prieuré,** 7 Place Chapitre, tel: 9025-1820, fax: 9025-4539. Sumptuous restaurant and hotel amid rose gardens, expensive.

Hotel: **Atelier,** 5 rue de la Foire, tel: 9025-0184, fax: 9025-8006. Old-fashioned, comfortable hotel, moderately priced.

Take the D980 north out of Villeneuve. After Roquemaure, get on the D976, cross the Rhône, go right on the D17 to **Chateauneuf-du-Pape,** where you may taste one of the prestigious wines of the Rhône Valley. The little **Tools of the Winegrower Museum,** located in a cellar, is instructive on the process. Leave here on the D68 to Orange.

Wine tasting: **Château de Mont-Redon,** tel: 9083-7275; closed Saturdays and Sundays and from 12 to 2 P.M.

Restaurant: ***Pistou,** 15 Rue Joseph-Ducos, tel: 9083-7175; closed for dinner Mondays, Tuesdays and Wednesdays. Rustic, family-run restaurant, moderately priced.

Orange

This old Roman city with its vestiges of a distinguished past also played an active role in the Reformation. As a Protestant stronghold it was here that the Orange-Nassau royal house was born; its descendants have reigned over England and still do in the Netherlands.

Tour

Every road into Orange takes you directly to the **Antique Theater,** where an annual music festival takes place. It is the best preserved of Roman theaters anywhere in the world. Take Rue Caristié from the theater for a walk through the **old part of town.** On the other side of the city, Rue de l'Arc-de-Triomphe will lead you to the **Roman Arch,** built in the year 20 B.C.

Tourist Info: Cours Aristide-Briand, 84100 Orange, tel: 9034-7088.

Wine tasting: **Château Saint-Estève,** Route de Sérignan Uchaux, tel: 9041-6238; closed Sundays and from 12 to 2 P.M.

Restaurants: **Atrium,** 5 Impasse du Parlement, tel: 9034-3417. Pleasant outside terrace, fish specialties, moderately priced. **Au Goût le Jour,** 9 Place aux Herbes, tel: 9034-1080; closed Thursdays except in July and August. Regional specialties.

Accommodations: **Arène,** Place de Langes, tel: 9034-1095, fax: 9034-9162. Extremely pleasant, comfortable hotel near the Roman Arch, medium-priced. **Mas des Aigras,** 2 kilometers from town on N7, tel: 9034-8101. Lovely provençal farmhouse, medium-priced.

Vaison-la Romaine

The D975 wends its way to romantic Vaison-la-Romaine. This Celtic capital was occupied by the Romans at the end of the second century B.C. Both the excavations in the lower town and the little streets of the upper town across the river deserve a visit.

Tour

Start with the lower town and the **Puymin Quarter.** Among the treasures here are the **antique theater,** the **mu-**

seum, and the **Messii House.** The museum contains the archaeological finds from the excavations.

Across Avenue du Général-de-Gaulle is a second series of Roman excavations, the **Villasse Quarter.** The **House of the Silver Bust** and the **Dolphin's House** are of interest.

On leaving this quarter go right and right again on Avenue Jules Ferry which will take you to the **Our Lady of Nazareth Cathedral,** one of the lovely Romanesque churches of Provence.

A walk through the medieval **high town** on the other side of the river is a delight not to be missed.

Tourist Info: Place Chanoine-Sautel, 84110 Vaison-la-Romaine, tel: 9036-0211.

Puymin Quarter: 9 A.M. to 5 P.M., 6 P.M. in summer.
Villasse Quarter: Same as above.

Wine Tasting: **Cave des Vignerons,** Rasteau, tel: 9046-1043, 8 A.M. to 12 noon and 2 to 6 P.M.

Hotel-Restaurants: *Fête en Provence, Place du Vieux-Marché, tel: 9036-3643. Closed Wednesdays all day and Thursdays for lunch (except in July and August) and from November to Easter. Charming house, interesting menu, moderately priced. Rooms available, medium-priced. **Beffroi,** Upper Town, tel: 9036-0471, fax: 9036-2478. Several 16th-century homes joined together, view for miles around, beautifully decorated, good restaurant, moderately expensive. Half-pension available.

Carpentras

Take the D938 to Carpentras. Off to your left along this route you will have wonderful views of Mount Ventoux and villages clinging to hillsides. Carpentras also has a papal past in that it was here that Clement v and others retreated from Avignon. With Cavaillon, l'Isle-sur-Sorgue and Avignon, Carpentras was one of the few cities admitting Jews to residence prior to the French Revolution. The gates to the Jewish "quarry," as it was called, were closed every night.

Surrounded by irrigated farmland and vineyards, Carpentras is known for its tomatoes and grapes. It is also the truffles capital of Provence. An Offenbach Festival takes place from July 15 to August 15.

Tour

Take the Rue Porte-Orange to the former **Saint Siffrein Cathedral,** a good example of southern Gothic. Enter the church from its right-hand side through the so-called Jewish door; this was the door used by those converting to Catholicism on entering the cathedral for their baptismal rites. In a chapel to the left of the choir a number of statues sculpted in wood and other artifacts are displayed.

Next door to the church, the **former episcopal palace,** now a law court, is open to visitors. Just behind it are a Roman **triumphal arch** and the ruins of the **Romanesque cathedral** which preceded Saint Siffrein.

Go left on leaving the ruins and turn right on Rue d'Inguimbert. Take the first left to the oldest active **synagogue** of France, built in the late 14th century and still in use. Notice the old matzoh ovens in the ground-floor kitchen and the basin for ritual bridal baths used on the eve of weddings.

A walk around the town is always pleasant. At the southern exit of Carpentras is the **Hôtel-Dieu** or hospital, well worth a visit. Its **pharmacy-museum** contains a fine collection of porcelain jars.

Tourist Info: 170 Avenue Jean-Jaurès, 84200 Carpentras, tel: 9063-0078.

Episcopal palace: Guided visits mornings and afternoons; see Tourist Office.

Synagogue: 9 A.M. to 1 P.M. and 2 to 6 P.M. except Saturdays; until 7 P.M. in summer.

Hôtel-Dieu: Mondays, Wednesdays and Thursdays from 9 to 11:30 A.M.

Secondhand Market: Rue Bidault, Friday mornings.

Wine Tasting: **Cave des Roches Blanches,** Mormoiron, tel: 9061-8007; closed Sundays and from 12 to 2 P.M.

Specialties: **Candy shops:** Confiserie Bono, 26 Rue de la Sous-Préfecture; Confiserie Daussy, 83 Rue Porte-de-Mazan.

Restaurants: *Orangerie, 26 Rue Duplessis, tel: 9067-2723; closed Saturdays for lunch. Pleasant outside terrace and interesting menu, moderately priced. **Vert Galant,** 12 Rue Clapies, tel: 9067-1550; closed Saturdays for lunch and Sundays. Inventive cuisine, moderately priced.

Accommodations: **Fiacre,** 153 Rue Vigne, tel: 9063-0315. Pleasant 18th-century residence, moderately priced. **Hermitage,** Pernes-les-Fontaines, 6 kilometers south on the N938, tel: 9066-5141, fax: 9061-3641. Surrounded by trees and garden, quiet, comfortable hotel, moderately priced.

Fontaine-de-Vaucluse

Continue on the N938 and just before l'Isle-sur-la-Sorgue turn left on the D25 for Fontaine-de-Vaucluse. The **fountain** is fed by an underground river, one of the swiftest in the world during the winter and spring months. At the exit to the amazing grotto, sound and light shows are organized during July and August. The **Underground World of Norbert Casteret** consists of a fascinating speleological collection. Next door, **Vallis Clausa** is a paper mill where one can witness the old hand techniques of papermaking.

The Italian poet Petrarch sojourned here in the 14th century. At **Petrarch and Laura's House** are documents concerning Petrarch's stay in the region and his sublime love for the unattainable Laura.

The **Museum of Restrictions,** located along the river, contains a curious collection of objects relating to wars and the restrictions they impose, in particular rationing.

Tourist Info: Chemin de la Fontaine, 84800 Fontaine-de-Vaucluse, tel: 9020-3222.

Norbert Casteret Museum: Chemin de la Fontaine, 10 A.M. to 12 and 2 to 6 P.M.; closed Mondays and Tuesdays except in June, July and August and from mid-November to end of January.

Vallis Clausa: 9 A.M. to 5 P.M., summer months only.

Petrarch and Laura: 10 A.M. to 12 and 2 to 6 P.M.; closed Tuesdays and January and February; weekends only from beginning of March to mid-April and mid-October to end December.

Restrictions Museum: Chemin de la Fontaine.

Hotel-Restaurants: **Hostellerie du Château,** Quartier Petite-Place, tel: 9020-3154; closed Monday evenings and Tuesdays. Dining at the riverside, moderately priced. Rooms available. **Parc,** Les Bourgades, tel: 9020-3157. Small hotel and restaurant on the river, moderately priced.

Gordes

Take the D100A, turn left on the D100 and right on the D110, then left on the D2 to Gordes, perched proudly on its hilltop taking in the view. The **Renaissance château** shades a daily market of local products. Here, as well as in the shops of the narrow streets, wares of potters and jewelers from the region are found. The castle plays host to the **Vasarely Museum,** a permanent collection by the artist, and occasional temporary exhibits.

On the D2 road coming up to Gordes, just before the village, is a turn-off for the **bories,** shelters made of flat, unmortared stone. These ingenious constructions have been used since neolithic times and until the early 20th century as housing units for man, beast and food.

From the village of Gordes take the winding D177 to the **Sénanque Abbey,** one of the most perfect Romanesque edifices in France. Surrounded by scrubland and fields of lavendar, this Cistercian edifice is both harmonious and remote. A **Saharan Museum** is located in the abbey.

Tourist Info: Place du Château, 84220 Gordes, tel: 9072-0275.
Vasarely Museum: Château, 10 A.M. to 12 noon and 2 to 6 P.M. except Tuesdays.
Sénanque Abbey: 10 A.M. to 12 noon and 2 to 6 P.M.

Hotel-Restaurants: **Bastide de Gordes,** tel: 9072-1212, fax: 9072-0520; closed Mondays, Tuesdays for lunch, and from mid-November to mid-December. Former convent become attractive hotel with exceptional panorama, very inventive provençal cuisine, moderately expensive. **Bories,** Route de l'Abbaye Sénanque, 2 kilometers on the D177, tel: 9072-0051, fax: 9072-0122; closed December and first two weeks of January. Demi-pension. Lovely rooms, some in authentic *bories,* swimming pool, expensive. **Gacholle,** Route de Murs, 2 kilometers on the D15, tel: 9072-0136, fax: 9072-0181. Comfortable rooms, sauna and pool, moderately expensive. Restaurant, moderately priced. **Mayanelle,** Rue Combe, tel: 9072-0028; closed Tuesdays and January and February. Lovely panorama and good food, medium-priced. Rooms available, moderately priced.

Lubéron

For those who have the time, an interesting side visit from Gordes is the Lubéron range with its charming villages: **Roussillon, Bonnieux, Ménerbes** and **Oppède-le-Vieux.** After descending Gorde's steep slope take the D2 to the left for about five kilometers until the D102 turn-off for Roussillon, a spectacular pale rose and ochre-colored village clinging to a mountainside. Outside the village to the south, pick up the D104 to the left and almost immediately the D149 to the right. It will drive you all the way to Bonnieux. The **Bakers' Museum** here is an interesting stop. Then take the D3 and

the D109 to Ménerbes and from there the D188 to Oppède-
le-Vieux. The D176, D29 and D2 will take you to Cavaillon,
a market town, and the D973 back to Avignon.

Roussillon
Restaurant: ***Val des Fées,** Rue Richard-Casteau, tel: 9005-
6499; closed Wednesdays, Thursdays and November 15 to
February. Overlooking the village, inventive, pleasurable
southern cuisine, moderately priced.

Hotel-Restaurant: **Mas de Garrigon,** Route de Saint-Sat-
urnin-d'Apt, tel: 9005-6322, fax: 9005-7001; closed Sunday
evenings, Mondays and from November 16 to December 17.
Delightful provençal charm, view of valley and mountains,
pool, horses, fine cuisine, half-pension required in season,
expensive.
Hotel: **Résidence des Ocres,** Route de Gordes, tel: 9005-
6050. Typical provençal home, calm, terrace and garden,
moderately priced.

Bonnieux
Hotel-Restaurants: **Aiguebrun,** D943 between Lourmarin
and Apt, Domaine de la Tour, tel: 9074-0414; closed Wednesdays and end November to Easter. Tranquility on the river,
simple charm and delicate cuisine, half-pension required, expensive. **Prieuré,** Rue Jean-Baptiste-Aurard (below ramparts), tel: 9075-8078; closed November 15 to February 15
and for lunch on Tuesdays, Wednesdays and Thursdays from
July to September. Peaceful surroundings in old priory, renovated with taste, moderately priced restaurant, medium-
priced hotel.

Ménerbes
Hotel-Restaurant: **Roy Soleil,** Route des Beaumettes, Le
Fort, Route D103, tel: 9072-2561, fax: 9072-3655. Charm,
quiet, pool and agreeable dining, moderately expensive.

Some Useful Words and Phrases

brown	**marron, brun** (m)
dark	**foncé(e)**
excavation	**fouille** (f)
to increase	**augmenter**
light	**clair(e)**
mill	**moulin** (m), **usine** (f)
to name, to nominate	**nommer**
to produce	**produire**
product	**produit** (m)
purple	**pourpre, violet** (m)
to settle	**coloniser, s'installer**
tan	**beige, bronzage** (m)
yellow	**jaune** (m)

Je cherche des bas marron foncé. (I am looking for dark brown stockings.)

Elle aime les couleurs claires. (She likes light colors.)

Cette usine produit des tissus de première qualité. (This factory produces top quality fabrics.)

Ses produits sont vendus dans le monde entier. (Its products are sold in the entire world.)

Leur production a augmenté cette année. (Their production increased this year.)

CHAPTER 18

The Southwest

The southwest of France was long a land of revolt and contradiction. French history books would say "heresy."

The first trouble to be documented occurred in 218 B.C. during Hannibal's trek from North Africa across Europe with an army of men and elephants to attack Rome. He traversed Spain, then started through Gaul. In an attempt to bar the way to the Carthaginian general, Rome called upon the Gallic tribes of the Southwest to set up a barrage against the invading army. The tribal assembly refused to go to war in Rome's stead, signing, on the contrary, an agreement with Hannibal that he be treated as a guest. According to this contract, if the inhabitants of the region had reason to complain of his soldiers, their deeds would be judged by Hannibal and his lieutenants. Should his army have cause to complain, judgment would be left to the Gallic women.

Another major contradiction appeared in the 12th century, at roughly the same time that the Cistercians were countering the Cluniacs in Burgundy. A movement of religious dissidents, the Cathari—from the Greek word *catharsis* meaning purification—evolved a doctrine of good and evil. The Cathari church was essentially a grassroots movement dedicated to a revival of Christianity in its "purest" form. Rejecting certain rites and the pomp of the established church, emulating Christ while refusing to recognize him as a divinity, the Cathari incurred the wrath of Catholic officialdom. Rome called for crusades against them, which produced bloodbaths of in-

259

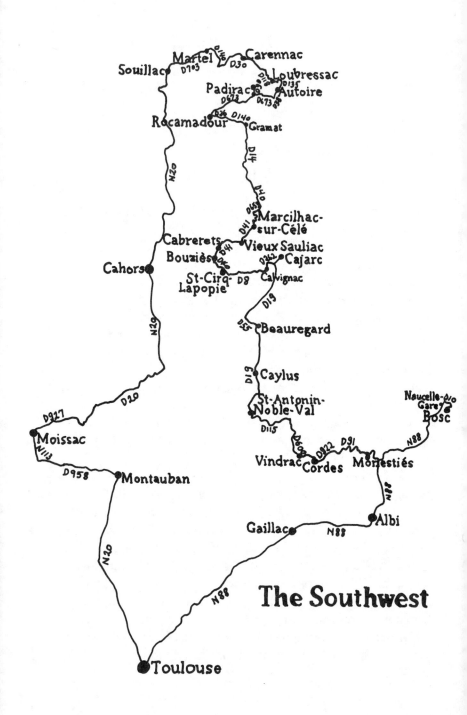

The Southwest

calculable dimensions followed by an inquisition. The new church was destroyed and the Capetian monarchs of France, Louis VIII and Louis IX (Saint Louis), took advantage of the situation to gain control of a prosperous and independent region.

That unique southwest spirit did not die, however, and in the 16th century it allied itself with the Protestant revolt. Once again a message of purification spread through the region. Religious strife followed and then subsided with the publication of the Edict of Nantes by Henry IV in 1598. With the revocation of the Edict in 1685, violence was revived. The devastation suffered by much of the Southwest was a direct cause of emigration to the New World. Pockets of Protestantism have, nonetheless, survived in the area until the present time.

The part of the Southwest we are concerned with goes by various names: Languedoc, Languedoc-Roussillon, Midi-Pyrénées. It covers a vast region extending from the Spanish border up to, but not including, Périgord in the north, and from Gascogne in the west to the Mediterranean.

Languedoc is in fact *langue d'oc,* the language of *oc,* spoken from Roman times until the 16th century when French became the official language. It resulted from the mixing of street Latin and the local tongue. This denomination covered a number of local dialects of southern France, including Provençal, all of which stood in opposition to the *langue d'oïl,* the language spoken in northern France. Both *oc* and *oïl* mean **yes,** *oc* coming from the Latin word for **this:** *hoc.* There have been periodic revivals of interest in the old language, which was incidentally that of the medieval troubadours.

We can obviously cover only a small part of such a large territory; making choices is difficult for the sights to be seen are myriad: Romanesque and southern Gothic churches, monasteries and bastides, villages which cling to mountainsides and cliffs, others which stretch lazily along river banks, austere cities and playful ones, market centers and vineyards, spectacular mountain marvels and caves, rivers, canals, the sea. . . .

Toulouse

The center of this tremendous hunk of France is Toulouse, a city built of brick. It gives off reddish hues, sometimes pink or rose, other times crimson or magenta. It is a southern European city, a bit Provençal, somewhat Hispanic and a dash Moorish. It is also an old city, originally Celtic, later Roman intellectual center for the region. In the 5th century it became the capital of the Visigoths before the latter were defeated by Clovis and pushed back into Spain. It then came within Charlemagne's empire. From the 9th to the 13th century Toulouse and the region were governed by the Raymonds, a dynasty of counts assisted by councilors called *capitouls*.

In 1208 Pope Innocent III excommunicated the Cathari leader Raymond VI and launched a crusade against his people. From northern France and Germany came thousands of crusaders looking for absolution for their past deeds . . . and spoils for their present ones. It was left to Raymond VII in semi-defeat to dismantle the ramparts of Toulouse and give his daughter in marriage to the brother of the king of France. During the wars of religion, Toulouse remained loyal to the Church.

At the beginning of the 16th century Toulouse became the center for the pastel trade. Although of short duration—some sixty years—it accounted for much of the city's prosperity. Pastel, a blue dye replaced in 1560 by indigo, is once again being produced for use in cosmetics and dyes.

Toulouse has long played a central role in aviation. It served as the departure point for the first postal routes between France, Africa and South America. An initial test flight took place here in December 1918; a permanent link-up with Morocco was established in 1919, with Dakar in 1925, and South America in 1930. The names of such legendary heros as Mermoz and Saint-Exupéry are linked to that exhilarating adventure.

Toulouse's experience with aviation did not, however, stop there. Since World War II it has been at the core of France's aeronautics industry. Airbus Industrie and Aérospatiale are located here, as well as the Centre National d'Etudes Spatiales which is behind the Hermès Project of an inhabited spaceship to be launched in 2001. Much other advanced technology, linked to space and aeronautics, is developed in Toulouse. The importance of training can be understood with a single statistic: one out of every six inhabitants of Toulouse is a student. The total population figure is about 360,000.

This is one of the few French provincial capitals that does not close down at night. Café life is inviting, the little restaurants in the center of town are good and inexpensive. It is a city one remains enamored of. Ask any Toulousan!

Tour

At the center of Toulouse is the **Capitole,** the city hall, named after the councilors of the Middle Ages. In the courtyard is a statue of Henry IV. The 16th-century donjon on the other side of the back garden is now the seat of the tourist information bureau. On the square in front of the Capitole, an organic produce market takes place on Tuesday mornings and a general produce market on Wednesday mornings. (If you are driving, avoid the underground parking garage here; it is expensive and you must have exact change in coins in order to exit.)

Leave the square on Rue Romiguières. At Rue Lakanal turn left for the **Jacobins,** a Dominican church and convent begun in 1230 which served as Toulouse's first university. The Dominicans, a mendicant and teaching order, had been founded in 1215 with the intention of providing an answer to the Cathari.

This brick church was the first example of post-Romanesque southern monastic architecture. It consists of a long nave terminated by three bays and is without a transept. More austere than the monastic architecture of the north of France, even military in aspect, it is nonetheless Gothic. The tiered, receding belfry is typical of church towers of the region. The effect of leaves and birds in stone against the ribboned brick of the portal is stunning.

The inside of the church is glorious: the nave consists of a line of central pillars, the seven pillars of wisdom; the last of them terminates in a palm-fan vault of twenty-two ribs of indescribable delicacy. The division of the nave into two parts served to separate the monks from the faithful. Many churches of the region contained two naves, the purpose being to prevent the monks from being seen by the parishioners, all the while being heard. Shades of rose and ochre filter the light from the stained glass. The rose windows date from the 14th century.

From the front of the church go through to the cloister, recently restored. In ancient times it served as a medicinal plant garden. Through the door at the far corner is the former dining hall of the convent, now used for temporary exhibits. Between the hall and the church is the muraled Saint Antonin Chapel and the capitular room, which plays host to a series of concerts in summertime.

Go right on leaving the Jacobins and take Rue Gambetta to the right. At Number 1 is the former **home of Jean de Bernuy,** one of the pastel fortunes. In the second court is the Tower of Pride of which some thirty exist in Toulouse. Their function was singularly social, the indication that the master of the house had been named councilor, *capitoul*. They might contain wardrobes or archives, even munitions.

Continue on to the **Garonne River.** The walk to the Pont Neuf, at left, is pleasant. It was once a covered bridge with water spurting from its gills. Turn left into Rue de Metz. Just before Rue de la Bourse is the 16th-century **Renaissance town house** of another pastel giant, Pierre d'Assézat. His was certainly the most elegant residence of Toulouse. One side of the courtyard was never completed: Assézat, having converted to Protestantism, was ruined and forced into exile.

Our walk continues on Rue des Marchands, then Rue de la Trinité and Rue Croix-Baragnon. There are a number of antique dealers in this quarter. At Number 15 is the oldest house in Toulouse, dating from the 13th century. Turn left on Rue d'Alsace-Lorraine in front of the Chamber of Commerce. After Rue de Metz you will come to the **Augustinian Museum.**

This former convent has been converted into a classic art museum of interest and beauty: among the masterpieces are Romanesque sculpture from the abbeys and churches of Toulouse. Also on display is an excellent collection of paintings which runs the gambit from the religious art of the 15th century to contemporary works by Hartung and Picasso. From the gardens on Rue de Metz one has an excellent view of the old convent church.

Retrace your steps on Rue de Metz. At **Rue des Changes,** an old Roman artery, turn right. The Hôtel de Brucelles, **Number 19,** has an elegant tower, **Number 16** a picturesque courtyard, wood staircases and galleries from the 16th century. On this street, Rue Saint-Rome and their side streets are a variety of restaurants, cafés and boutiques alongside or within the Gothic and Renaissance homes.

Cross Place du Capitole and enter Rue du Taur. The extraordinary fortified facade on the right is that of **Our Lady of Taur Church.** At **Number 49** glance at the courtyard and the paintings on the vaults at the entrance.

The **Saint Saturninus Basilica** at the end of the street is the largest Romanesque church in Europe and contains more relics than any other in France. The original structure was a sanctuary for the tomb of Saint Saturninus, the first bishop of Toulouse (250 A.D.). Over the centuries the number of relics increased and, consequently, the number of pilgrimages. The little basilica received visitors from all over Europe. It then served as a relay station on the road to Santiago de

Compostela. Work on a new, larger basilica began in 1080 and was completed in the 14th century. The architects Viollet-le-Duc and Baudot were successively in charge of its restoration in the 19th century.

The chevet of the church, composed of staged roofs over chapels, and a single belltower is outstanding. Especially expressive are the tympanums and capitals of the portals. For a Romanesque church, Saint Saturninus is immense. Inside, the capitals, murals and bas-reliefs of the transept and deambulatory are particularly noteworthy.

On Saturdays and Sundays Saint Saturninus is circled by a **flea market.**

The **Saint Raymond Museum** of archaeology is located in front of the basilica. It contains one of the best collections of Roman sculpture in France (ground floor) beautifully arranged. In addition, a great number of everyday objects are on show. The second floor is devoted to applied art objects from the beginning of time until the 8th century: coins, oil lamps, jewelry, pottery, and the like.

Train from Paris: Gare d'Austerlitz or Gare Montparnasse (change in Bordeaux): 8 hours (TGV part of the way).
Plane from Paris: 1 hour, Air Inter.
Tourist Info: Donjon of the Capitole, 31000 Toulouse, tel: 6123-3200, 17 Allées Jean-Jaurès, tel: 6162-7621.

Capitole: 8:30 A.M. to 5 P.M.; closed Saturdays and Sundays from October to June.
Jacobins: 10 A.M. to 6:30 P.M. and 2:30 to 6:30 P.M. on Sundays and holidays.
Augustinian Museum: 10 A.M. to 6 P.M. fron June 1 to September 30, until 5 P.M. rest of year; 2 to 9 P.M. on Wednesdays; closed Tuesdays and holidays.
Saint Raymond Museum: 10 A.M. to 6 P.M. in summer, 5 P.M. other months.

Restaurants: The following are pleasant, neighborhood establishments serving local specialties, located on Rue des Changes or the little streets to the left and right of it, inexpensive: *Auberge Louis XII. *Coq Hardi. *La Corde. *Maison Louis XIII. *Place du May. Barreau de Toulouse, 10 Rue des Moulins, tel: 6125-2552; closed Sundays. Located in former bakery, inventive cuisine, moderately priced. Bibent, Place du Capitole, elegant café, fine, classic cuisine, medium-priced. *Caves de la Maréchale, 3 Rue Jules-Chalande, tel: 6123-8228. Attractive upstairs room and wonderful brick cellar, quality buffet luncheon, moderately priced. Claude Ribardière, 21 Boulevard Duportal, tel: 6113-9112; closed Saturdays for lunch and Sundays. Elegant décor and interesting menu, medium-priced. Colombier, 14 Rue Bayard, tel: 6162-4005; closed Saturdays, Sundays and August. Fine regional dishes by former cook on the *France* (now the *Norway*), moderately priced. *Côte de Boeuf, 12 Rue Gestes, tel: 6121-1961; closed Mondays and August. Family-type restaurant, steak special, moderately priced. Jardins de l'Opéra, 1 Place du Capitole, tel: 6121-8266, fax: 6123-4104; closed Sundays and holidays and August. Part of Grand Hotel, top-rated restaurant of Toulouse, spectacular décor, expensive. Vanel, 22 Rue Maurice-Fontvieille, tel: 6121-5182, fax: 6123-6904; closed Sundays. Light, airy, inventive, moderately expensive.

Accommodations: Beaux-Arts, 1 Place du Pont-Neuf, tel: 6123-4050. View on the river, pleasantly decorated, art shows in residence throughout the year, medium-priced. Capoul, 13 Place du Président Wilson, tel: 6110-7070, fax: 6121-9670. Grand hotel, international standing, art déco fittings, moderately expensive. Clocher de Rodez, 14–15 Place Jeanne-d'Arc, tel: 6162-4292, fax: 6162-6899. Newly renovated, well placed, moderately priced. Grand Hôtel de l'Opéra, 1 Place du Capitole, tel: 6121-8266, fax: 6123-4104. Magnificent luxury hotel, charm, comfort, sauna, steam baths, expensive. Junior, Rue du Taur, tel: 6123-9867. Conveniently located in pedestrian street, moderately priced.

Mermoz, 50 Rue Matabiau, tel: 6163-0404, fax: 6163-1564. Peaceful, spacious, pretty rooms, medium-priced.

Gaillac

Leave Toulouse on the N88 for Gaillac. This small town on the Tarn has given its name to one of the oldest wines in France; there are those who claim this region has produced wine since 300 B.C. The Romans, we know, drank Gaillac vintages. In the 13th century the Benedictine monks of Saint Michael's Abbey tested, grafted and perfected their vines until they were satisfied they had elaborated the finest sacramental wine, one which would be celebrated abroad. They then established a charter defining production standards for Gaillac, laying down the law for the choice of land and vines, even for the wood of the kegs.

Gaillac produces red, white, rose and sparkling wines. The latter, called mauzac, is exported to the United States. Robert Plageoles, one of the region's most vocal winegrowers, insists that mauzac is champagne's ancestor. He also maintains that Gaillac is capable of competing with the finest Bordeaux.

Saint Michael's Abbey, worth a stop, is now the seat of the Gaillac Wine House, representing the region's producers.

Wine tasting: **Robert Plageoles et Fils,** Domaine des Tres Cantous, Route D922 towards Cahuzac-sur-Vère, tel: 6333-9940.

Albi

Go back to the N88 for Albi. This city is so closely identified with the Cathari revolt that the term Albigenses or Albigeois has become synonymous with Cathari. The new church attracted people from all walks of life; it was joined by rich and poor. The army of crusaders who descended upon the region at Pope Innocent III's beckoning massacred entire villages and towns, pillaged dwellings and ravaged property. Begun in 1208, the crusades lasted until 1229. The inquisition, the burnings at the stake which followed, continued for another fifteen years.

The bishops named by Rome during this troubled period and thereafter wielded tremendous power. Bernard de Combret, bishop from 1254 to 1271, undertook the construction of the Berbie episcopal palace. Bernard de Castanet, bishop from 1276 to 1308, launched the Saint Cecilia project. Both were intended as grandiose in order to underscore the supremacy of the Roman Catholic Church and enhance its prestige, which perhaps accounts for the solid, military aspect of **Saint Cecilia.**

The entrance is majestic; it is the only decorative note on the austere facade. The interior was, in its beginnings, sober too: a long nave without transept in the style of southern Gothic, bays all the way round. At the end of the 15th century, Bishop Louis I d'Amboise decided to build a rood screen to shield a choir which would occupy one-half the church. The screen is lace worked in stone. Before the French Revolution ninety-six statues decorated it; six remain.

The statues which surround the choir, in the deambulatory, are exquisite representations of figures from the Old Testament: Gothic realism and expressiveness at its height. They were executed by artists from Burgundy. The apsidal stained glass windows of brilliant blue date from the 14th century.

Under the grand organ note the mural in tempura of the Last Judgment. The lovely murals of the vault were executed by Italian artists in the 16th century. Take a last look around Saint Cecilia; there is a sensuous aura to this edifice.

The **Berbie Palace** which serves as backdrop for the **Toulouse-Lautrec Museum** was built as an episcopal residence and was initially a fortress and donjon. Over the years, in particular after the promulgation of the Edict of Nantes in 1598, the military character of the palace was gradually sublimated.

The Toulouse-Lautrec collection is the most complete in existence, some 600 works in all. It represents a clear panorama of the artist's work: from the portrait of his mother when he was sixteen to his last painting (1901) of the hands of two men called *Medical School Examination.* The collection is especially revealing of Lautrec's ability at poster design and graphics; he has been called the world's first ad-man.

From Place Sainte-Cécile take Rue Mariés to the **Saint Salvy Church,** named after the lawyer-become-monk who introduced Christianity to the region. The Romanesque church started here in the 11th century was interrupted by the Abligenses interregnum; when resumed, it was in the Gothic style.

Before leaving Albi take Quai Choiseul down from the Berbie Palace and cross the river on the **Old Bridge.** From the opposite shore the view of Saint Cecilia is spectacular. At night it is illuminated.

Tourist Info: Palais Berbie, Place Sainte-Cécile, 81000 Albi, tel: 6354-2230.

Toulouse-Lautrec Museum: 10 A.M. to 12 noon and 2 to 6 P.M. from April 1 to September 30; from 9 A.M. in July and August; closing at 5 P.M. and on Tuesdays from October 1 to March 31.

Restaurants: **Jardin des Quatre Saisons,** 19 Boulevard Strasbourg, tel: 6360-7776; closed Mondays. Good food at reasonable prices, flowers and greenery, moderately priced. **Moulin de la Mothe,** Rue Mothe, tel: 6360-3815; closed Sunday evenings, except July and August, and Wednesdays. On the riverside, local specialties, moderately priced.
Hotel-Restaurants: **Altéa,** 41bis Rue Porta, tel: 6347-6666, fax: 6346-1840. Efficient, modern rooms with spectacular view of river and Saint Cecilia, pleasant dining room, medium-priced. **Chiffre,** 50 Rue Séré-de-Rivières, tel: 6354-0460, fax: 6347-2061. Quiet street, comfortable, good table, medium-priced. **Hostellerie Saint-Antoine,** 17 Rue Saint-Antoine, tel: 6354-0404, fax: 6347-1047. Elegantly modern,

beautifully decorated, view on gardens, fine cuisine, moderately expensive. **La Réserve,** Route de Cordes, 3 kilomètres on D600, tel: 6347-6022, fax: 6347-6360. On the banks of the Tarn, stylish residence and park, individualized rooms, delicate cuisine, calm, expensive.

Bosc

Once again, take the N88, this time north towards Rodez. The scenery varies. The road passes through some old mining towns, then forest and, further on, plateau country with slate-roofed houses constructed from dark volcanic stone. At Naucelle-Gare turn right on the D10. Road signs indicate the way to the **Bosc Château,** about three kilometers south.

You will know this is not an ordinary visit when you approach the château. A small sign requests that you advance to the house entrance and ring the bell, which you will see is a thin chain with a metal hook on which to pull in order to procure a tinkle from some bells up above. In the event there is no reply, a similar bell chain exists in the courtyard.

An aristocratic head of gray hair, green eyes, high cheekbones and a strong hooked nose may appear in one of the upper windows, then descend to admit you to the **Toulouse-Lautrec family museum.** Your guide may well be, as mine was, Nicole Bérengère Tapie de Celeyran, the painter's cousin. Lautrec, as she calls him, died in 1901 so she could not possibly have known him. She has, however, been devoted throughout her life to the task of conserving the memory of the artist.

This unpretentious, rustic manor house was often home to Lautrec and his many cousins. He spent most every summer here and visited at least once a year all his short life; he was 37 when he died. The rooms you will visit pay witness to a fashionable life style, antiquated but touching; much memorabilia has been conserved. In the room where Lautrec slept on his visits you will see the sailboat he whittled when bedridden after his first accident. Both he and his mother spoke fluent

English. Notice the children's picture books *Funny Pictures* and *The Three Jovial Huntsmen.*

Mademoiselle de Celeyran has numerous anecdotes to recount: "He was an observer of the human comedy," she recalls.

Château visit: 9 A.M. to 12 noon and 2 to 7 P.M. every day.

Monestiés

Return to the N88, taking it to the left back to Carmaux. Turn right on the D91 and take the D91A into Monestiés. In the **Saint Jacques Chapel** just off the main road, a five hundred-year-old *Entombment of Christ* has just been restored to its original splendor. Ring the bell of the house next door to the chapel. A very knowledgeable person will arrive to unlock, provide explanations and collect a few francs.

In 1490 Louis I d'Amboise, Bishop of Albi, dedicated, in his summer residence of Combefa Castle now in ruin, this startling Entombment composed of twenty life-sized figures. Ten of the painted statues are standing on either side of the tomb. They face the viewer, naturally expressive in their suffering. The resemblance to the Burgundian sculpture of Saint Cecilia is evident; they could possibly have been executed by the same artists, who remain nameless. It would seem that the stone for this representation was cut locally.

Take a walk around the medieval stone village on leaving the chapel. Visit the old **church** with its belfry and exterior Romanesque tower so typical of the architecture of the region. In the dimly lit church, with flowers and plants throughout, plaques near the entrance remember those killed in France's 20th century wars. A small fortified château and bits of rampart are still standing.

Cordes

The D91 will take you along the narrow Cérou River. Note the pretty vine-covered village of Salles built from the stone of its quarries. Go left on the D922.

Cordes in its entirety, perched on the top of a monticule, has been entered in the register of historic monuments. It is also "one of the most beautiful villages of France." Founded in 1222 during the war against the Cathari by Count Raymond VII of Toulouse, the fortified village was conceived as an outpost against the crusaders. The inquisition which followed was particularly vicious.

The latter part of the 13 and the 14th centuries were prosperous, however, thanks to the cloth and tannery trades. Fabric woven by the peasant population was then dyed in the blues of pastel and the yellows of saffron. For the French this was the *pays de cocagne* or cockaigne, the land of milk and honey. The fine mansions in Grande Rue and Rue Voltaire, designed by Italian artisans, date from that era. In the 16th century fortunes were reversed and in 1631 the town was decimated by the plague. A short reprieve occurred in 1870 with the arrival of Swiss embroidery machines, an industry which collapsed totally after World War I. Until the war, only men worked the machines, the women and children's task being to thread the needles. Mobilization changed that pattern and the women of the village kept the machines operating. Cordes' principal industry today is the tourist trade.

Among the fine homes built of stone from the quarries at Salles is that now occupied by the **town hall** and the local tourist office. The **market hall** built in 1271, originally the cloth market, is dedicated to Saint Bartholomew, the tanners' saint. **Saint Michael's Church** on Rue de la République warrants a stop if only for the lovely rose window and the organ. The watchtower antedates the building of the church, often the case in this region.

Tourist info: Grande Rue, 81170 Cordes, tel: 6356-0052.

Restaurant: ***Auberge de la Cité,** Place de la Halle, tel: 6356-1559. Regional specialties, inexpensive.
Hotel-Restaurants: ***La Chevance,** Porte des Ormeaux, tel: 6356-1465. Rooms with view, moderately priced. **Grand**

Ecuyer, Rue Voltaire, tel: 6356-0103, fax: 6356-1699; closed Mondays except July and August and October 15 to March 15. Former hunting lodge of Raymond VII, period furniture, cuisine by a winner of "best French artisan" award, moderately expensive to expensive. ***Hostellerie du Vieux Cordes,** Rue de l'Eglise, tel: 6356-0012; closed January. Picturesque setting, pleasant atmosphere, moderately to medium-priced. ***Hostellerie du Parc,** Route des Cabannes, 1 kilometer on D600, tel: 6356-0259. Quiet, comfortable residence surrounded by cedar trees, good food, moderately priced.

Take the D600 past Cabannes to **Vindrac.** Follow the signs to the **Tools Museum** located in an old mill. It possesses a very complete collection of old tools and utensils, many evoking trades long extinct. Before leaving ask the curator to show you the old bread oven. Open 3 to 8 P.M. every day.

Saint-Antonin-Noble-Val

Return to the D600 north. The road passes forest and farms; at the Aveyron River turn left on the D115. The views of the valley on one side and the cliffs on the other will enchant you along the way to **Saint-Antonin-Noble-Val.** This is a pleasant little town known for its spring water. Walk through the narrow streets, take a look at the **market place** and the **archaeological and folklore museum.** The latter is located in the former council hall remodeled by Viollet-le-Duc in the 19th century by the addition of a curious Tuscan watchtower.

Tourist info: Town Hall, 82140 Saint-Antonin-Noble-Val, tel: 6330-6347.

Museum: Afternoons, except Tuesdays, in July and August; Saturdays only, 3 to 4 P.M., other months.

Accommodations: ***Viollet-le-Duc,** Place de la Halle, tel: 6368-2100. Charming hotel recently renovated, moderately priced.

Caylus

The winding, scenic D19 will bring you into Caylus. Park near the **church.** The strong, simple architecture, topped by a heavy stone steeple is impressive. Perhaps the screeching red of the door will have toned down by the time you get there. Is there still grass growing on the tiled roof?

The church is particularly well proportioned and beautifully simple with its balustrade in stone and forged iron. The wooden statue of Christ is by Zadkine.

Climb **Rue Droite** up to the market place. There is a nice pottery shop on the way, La Hulotte, with a wide choice and good prices; also, a number of interesting medieval houses, one with wolf gargoyles on the facade. Glance behind you and between the houses for a glimpse of the green hills around.

The **market hall** is covered by a slate roof. The holes carved in the stone table barrier were used for measuring grain. Note also the charming town hall, called the Common House. Take the street alongside the restaurant on the square. At the top is a hairdresser who distinguishes himself in English as "qualified."

Tourist Info: Rue Droite, tel: 6367-0028; Town Hall, tel: 6367-0617.

Hotel-Restaurant: ***Renaissance,** Avenue du Père Huc, tel: 6367-0726. Hearty food, good-sized portions, moderately priced.

Saint-Cirq-Lapopie

From Caylus there is a wonderfully picturesque road, the D19, through Lacapelle-Livron, Les Tourettes and **Beauregard** and its market square. It travels through oak forests lined with moss-covered stone walls. From Beauregard take the D55 left towards Varaire and just before arriving there, pick up the D19 north through Limogne-en-Quercy. Cross the one-car bridge over the River Lot to **Cajarc.**

A brief stop here is agreeable. Go down by the riverside to

the *Plan d'eau*. See also the little square in the center of a town made famous by a former president of France, Georges Pompidou, who had a country estate here. There is a small contemporary European **arts center** named after him open from 10 A.M. to 12 noon and 2 to 6 P.M. from May to November, except Tuesdays.

Turn back, out of Cajarc. The D19 will take you quickly into the D262 which travels along the right or northern bank of the Lot. At the entrance to Larnagol, also charming, take the bridge across to Calvignac, 200 inhabitants on a wedge over the river! Continue along the river on the D8 from which you can see La Toulzanie on the other side. The D8 will take you into **Saint-Cirq-Lapopie,** another of "the most beautiful villages of France," also declared a national historic monument.

As you will quickly realize Saint-Cirq-Lapopie occupies a strategic location. It seems probable that a Gallic tribe settled here long ago and the Romans occupied it later. The château above the village was built by a local feudal lord La Popie during the Middle Ages. Until its total destruction in 1580 on orders from the future Henry IV, control of this seemingly insignificant burg was the object of fierce battles at various key moments in history: first in the 8th century, then in 1198 when Richard the Lion Heart made an unsuccessful attempt to capture it. During the Hundred Years War it again came under attack from the British and during the wars of religion the Huguenots battled to gain control of the town.

Meander, stop, start, turn your head right, turn left, eyes a-goggle. The rooftops of burgundy tile have mellowed into shades of brown, stone is light gray and ochre. The roof tiles are flat on the sides and rounded at the edges giving the impression of turned up roof ends. Climb to the top and survey it all from the ex-castle: the village, the river at the foot of white and gold cliffs, the locks, the fields. The Farrel Potts of Atlanta writing in the tourist office visitors' book, put it this way: "So glad we kept on driving!" Yes, indeed.

The crafts shops now occupied by painters, potters and leather artisans were once those of wood turners who specialized in spigots for wine kegs. On the village square is the little Rignault Museum of local and Chinese objects.

Tourist Info: Village square, 46330 Saint-Cirq-Lapopie, tel: 6531-2906.

Rignault Museum: 10 A.M. to 12 noon and 2 to 6 P.M. from April 1 to November 1, except Tuesdays.

Hotel-Restaurants: *Auberge du Sombral, tel: 6531-2608; closed Tuesday evenings and Wednesdays except during school holidays. Delightful small inn, pleasantly decorated rooms and attractive dining room with fine regional cuisine, moderately priced. Pelissaria, tel: 6531-2514, fax: 6530-2552. Dinner only. Restaurant closed Thursdays. Tasteful, original rooms with fine views and rustic antique furnishings, creative cuisine, moderately priced restaurant, medium-priced accommodations.

Bouziès

Take the spectacular cliff road, the D40, down to Bouziès on the water. This sweet town of 70 inhabitants is the departure point for promenades on the river. Between here and Luzech, to the west of Cahors, 65 kilometers of river are now navigable through fourteen locks.

Houseboats, canoes and bicycles are for hire here. A one-hour riverboat excursion, with French commentary, is also a pleasant way to get the feel of the river; pass through a lock and admire the serene, picturesque landscape. At river level a trail carved out of the stone cliffs centuries ago allowed for the passage of cargo and boatsmen to different water levels. The first locks were dug and imbedded in 1664. Until the 1870s when railway transport took over, the Lot was the commercial thoroughfare for the region. The locks gradually became unusable. They are now, one by one, being overhauled and each year more of the river is opened to navigation.

Boat rides: Les Falaises. Sailings at 11 A.M. and 3, 4:30 and 7 P.M.

Hotel-restaurant: *Les Falaises, tel: 6531-2683, fax: 6530-2387. Small resort on the river, swimming pool, tennis, boating, nature walks, good food, moderately priced.

Célé Valley

On leaving Bouziès cross the Lot and go right for one kilometer. When you reach the D41 turn left and follow the Célé River Valley. At **Cabrerets,** a 14th-century castle is poised to dive into the river some eighty feet below. Nearby are the prehistoric caves of **Pech Merle,** open to the public. Inhabited 10- to 20,000 years ago, they were discovered in 1922 by two fourteen-year-old boys. Mammoths and bison drawn in black cover the wall of one cave; other drawings, as yet undeciphered, another. In an upper grotto, natural seepage has created interesting shapes and columns in astonishing tones of rust and white. In other galleries are drawings of a bear's head, silhouettes of horses and again incomprehensible graffiti. The **Amédée-Lemozi Museum** exhibits in didactic fashion objects uncovered in the caves.

Continue on the D41 from Cabrerets. You will pass Liauzu, a hamlet of a few houses backed into the cliff. A few miles on you will see Sauliac, of 100 inhabitants, half way up the stone barrier. The houses are of light colored stone with dark tile roofs like those in Saint-Cirq-Lapopie. If you are courageous (and you will be rewarded) take the little road up to **Vieux Sauliac.** Leave the car and walk until you arrive at a view of rare beauty encompassing a castle, fields and the river. The caves above Sauliac served as refuges in times of war.

The D41 then wends its way to **Marcilhac-sur-Célé.** Go towards the water and you will discover the remains of a once prosperous and powerful **abbey.** Over the portal, the tympanum of the Last Judgment surrounds an expressive Christ (10th century). To the left, open to the winds, is a majestic square Romanesque narthex. The church to the right is in flamboyant Gothic. Its murals represent the apostles; the woodwork, the life of Christ. To the right, out of the narthex, is a path which leads around other remains of the old abbey. The guardian is deaf and mute but you will have no trouble understanding him!

From here, take leave of the river valley on the D14. Turn right on the D653 and, one kilometer on, left on the D40 to Espédaillac. On leaving the town, pick up the D14 again to Gramat. There, go left on the N140, then left on the D36, through the Monkey Forest, to Rocamadour. There are actually some 150 Barbary apes, an almost extinct species, living here.

Cabrerets
Pech Merle and Museum: 9:30 A.M. to 12 noon and 1:30 to 5:30 P.M. from Easter to November 1.

Hotel-Restaurants: **Auberge de la Sagne,** Route des Grottes de Pech-Merle, tel 6531-2662; closed October through April. Flowers, trees and comfortable rooms, regional cooking, moderately priced. **Grottes,** tel 6531-2702; closed October 1 to May 14. Peace and quiet with a view of the river. Inexpensive to moderately priced.

Espédaillac
Restaurant: **Auberge Beauville,** good regional fare, moderately priced.

Gramat
Hotel-Restaurant: **Lion d'Or,** 8 Place de la République, tel: 6538-7318, fax: 6538-8450; closed Mondays from November to March and December 15 to January 15. Recently renovated rooms with views, delicate regional cuisine, medium-priced.

Rocamadour

The beginnings of Rocamadour are lost in legend. The original site, a cave in the cliff, possibly served as a place of worship before Christianity. In about the year 1000 a small chapel was constructed in the grotto. Remains discovered in the 12th century under the chapel are thought to have been those of a hermit. However, throughout the countryside, the story spread that the skeleton belonged to one of Christ's disciples. Miracles were reported to have occurred there.

In short time Rocamadour attracted as many pilgrims as Jerusalem or Rome. On days of atonement, from 15- to 30,000 people camped on the plain beneath. The king of England, kings and queens of France, saints and public figures arrived in Rocamadour to kneel at the Virgin Mary's feet. Crusaders left northern Europe for Spain to battle the so-called infidels, the Muslims, with the banner of Rocamadour in the lead. Penitence for the Cathari often required a pilgrim-age to the Chapel of the Virgin, the penitent arriving on foot and mounting the steps on their knees, after which they were put in irons and chastised on the altar of the chapel. Repen-tents were then provided with a statement attesting to their purification and sent on their way.

With notoriety came prosperity. Control of the church was fought for between dioceses. During the Hundred Years War the English pillaged the sanctuaries. During the wars of reli-gion the Protestants tried to destroy them. They also came under attack at the time of the French Revolution. In the last century, restoration was begun. Once again pilgrims are making their way to Rocamadour. Tourists, too!

Tour

Rocamadour clings to the mountainside, glued to it and locked in. The approach is spectacular.

Leave your car in the parking lot and make your way along the main street, Rue de la Couronnerie, lined with souvenir shops. For the fervent, there are a total of 233 steps going up. The rest can take the elevator. The first level, after 143 steps, was that formerly occupied by the canons' living quarters, now converted into stores and hostels. From here another stairway leads to **Saint Amadour Square,** off of which are seven sanctuaries. This is the holy city, at the median level.

The **crypt or Saint Amadour Chapel** is a single undecorated nave without transept or apse, exquisite. The **Saint Savior Basilica** is a marvelous low-ceilinged, heavy-pillared Romanesque structure. It was fitted out with wooden galleries in the 19th century. The space exudes an aura of religion. Richly colorful frescos line parts of **Saint Michael's Chapel.**

Another staircase leads to **Notre Dame Chapel,** its walls darkened by the smoke of centuries of tapers. Here is the miraculous Virgin, known as the Black Virgin, sculpted in wood in the 12th century. Also here is a 9th century bell which, story has it, used to ring each time the name of the Virgin of Rocamadour was cited by people in danger. The presence of numerous boat models is due to the popularity of Rocamadour among sailors from Brittany.

Below the sanctuaries, the **Museum of Sacred Art** is dedicated to the French composer François Poulenc who wrote his *Litanies to the Black Virgin* after a visit to Rocamadour in 1936.

A path climbs to the top, to the ramparts of the old fort and the chaplains' residence, built in the last century. The view is exceptional from here. Close by is a **training and reproductive center for birds of prey** which organizes daily demonstrations.

Rocamadour is illuminated at night.

Tourist Info: Town Hall, 46500 Rocamadour, tel: 6533-6259.

Crypt and Chapels: Guided visits every day except Sundays. *Museum:* 10 A.M. to 12:30 P.M. and 2 to 6 P.M. from Easter to November 1.

Illuminations: April 1 to October 31.
Birds of Prey Shows: Mornings and afternoons from Easter to November 1.
Candle Procession: August 14.

Hotel-Restaurants: ***Château et Relais Amadourien,** Route du Château, 1.5 kilometers from town, tel: 6533-6222, fax: 6533-6900; closed November 11 to March 27. Comfortable, quiet hotel, tennis, moderately to medium-priced. **Château de Roumégouse,** Route 140, 4 kilometers towards Gramat, tel: 6533-6381, fax: 6533-7118; closed October 26 to April 12. Superb château surrounded by woods, renovated and tastefully decorated, pool, fine cuisine with regional products, moderately expensive. **Grand Hôtel Beau Site,** in town, tel: 6533-6308, fax 6533-6523. Perfect family-run hotel, comfort, conveniences, view, innovative regional cuisine, medium-priced. **Panoramic,** L'Hospitalet, tel: 6533-6306, fax: 6533-6926; closed November 1 to February 15. View, shaded terrace, regional specialties, moderately priced. ***Sainte-Marie,** Place Senhals, tel: 6533-6307, fax: 6533-6908; closed October 21 to March 31. From the terrace a wonderful view, regional dishes, moderately priced. **Vieilles Tours,** Lafage, 2 kilometers west on D673, tel: 6533-6801, fax: 6533-6859; closed November 6 to April 14. Painter's lovely master farmhouse, comfortable, tastefully arranged rooms, good family-style table, moderately priced.

Dordogne

If you have a day to spare, the ride from Rocamadour to Souillac through a bit of Dordogne is most satisfying. Leave the pilgrim city on the D673. Go left on the D90 to **Padirac.** The **grottos** are bewitching. Take a ride on the underground river, some 360 feet below the land surface. Visit the great halls of stalagmites, the giant stalactite and the emerald lake, truly enchanting.

Go back to the D673 and go left to the D38 and left again for **Autoire.** Awaiting you are majestic old homes of yellow stone covered with burnt orange tiles and little towers that sprout from the rooftops. From the terrace near the pretty Romanesque church there is a good view of the surrounding countryside.

Continue on the D135 to **Loubressac** which, says the road sign, is a village of flowers. It is in fact more than that: from its perch above the river, it dominates the valley. The **château** occupies a wonderful spot at the edge of town.

Leave here on the D118. Just before the Bave River, turn left on the D30 for **Carennac.** Take the old bridge to "one of the most beautiful villages of France," inhabited by less than 400 people. Once again, pale yellow stone and brown tiles and turrets. And this time, wood balconies and flower pots. The **church** contains interesting details: wood sculpture, a 16th-century entombment, murals of the Evangelists, a Romanesque vaulted cloister.

The river road out of Carennac will take you to the N140. Go right into **Martel,** the city of seven towers. Enter the old town on foot. Take Rue du Four-Bas to **Saint Maur's,** partially fortress, partially church. The Romanesque tympanum is a portrayal of the Last Judgment. Inside are some lovely stained glass windows. From the church take Rue Droite. Turn right at the 12th-century **Fabri House**; you will soon arrive at Place des Consuls in the center of which is a handsome **market place.**

The D703 will take you to **Souillac.** Of the former Benedictine abbey which transformed this region from marshes into arable land there remains only **Saint Mary's Church,** containing a famous sculpture story of the life of the monk Theophilus. It was placed originally over the outside portal. However, during the wars of religion, the abbey was attacked by Protestants and the sculpture was brought into the nave of the church for safekeeping. It is still there today.

Take a walk around the outside of the church. The three amazing flat domes are reminiscent of Saint Sophie's in Istanbul.

In front of the abbey is a joyful **Mechanical Toys Museum.** The one thousand mechanical toys and instruments here are a show in themselves, a show which functions with the help of a modern robot.

Padirac

Grotto: 9 A.M. to 12 noon and 2 to 6:30 P.M. from Easter to second Sunday of October; 8 A.M. to 7 P.M. in August. Tour: 90 minutes.

Hotel-Restaurant: *Padirac, at the chasm, tel: 6533-6423, fax: 6533-7203; closed from October 12 to March 31. Tranquil, conventional establishment, regional cooking, moderately priced.

Loubressac

Accommodations: **Château de Gamot,** tel: 6538-5205 §-5850. Lovely private home offering bed and breakfast, medium-priced.

Carennac

Hotel-Restaurants: *Auberge du Vieux Quercy, tel: 6538-6900, fax: 6538-4238; closed Mondays off season and November 15 to February 15. Quiet, attractive rooms, simple, regional cuisine, moderately priced. *Fénelon, tel: 6538-6767; closed Fridays and for lunch on Saturdays from October to Easter. Annual closing January 6 to March 10. Another quiet establishment on the river, regional dishes, moderately priced.

Souillac

Mechanical Toys Museum: 10 A.M. to 12 P.M. and 3 to 6 P.M. except Mondays, from April through October; 10 A.M. to 7 P.M. every day in July and August; afternoons only, except Mondays and Tuesdays, from November through March.

Hotel-Restaurants: *Granges Vieilles, 2 kilometers on Route de Sarlat, tel: 6537-8092; closed January 2 to February 15. Quiet residence and pleasant grounds, regional specialties, medium-priced. *Ambassadeurs, 12 Avenue du Général-de-

Gaulle, tel: 6532-7836; closed December 20 to January 20. Fine neighborhood atmosphere and regional cooking, moderately priced. **Vieille Auberg,** Place de la Minoterie, tel: 6532-7943, fax: 6532-6519. Calm, view, and delectable recipes from the past, moderately priced.

Cahors

The N20 will take you straight into Cahors. Situated on a small peninsula surrounded by the Lot River on three sides—in French this is called a curl in the river—the location was chosen for settlement because of the natural founts at this point. They are still supplying the city with water.

Bustling market town and provincial capital, it was, back in the 13th century, the dominant financial capital of Europe. Cahors' bankers lent money to the pope, to kings and merchants from Scandinavia to the Orient. In the slang of the times, the word *cahorsin* was the equivalent of usurer. Pope John xxii, native of Cahors, set up a university here in 1332; its reputation surpassed that of Toulouse.

The Hundred Years War finally provoked the city's decline, through no fault of its people, however. Undefeated in battle against the English, it was delivered to the enemy by the king of France. Cahors further suffered at the time of the Reformation when its population was sharply divided. In 1560 Protestants were massacred, in 1580 they sought revenge and pillaged the city.

Tour:

The best way to begin the visit of Cahors is to traverse the town lengthwise, down Rue de la Barre and Boulevard Gambetta to the riverside. Then turn right and advance slowly along Quai Cavaignac and Allée des Soupirs for a long look at the **Valentré Bridge.** This magnificent military structure, started in 1308, took over fifty years to complete. The central tower functioned as an observation post, the towers at either end served to block passage.

Go back up Boulevard Gambetta to the Allées Fénelon and the tourist information center where there is ample public parking. From there set out on foot.

Take **Rue du Docteur-Bergounioux** across from the Allées Fénelon. You will pass an interesting Renaissance home, Number 40, in the Italian style. When you reach Place Saint-Priest note the old wood staircase, known as a Toulousan stairway. Continue on **Rue Lastié.** You will notice the widespread use of brick, the reason being that local stone was too hard to sculpt. These timbered houses were what might be called the prefabs of the 15th century: the wood and brick frames were prepared in advance and then the entire block was lifted into place. Given the difficulty and the expense of stone sculpture, the carved doorways you will see from time to time were the success symbols of the era.

At Rue Saint-Urcisse turn left past the 12th-century Saint-Urcisse's Church. It is presently undergoing restoration. At the end of the street, turn right towards the river for the **Roaldès House,** an attractive home with a lovely facade. Pass behind the cathedral to Olivier-de-Magny Square, then go round to the front of **Saint Stephen's.** You will notice some similarity between the low, rounded domes of Souillac and the cupolas here. Oriental in origin, they are common in Aquitaine, the region to the west of Cahors. Saint Stephen's has a fortresslike quality. The tympanum of the northside portal, worth noting, dates from the 12th century; other parts of the church are Gothic. Step down into the nave, its width and clarity are surprising, evoking theater rather than worship. The choir, however, with its stained glass and paintings reverses that first impression. To the right of the choir is a doorway into the flamboyant Gothic cloister. Despite its deterioration, the sculpture work here is still remarkable.

Outside the cathedral, on Wednesday and Saturday mornings, there is a fabulous **market** of local farmers' produce. On Sundays it becomes a flower market. Cahors is known for its goose-and duck-liver pâtés, truffles, wild mushrooms, wines, cabécou cheeses, nut pastries. . . The annual truffles, goose and duck-liver market holds sway on Saturdays from November 1 to March 31.

Take Rue Nationale, along which are a number of interesting old residences, back to Rue du Docteur-Bergounioux.

Tourist Info: Place Aristide-Briand, 46000 Cahors, tel: 6535-0956.

Roaldès House: Mornings and afternoons from mid-June through September.

Restaurants: **Balandre,** 5 Avenue Charles-de-Freycinet, tel: 6530-0197, fax: 6522-0640; closed Sunday evenings and Mondays off season and February. It has 1900s décor for good traditional cuisine, moderately priced. **Marco,** *Lamagdelaine,* 7 kilometers north on D653 towards Figeac, tel: 6535-3064; closed Sunday evenings and Mondays from September 15 to June 1. Lovely vine-covered restaurant, cuisine based on fresh, local products, medium-priced.

Hotel-Restaurants: **Château de Mercuès,** *Mercuès,* 7 kilometers north on N20 and D911, tel: 6520-0001, fax: 6520-0572; closed November 15 to March 15. Exquisite castle on cliff overlooking the Lot River, beautifully decorated, comfortable rooms, pool, fine cuisine, expensive to luxury prices. ***Clos Grand,** Route de Luzech, Labéraudie, 4 kilometers across river on D8, tel: 6535-0439. Closed Friday evenings and Saturdays for lunch during winter. Quiet, comfortable, pleasant terrace, typical regional dishes, moderately priced.

Moissac

After leaving Cahors on the N20, about 25 kilometers to the south you will come to the D20 turn-off. Go through Molières and just beyond Lafrançaise, after a spectacular view of the Tarn River, get on the D927 to Moissac. The grapes grown in this region, called chasselas, are for eating, not making wine.

The former abbey at Moissac was founded in the 7th century. In the 11th century it joined the Cluniac order, after which its influence spread and it prospered. Occupied and severely damaged by the English during the Hundred Years War, it suffered additional destruction during the wars of religion and the Revolution.

The extraordinary **cloister,** which dates from the end of the 11th century, is one of the jewels of the region; it exhibits harmony of color in different shades of marble, delicacy of arcades and columns, variety of sculpture, and elegance of a single cedar. From the narthex a staircase leading to the floor above allows for an overall view of the cloister.

The south portal of **Saint Peter's Church** (early 12th century) rates as one of the masterpieces of Romanesque art. The tympanum represents an apocalyptic vision of the universe as depicted by Saint John. The narthex, the nave and the chapels are interesting for their architecture and sculpture. The 12th-century statue of Christ to the right of the organ is particularly noteworthy.

Tourist Info: Place Durand-de-Bredon, 82200 Moissac, tel: 6304-0185.

Hotel-Restaurants: *Pont Napoléon, 2 Allées Montebello, tel: 6304-0155; closed Sunday evenings and Mondays and January. View of bridge and the Tarn, traditional in the best sense, moderately priced. **Relais du Moulin de Moissac,** tel: 6304-0355, fax: 6304-2458. Peaceful, well-run establishment, pretty grounds, medium-priced.

Montauban

Drive out of Moissac on the N113. Take the D958 over the canal to Montauban, Ingres' birthplace. Montauban, too, is a city of reddish hues, built of brick and laid out according to a plan. It is particularly remembered for its part in the wars of religion and its role as the last Protestant outpost.

The first attempts of the monarchy to overpower the reformers' revolt were a failure and in 1570 it was recognized officially as one of the Protestant strongholds. The assemblies of the Reformed Church of France were held here. Nonetheless, in 1621, Louis XIII marshaled an army of 20,000 men and attacked Montauban. The population resisted and king and army were forced to withdraw. They returned, however, in 1628 and gained entrance into the city. The Huguenots were spared their lives but the city's fortifications were destroyed.

Tour:

Cross the Tarn River on the **Old Bridge,** another fortified structure built in the same period as the Valentré Bridge of Cahors. Immediately to your right is the former episcopal palace, now the **Ingres Museum.** It houses the richest collection of Ingres' work anywhere in the world, some 4,000 drawings and thirty paintings, most of which were bequeathed by the painter to his native town.

The decorative second-floor rooms provide a magnificent background for Ingres' art. Also here are a number of works by Delacroix, Géricault, David and others. On display, among Ingres' personal effects and drawings, are his violin and paint box. On the third floor, 14th- to 18th-century paintings from Ingres' personal collection are exhibited.

The ground floor of the museum is dedicated to another native of Montauban, Bourdelle. Among pieces of his sculpture are portraits of Beethoven, Rodin and Ingres. The vaulted rooms on the lower level are devoted to archaeology, folklore and temporary shows. On the square outside the museum, the imposing bronze of a dying centaur is also by Bourdelle.

On the other side of the fortified Saint Jacques' Church is **Place Nationale** surrounded by ingenious brick arcades and subtle red-toned buildings. A colorful **market** is held here every morning. On Wednesday and Friday mornings from November to February the specialties are goose- and duck-livers, tureens and pâtés.

Tourist Info: Place Prax-Paris, 82000 Montauban, tel: 6363-6060.

Restaurant: ***Ventadour,** 23 Quai Villebourbon, tel: 6363-3458; closed Saturdays for lunch, Sundays and August. Attractive settings and view, regional specialties, medium-priced. **Hotel: Midi,** 12 Rue Notre-Dame, tel: 6363-1723, fax: 6366-4366. Centrally located, moderately priced.

Hotel-Restaurants: **Cuisine d'Alain and Hôtel d'Orsay,** across from RR station, tel: 6366-0666, fax: 6366-1939; restaurant closed Sundays and for lunch on Mondays. Montauban's finest chef, moderately priced rooms, medium-priced restaurant. **Hostellerie les Coulandrières,** Route de Castelsarrasin, 3 kilometers west on D958, tel: 6367-4747, fax: 6367-4645. Pleasant, modern rooms, garden and pool, medium-priced. ***Trois Pigeons,** 4 Avenue du Deuxième-Division-d'Infanterie, tel: 6366-4646, fax: 6320-2658. Recently renovated, spacious rooms, regional dishes, moderately priced.

Some Useful Words and Phrases

to bathe, to take a bath	**se baigner**
beginning	**début** (m)
cheek	**joue** (f)
to contain	**contenir**
to dress, to get dressed	**s'habiller**
dye	**teinture** (f)
embroidery	**broderie** (f)
to establish	**établir**
faithful	**fidèle**
flight	**vol** (m)
to get up, to rise, to stand up	**se lever**
to marry, to get married	**se marier**
nose	**nez** (m)
organic produce	**culture biologique** (f)
prosperous	**prospère**
to shower, to take a shower	**se doucher**

to suffer	**souffrir**
to training	**formation** (f)
to wash	**se laver**

Je vais me doucher. Je vais prendre une douche. (I am going to shower. I am going to take a shower.)

Nous devrions nous lever à sept heures. (We should get up at 7.)

Je voudrais me laver les mains. (I would like to wash my hands.)

Nous voudrions nous laver les mains. (We would like to wash our hands.)

Nous voudrions laver la voiture. (We would like to wash the car.)

Ils se sont mariés l'année dernière. (They got married last year.)

Il prend son bain. Il se baigne. (He is taking a bath. He is bathing.)

Je me suis baignée dans la mer. (I swam in the sea.)

Habillons-nous et partons. (Let's get dressed and leave.)

The reflexive form of an infinitive is formed with the prefix **se,** example: **se doucher**/to shower or to take a shower. Literally translated it would be: to shower oneself.

present tense
je me douche	**nous nous douchons**
tu te douches	**vous vous douchez**
elle, il se douche	**elles, ils se douchent**

past tense
| **je me suis douché(e)** | **nous nous sommes douché(e)s** |

tu t'es douché(e)   vous vous êtes douché(e)s
elle, il s'est douché(e)   elles, ils se sont douché(e)s

<u>future tense</u>
je me doucherai   nous nous doucherons
tu te doucheras   vous vous doucherez
elle, il se douchera   elles, ils se doucheront

CHAPTER 19

Western Loire

Most tours of the Loire Valley start around Orléans and end in or near Tours. Why is difficult to explain since the Loire continues to flow westward, becoming even wider, lazier and more beautiful. It continues to be lined with impressive châteaux and churches. The mouth of the Loire River opens onto a part of the Atlantic coast that boasts some of the most perfect bays and inviting island havens. Furthermore, its coastline is sheltered by Brittany and warmed by the Gulf Stream, all of which is reason enough to wish to become acquainted with a little known area of France.

Add to this the fact that the history of the Western Loire includes a number of powerful and intriguing episodes, the first being the dolmens and menhirs of uncertain meaning left behind by populations who inhabited the region during the fourth millennium B.C. They were not the first inhabitants of the region for human activity has been discovered going back to the Stone Age.

The impact of the religious wars of the 16th and 17th centuries was especially brutal here. The Protestant churches reacted to early persecutions by strengthening cohesion amongst craftsmen, the weavers in particular, and aristocrats. It is significant that the edict published by Henry IV putting an end temporarily to the war between Huguenots and Catholics was signed in Nantes, one of the principal cities of the Western Loire. When warfare resumed in the 17th century, Protestants had no recourse but to convert or flee.

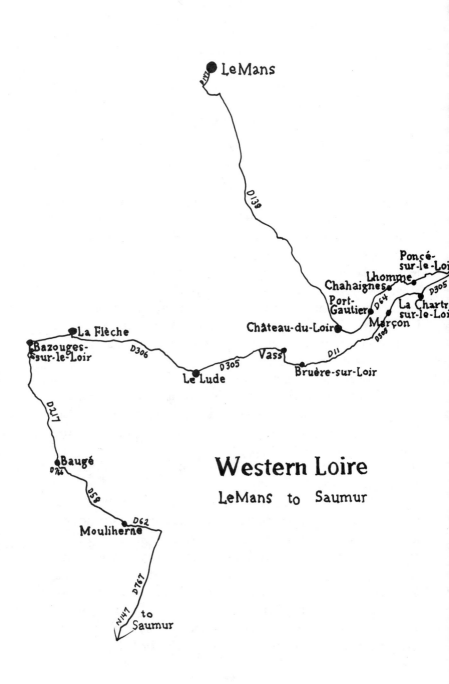

Western Loire

LeMans to Saumur

Nantes, the last harbor on the Loire River, is also an ocean port. As such it played a key role in the slave trade, being one of the main European links in the triangle between Africa, the New World and the Old. The fortunes amassed by shippers and traders active in the buying and selling of human flesh, rum, wood and agricultural produce accounted for the dubious prosperity of the city in the 17th and 18th centuries.

The Western Loire was also the site of France's last civil war. Briefly stated, a deeply religious and pro-royalist population took up arms, beginning in 1793, against the new Republic. Defeated in 1804, the insurrectional groups—called in one area Vendéens and in another Chouans—did not totally fade out, and as late as the 1830s fighting would sporadically erupt against the powers that were. The history of this period is both complicated and delicate, fraught with misunderstandings, ignorance and incompetence. The result has been deep-seated resentment which, on occasion, is clearly expressed.

In the rural areas behind the Loire Valley, small, family farms are the rule rather than the exception. The churches are active, Catholic schools are numerous. Crosses posted in fields, at a bend in the road, at certain intersections are reminders of events—an ambush, perhaps a battle—which occurred two centuries ago.

The cities and towns along the river valleys and the coastline are among the friendliest of France. Living is good in the Anjou where the wine sparkles and the white stone shines. The great medieval fortresses of Saumur, Angers and Nantes, the old city in the heart of Le Mans, and the Atlantic resorts beckon.

NOTE that the itinerary which follows could be divided into two. Le Mans and the Loir Valley from Poncé-sur-le-Loir to Bazouges-sur-le-Loir would constitute one trip, and Saumur to Sables-d'Olonne and/or La Baule a second one.

Le Mans

Le Mans is the capital of the province called Maine from which the State of Maine took its name at a time when the French province was governed by the English.

The hilltop overlooking the Sarthe River has been inhabited for six thousand years. A menhir attests to this fact. The Romans built a city here some fifty years before our era. In 270 A.D. the hill was surrounded by the protective wall you see today along the river. The city continued to develop within its fortifications throughout the Middle Ages. Admittedly, the town that has grown up around the medieval center is best traversed quickly. The hilltop itself is very much intact and splendid!

Before the Revolution Le Mans was noted for its black woolen muslin used by the clergy and the legal profession, as well as for the wax candles it supplied to Versailles. In the second half of the 19th century it became the center for the production of railway cars by the Bollée family. In fact, it was one of the latter's descendants who invited Wilbur Wright to Le Mans in 1908 to prepare a new prototype and do trial runs on his invention. Wright's Kitty Hawk experiment did not attract the attention he had hoped for. Quite the contrary in Le Mans on August 8, 1908, and thereafter, when he took to the air from grounds which have since become the 24 Hour Race Track.

The first twenty-four hour automobile race took place in 1923. This annual event has now been augmented to include other twenty-four hour races at different times of the year (motorcycles, trucks, reduced models, etc.). Today Le Mans is a major center for headquarters of insurance companies.

Tour

Boulevard de la Gare, outside the railway station, goes left down to the river. Turn right along the quay, pass three bridges and you will come to the **Gallo-Roman ramparts:**

sections of wall link eleven great towers of reddish brick and white stone with geometric design insets. They are magnificent timeworn structures, leaning inward to the city.

At the fourth bridge, the Yssoir, enter the old town on **Rue Wilbur Wright.** Go left on **Rue des Chanoines.** At Number 1 is Saint Paul's House in the style of the Italian Renaissance. Number 1 **Place du Cardinal-Grente,** in front of the cathedral, is also a Renaissance residence.

The nave of **Saint Julian's Cathedral** is essentially Romanesque, the chancel is luminous Gothic. Surrounded by its exemplary stained glass windows dating from the 12th century, this part of the church is unique and grand. The 16th century tapestries on the pillars recount certain of Saint Julian's exploits. In the last chapel of the transept, note the two impressive tombs facing each other.

On leaving the cathedral, take time to visit the **menhir** along the wall to your left. According to custom, a touch of the hand on the little cavity on its surface guarantees good luck. Pass the portal on this side of the church with its statue-columns. Go on to the grandiose chevet composed of a multitude of flying buttresses like those of no other Gothic church.

Leave this area on **Rue de la Reine-Bérengère.** You will pass the Ave Maria House at Number 7 and Leprince House at Number 14. The **Queen Bérengère Museum,** Numbers 7 to 11, is composed of three remarkable timbered houses. The highlights of the museum are the imaginative baroque chapel retables from the 17th century. Also noteworthy are the pewter objects and the faience for which the region is well known.

At the corner of Rue du Pilier Rouge and Grande Rue stop for the wonderful **red pillar.** You will see other such sculpted cornerstones at intersections. Continue on **Grande Rue.** Number 71 with its sculptured facade and signs of the zodiac was commissioned by a doctor-astrologer in the first half of the 16th century.

Go right in **Rue Saint-Pavin-de-la-Cité.** Number 18 was sold in 1622 in order to finance an expedition to Canada.

Continue out to **Rue de Vaux** for the view over the Sarthe. Go back on **Rue Saint-Honoré** which will take you to **Place Saint-Pierre.** Backtrack to **Grande Rue,** turn left on **Rue Godard** which leads out of the old town. There you might wish to circle left to **Place du Jet-d'Eau** at the foot of the cathedral.

Six kilometers south of Le Mans is the **24 Hour Race Track.** The race takes place on a weekend in the second half of June; the track is open to visitors throughout the year. The permanent Bugatti circuit is two and one-half miles long. The 24 Hour track measures about eight miles. To reach there, go back along the quay towards the railway station. Stay on the river road which will become the D147. At the traffic circle keep left and follow signs to the **Automobile Museum,** which is also the entrance to the 24 Hour Race Track. The museum collection contains about 150 famous racing and antique cars.

Train from Paris: From Gare Montparnasse (TGV) 50 minutes.

Tourist Info: Hôtel des Ursulines, Rue de l'Etoile, 72000 Le Mans, tel: 4328-1722.

Queen Bérengère Museum: 7–11 Rue de la Reine-Bérengère, 9 A.M. to 12 noon and 2 to 6 P.M.
Automobile Museum: 24 Hour Circuit, 9 A.M. to 12 P.M. and 2 to 7 PM., except Tuesdays, from Easter to October 15; until 6 P.M. the rest of the year.

Restaurants: **Ciboulette,** 14 Rue de la Vieille-Porte, tel: 4324-6567; closed Saturdays, Sundays and August. Charming décor in the Old Town, fine seasonal menus, medium-priced. **Feuillantine,** 19bis Rue Foisy, tel: 4328-0038, fax: 4377-1628; closed Saturdays for lunch, Sundays and Christmas holidays. Mirrors and greenery, interesting cuisine, moderate to medium-priced. **Grenier à Sel,** 26 Place Eperon, tel: 4323-2630; closed Sundays, Mondays and August. Attractive restaurant at entrance to Old Town, medium-priced.

Accommodations: **Central,** 5 Boulevard René-Levasseur, tel: 4324-0893, fax: 4324-2495. Quiet location, sauna and exercise room, moderately priced. **Chantecler,** 50 Rue Pelouse, tel: 4324-5853, fax: 4377-1628. Modern hotel, moderately priced.

Loir Valley

From the 24 Hour Race Track, continue on the N138 through Bercé Forest to **Château-du-Loir.** The spelling here is not an error for there are two rivers in the region: *la* Loire and *le* Loir. The first is a wide, graceful waterway, the second a fine, sinuous, romantic one. So much does the latter curve and wend that it is impossible to follow its banks by road. Rather, one meets up with it in a village, over a bridge. Each encounter is poignant.

Like most towns and villages of this *département* Château-du-Loir is beautifully adorned with flower beds, bouquets and pots of different sorts, depending on the season. The last time I passed by the town hall it was literally dripping with pink-orange geraniums. To the right is the Graslin Manor built in the 14th century. Across the way, all that remains of a medieval castle, the donjon, some cells and a very pleasant garden. The local church has character.

Hotel-Restaurant: *****Grand Hôtel,** Place de l'Hôtel-de-Ville, tel: 4344-0017. Traditional, moderately priced.

Go left on the D64 to **Port Gautier** placed romantically on the river. Continue on the D64 to **Chahaignes.** A few kilometers beyond the town is the Bénehard Château which possesses a monumental wine press, four centuries old. Then on to **Lhomme,** famous for is white Jasnières wine resembling sauterne. There is a small wine museum here next to the town hall. Continue on through Ruillé-sur-Loir to **Poncé-sur-le-Loir.**

This charming village warrants a more lengthy visit. The inside of the church is literally covered with 12th-century frescos and the promontory offers a wide vista of the village and the valley. Just below the church, a Renaissance château built in the 16th century boasts a wonderful staircase, a labyrinth garden and one of the most elaborate pigeon houses in France.

The craftsmen's center, in a mill at the entrance to the village, groups a number of different crafts: blown glass, pottery, weaving, woodwork, candlemaking, leatherwork, etc. At the other end of the village there is another glassblowing studio and an artisan who produces painted furniture.

Port Gautier
Accommodations: **Hôtel du Port Gautier,** tel: 4379-4492; closed Sundays off season, moderately priced.

Poncé-sur-le-Loir
Château: 10 A.M. to 12 noon and 2 to 6 P.M. from April 1 to September 30.
Bed & Breakfast: André Sevault, **La Tendrière,** tel: 4344-4527. Elegant town house, moderately priced.

Turn back on the D305 from Poncé. It will take you into **La Chartre-sur-le-Loir.** This village is known for its houses of white stone and its good white wine. From the ruins of the old castle there is a fine view of the countrywide.

Hotel-Restaurant: *Hôtel de France, 20 Place de la Ré-publique, tel: 4344-4016, fax: 4379-6220. Ivy-covered building set on magnificent square, charming restaurant, hearty food, old-fashioned rooms, moderately priced.
Bed & Breakfast: Madame **Travers,** 20 Place Carnot, tel: 4344-1025 and 4379-1213; closed January. Lovely manor, moderately to medium-priced.

On the D305 again, go west to **Marçon.** The key to the lovely church can be picked up at the local tourist office or at the neighbor's. See the sign at the entrance to the church.

Hotel-Restaurant: *Hôtel du Boeuf, 21 Place de l'Eglise,

tel: 4344-1312; closed Sunday evenings and Mondays off season. Traditional, moderately priced.

Stay on the D305 west, then pick up the D11 to Le Gué-de-Mézières. Continue on to **La Bruère-sur-Loir.** Its church diffuses wonderful light through Renaissance stained glass windows. Then go on to **Vaas.** The church here is a mixture of Romanesque and Gothic architecture. From it one can walk down to the river. Cross the bridge. On the right a lane leads to the **de Rotrou grain mill,** built in the 16th century and still operating. The tour carries a real lesson in breadmaking. Then go back to the D305 for **Le Lude**.

Despite its location, Le Lude is considered one of the Loire châteaux. Originally a fortress, it became a castle in the 15th century. It has the distinction of being a "live" château in several ways. First of all it is still a family residence and inhabited. Secondly, it is the backdrop for a magnificent sound and light show with live participants during the summer season. For an audience seated on the opposite bank of the Loir, 350 amateur actors and actresses from the region reenact the great moments of history in which Le Lude has played a role. The show terminates with the bang and splash of fireworks.

Leave the château on Rue d'Orée. Saint Vincent's Church, curiously shaped, possesses an admirable pulpit. At Place Neuve go right to the town hall. Leave here on Grande Rue. Take your right on Le Mail. In the hospice on the square is a little museum with an interesting collection of headgear from around the world.

Tourist Info: Place de-Nicolay, 72800 Le Lude, tel: 4394-6220, Easter-September.
Château: **Gardens:** 10 A.M. to 12 noon and 2 to 6 P.M. from April 1 to September 30. **Interior:** 2 to 6 P.M. from April 1 to September 30. **Sound & Light Show:** Friday and Saturday evenings at sunset from mid-June to early September.
Restaurant: *__Renaissance,__ 2 Avenue de la Libération, tel:

4394-6310; Closed Sunday evenings and Mondays. Attractive country inn, moderately priced.

Hotel-Restaurant: **Hostellerie du Maine,** 17 Avenue de Saumur, tel: 4394-6054. Pretty, ivy-covered edifice, traditional, moderately priced.

From Le Lude take the D306 to **La Flèche.** This small town has gained its reputation from the military academy established here. Originally created as a royal college by Henry IV who entrusted the Jesuits with its administration, it was converted into a military academy in 1762. Take note in passing that the people of La Flèche were among the first recruits to leave France in the 17th century to found Montreal.

From Promenade Foch take Rue Gallieni to Place Henri-IV, the town center. Take Rue Henri-IV to the Prytanée military academy, a secondary school with an enrollment of about 900 students. The grounds may be visited. The real jem is the chapel built by the Jesuits in the early 17th century in the bright white chalk stone of the region. It contains numerous decorative bays, an ornate choir and simple nave.

Leave the Prytanée to the left. After the pleasant Place du Marché-au-Blé, take Rue Vernevelle to the right. Note at Number 10 the Huger mansion designed by the architect Jacques Gabriel. Go right in Grande Rue and left in Rue Grollier to the gardens and donjon of the former Carmes convent and the town hall lodged in a ravishing ochre-colored château. The view and the atmosphere down by the river and near the bridge are delightful. It was from the little harbor on the river that the emigrants embarked on their journey to the New World.

Tourist Info: Hôtel de Ville, 72200 La Flèche, tel: 4394-0253.

Restaurants: **Fesse d'Ange,** Place du 8-Mai-1945, tel: 4394-7360; closed Sunday evenings, Mondays and August. Good quality, moderately priced.

Hotel-Restaurants: **Relais Cicero,** 18 Boulevard d'Alger, tel: 4394-1414, fax: 4345-9896. Beautiful 17th-century home, individually decorated rooms, regional cuisine, moderately expensive. *Relais du Loir,** 40 Promenade du Maréchal-Foch, tel: 4394-0064, fax: 4345-9815. Traditional inn, lovely dining room, moderately priced. *Vert Galant,** 70 Grande Rue, tel: 4394-0051, fax: 4345-1124; restaurant closed Thursdays. Attractive, regional cuisine, conventional hotel, moderately priced.

Out-of-Town: **Haras de la Potardière,** *72200 Crosmières,* D306 and left on D70 towards Bazouges, tel: 4345-8347, fax: 4345-8106. Stud farm and small château in middle of fields for calm, taste and comfort, medium-priced to moderately expensive.

From La Flèche the N23 takes you to **Bazouges-sur-le-Loir.** This is a delightful village. Its castle is nestled in a bend of the river and can be visited. The Romanesque church in the village, which dates from the year 1008, possesses wonderful painted vaults covered with twenty-four full figures, trees and flowers. The view from the river bridge is worth a stop and an amble.

Château: From July 1 to September 15, 10 A.M. to 12 noon on Tuesdays and Fridays; 3 to 5 P.M. Thursdays and Saturdays.

Hotel-Restaurant: *Moulin de la Barbée,** tel: 4345-3317; closed Monday afternoons and Tuesdays from October through March. Absolutely charming location, mill surrounded by water and ducks, rooms in the tower, medium-priced, restaurant moderately priced.

Leave Bazouges on the D70. Take the D18 to the left into **Baugé.** The countryside is pleasant: small farms, cattle grazing, orchards laden with apples and pears. It is hilly and wooded. This area, like Normandy, Brittany and Vendée, contains small fields, more often tree-lined or hedged than not. This type of landscape is called *bocage*.

Baugé is known for its Anjou or Lorraine cross brought back from the crusades in the 13th century and now exposed in the Girouardière Chapel. This double-barred cross is the same one adopted as his symbol by General de Gaulle during World War II and afterwards. Another visit of interest in this little town is the Saint Joseph Hospital's pharmacy which contains a priceless collection of faience pots from the 16th to the 18th century.

Out of Baugé you will quickly leave the D766 to pick up the D58 which skirts forestland and goes through **Mouliherne**. Note the curious torsaded belfry, one of four in the region. The supposition is that they represented carpenters' wishes to display dexterity, nothing more profound.

The D62 will take you to La Ganaudière. Take the D767 to the right. Go through Vernantes and Le Doreur. At Le Pré get on the N147 to Saumur.

In the region: **Château de la Grifferaie,** *Echemiré,* 5 kilometers east of Baugé on D766; tel: 4189-7025. Refined 19th-century castle of white stone surrounded by woods and a rose garden, delicate cuisine, medium-priced to moderately expensive.

Saumur

As you face the city, coming from the north, its silhouette informs you of a rich past: castle, stately homes, a tall cathedral, all stand out on the left bank of the Loire. Medieval first, Saumur was incorporated into Anjou territory in 1203, and later enclosed within walls. In the 14th and 15th century it was cherished by the Anjou dukes, in particular René, known as the king.

The town played an active role in the Reformation. For its most enterprising citizens the Reform was a means of curtailing the privileges of the abbeys which dominated the territory. In 1589 Saumur was declared officially a Protestant stronghold. The Protestant Academy founded in 1593 attracted students and theologians from all over Europe, and the city prospered. A dozen printers and bookshops functioned in Saumur during the 17th century.

The Catholics were not to be outdone and during those years they suceeded in establishing seven religious communities outside the city, as well as a school of theology. In 1685 Louis XIV closed the Protestant Academy and destroyed the house of worship. Estimates as to the number of Protestants to emigrate from Saumur vary. It is certain, however, that the city turned inward.

At the end of the 18th century the creation of a cavalry school in Saumur invested the city with a new role, that of the cavalry capital of France. Known as *Le Cadre Noir* because of the black uniform that cavalry instructors adopted—as opposed to the blue uniforms of other army instructors—the school continued to train French army officers in riding until 1969. The cavalry having now been totally replaced by armored divisions, its instructors have been detached to the National Riding School, also in the Saumur area.

Tour

Our tour of Saumur begins at Place de la Bilange, just over the Cessart Bridge on the left bank. Take Rue Molière which passes in front of the **town hall,** located on the site of the former Protestant Academy. Go around to the courtyard of the building, also interesting for its duplication of the original Gothic structure in neo-Gothic.

Go left on Rue des Puits-Neufs into the lovely square with trees and small fountain. Cross the square, go right on Rue de la Tonnelle and you will find yourself on **Place Saint-Pierre** in front of **Saint Peter's Cathedral.** Wonderful timbered houses from the 15th century have survived here, as well as some sedate stone structures built originally to house teachers, ministers and staff of the Protestant Academy. The small protruding upper towers are in fact staircases.

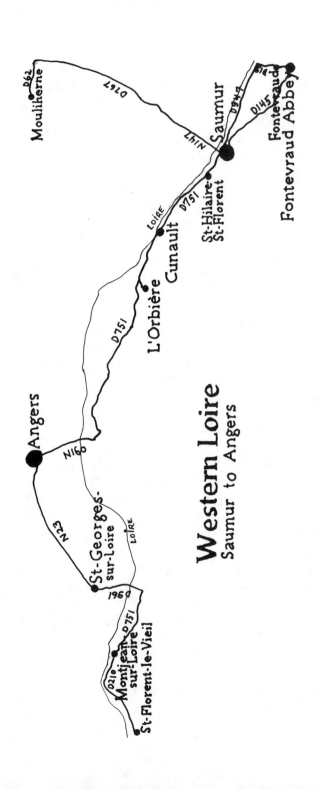

Western Loire
Saumur to Angers

Moulineherne
D62
D767
N147
Saumur
D947
Fontevraud
D145
Fontevraud Abbey
St-Hilaire-
St-Florent
D751
Loire
Cunault
L'Orbière
D751
D751
Angers
N160
N23
St-Georges-
sur-Loire
Loire
196 0
Montjean-
sur-Loire
D751
D210
St-Florent-le-Vieil

The cathedral presents a mixture of styles. Although construction began in the 12th century and was continued in the 13th, transformations were initiated in the 16th and 17th. Most noteworthy are the 15th and 16th century tapestries, in particular those in the apse. Try to envision them as they were before the yellows, greens and reds slipped and faded, leaving only blues and beiges.

Take Rue Fourrier, behind the church, and the Montée du Petit-Genève up to the **château.** The vista here is magnificent. The castle—very much the fairy tale image—was a favorite of Anjou's king René who tagged it his "castle of love." In the 17th century Louis XIV used it to intern prisoners. It later became a state prison and army garrison. Purchased by the city in 1906, it now houses three prestigious museums. In the waiting room, an impressive model of a processional barge is on display.

The **Museum of Decorative Arts** is noted for its ceramics collection, in particular French porcelain, its tapestries and religious art. The remarkable carpenter's studio in the north tower dates from the 4th century. The hall decoration and the presentation of all the objects are admirable.

The **Horse Museum** is located in the former officers' quarters under awesome timber-vaulted ceilings. The museum tells the story of the horse from antiquity to modern times, very complete and well-presented.

The **Figurine Toy Museum** is located in the old powder magazine of the château. It contains more than 20,000 figurine toys from the 19th and 20th centuries made of everything from wood and paper to lead and plaster.

Leave the château on Rue des Remparts and go down the Montée du Fort. Back at Place Saint-Pierre take **Grande Rue** to the left. At Numbers 4 and 6 is the residence used by the abbeys from Asnières when in town. Turn right on Rue du Petit-Mail. At Place de l'Arche-Dorée the **Protestant temple** built in 1842 displays the Tables of the Law retrieved from the first church destroyed in 1685.

Continue on **Rue des Païens** and right on **Rue du Prêche** and left on **Rue du Temple.** Lovely homes line all these streets. The manor at **33 Rue Dacier** was the residence of royalty when in Saumur. From Rue Dacier take **Rue Franklin-Roosevelt** back to Place de la Bilange.

Go left at the bridge, then left at Place Kléber. Go right on Rue Saint-Nicholas. You will come to the **Armored Tank Museum** which houses a unique collection of tanks from all over the world. Beyond here is the former Cavalry School and the **Cavalry Museum** which contains a fine collection of weapons, uniforms, cavalry equipment and mementos.

Tourist Info: Place de la Bilange, 49400 Saumur, tel: 4151-0306.

Château: 9 A.M. to 7 P.M. from June 15 to September 15; open Wednesdays and Saturdays in season until 10 P.M.; closed from 12 to 2 P.M. the rest of the year and at 5 P.M. in winter; closed Tuesdays throughout the year.
Museum of Decorative Arts: Same as château.
Horse Museum: Same as château.
Figurine-Toy Museum: 10 A.M. to 6 P.M. from July 1 to August 31; closed from 12 to 2 P.M. from April 1 to June 30 and in September; closed the rest of the year.
Armored Tank Museum: 9 A.M. to 12 noon and 2 to 6 P.M.
Cavalry Museum: 1 to 5 P.M. except Mondays; 9 A.M. to 12 noon on Sundays.

Wine tasting: **House of Saumur Wines,** 25 Rue Beaurepaire, 9 A.M. to 12:30 P.M. and 2 to 6:30 P.M.; closed Sundays all year and Mondays from October through May.

Restaurants: **Croquière,* 42 Rue du Maréchal-Leclerc, tel: 4151-3145; closed Sunday evenings and Mondays. Good regional specialties, moderately priced. **Délices du Château,** château courtyard, tel: 4167-6560, fax: 4167-7460; closed Sunday evenings and Mondays from October to May and all of December. Lovely setting, refined cuisine, medium-priced.

Ménestrels, 11 Rue Raspail, tel: 4167-7110; closed for lunch Sundays and Mondays, also Sunday evenings off season.

Accommodations: **Anne d'Anjou,** 32–33 Quai Mayaud, tel: 4167-3030, fax: 4167-5100; closed Christmas week. Elegant hotel on the Loire, medium-priced. **Loire,** Rue du Vieux-Point, tel. 4167-2242, fax: 4167-8880. Superb location across the river from town, calm, pleasant, medium-priced. **Roi René,** 94 Avenue du Général-de-Gaulle, tel: 4167-4530, fax: 4167-7459. Modern rooms, good view, moderately priced.

Out-of-town: **Croix de la Voulte,** Route de Boumois, *Saint-Lambert-des-Levées,* 3 kilometers on D229, tel: 4138-4666. Comfortable private residence used for the hunt centuries ago, total calm, medium-priced. **Prieuré,** *Chênehutte-les-Tuffeaux,* 8 kilomètres west on D751, tel: 4167-9014, fax: 4167-9224. Magnificent Renaissance manor overlooking the Loire, comfortable, peaceful, welcoming establishment with quality cuisine and wine list, moderately expensive to luxury prices.

Fontevraud-l'Abbaye

Leave Saumur, and head eastward on the D145, the inland road through forest to the famous abbey. Fontevraud was founded in 1101 by Robert d'Arbrissel, an errant priest and theologian who had been thwarted in his attempts to introduce Gregorian reforms in his Brittany diocese. Among the adepts who followed him and settled Fontevraud were a large number of lepers and women, many of whom were "repented sinners." For each group of followers, a separate convent was built. While not the first mixed religious community, it was perhaps the most original in that an abbess was placed at its head (recommended to be widowed).

Women from the most illustrious families soon joined the order. The most socially eminent were named abbess; many were of royal lineage. The Plantagenêt family, future kings of England, lent their prestige to Fontevraud. Louis XV sent his

four daughters to be educated there. Generous donations
were showered on the abbey. Gradually, the ideals of humility
and poverty which had guided its founder were ignored.

In 1790 the abbey was divided into lots and put up for sale.
Those parts which found buyers were soon dismantled. Those
that did not were turned into a penitentiary. It was only in
1963 that the prison was closed for once and all and the
property entrusted to the Ministry of Culture.

The acoustics at the church are so perfect that professional
records are made here, in particular of Gregorian chants. Concerts are organized regularly during the tourist season.

Restoration is in full swing and will doubtless go on for
several decades. The buildings already renovated are enough
to make Fontevraud a must for all visitors to the Loire Valley.

Tour

Of the five original institutions of the Fontevraud community, only three have survived: the women's monastery, the
infirmeries, and the lepers' priory. The men's monastery and
the repentent sinners' monastery were dismantled and sold
stone by stone.

Begin the tour with the abbey church. The simple facade
scarcely prepared one for the majesty and solemnity in waiting. Step down into the white stone nave: particularly long
and narrow, devoid of side aisles, covered with flattened
domes, adorned with lovely capitals and dimly lit. Ahead of
you is the choir: yellow light shines strongly on immense
pillars creating the impression of a distant Valhalla.

The two parts of the church are oddly joined. Actually they
were built separately. The choir was constructed first for the
men's monastery, the nave later for the women's; then a grill
was installed to separate the two. Imagine that this building
was, for roughly two centuries, a penitentiary with four floors
of cells!

The impressive recumbent figures in the transept are those
of Henry II of England, his wife Eleanor of Aquitania, their

son Richard the Lionheart, King of England, and their daughter-in-law, Isabelle of Angoulême, wife of their son John.

Continue on to the cloister, flamboyant Gothic and Renaissance. See the chapter house and the scriptorium which was the only room heated in the monastery. The frescos of the chapter house depict scenes from the gospel to which the various abbesses added their own portraits!

To the right of the scriptorium, go into the dining hall. The abbess, on her rare appearances, took sustenance on the upper balcony.

The fantastic building at the end of the dining hall was the monastery kitchen. Story has it that Eleanor of Aquitania brought back from the Orient at the time of the Crusades a number of modes and fashions. The fish-scaled roof of this edifice was one. Octogonal in shape, there were originally eight foyers plus one central foyer.

From here go through to the orange gardens, now planted with vegetables and herbs of medicinal value, labeled in French. Did you know that lettuce is recommended for insomnia because it contains a hypnotic substance, lactucarium? That leeks were domesticated in Asia Minor and are useful to combat obesity and for wasp and bee bites? Just rub some raw leek on the injured skin.

From the plant garden descend to the apple, pear and mulberry orchard. Then go around to the former lepers' quarters, now a charming restaurant and hotel. Once leprosy was eradicated, the buildings were turned into a rest home for nuns in the 17th century.

In the village of Fontevraud, **Saint Michael's Church** is well worth a stop. An 18th-century wooden gallery on stone pillars has been added to a 12th-century church. Several interesting white stone retables and other pieces of religious art from the abbey are sheltered here.

At the end of the lane of linden trees is the **Saint Catherine funeral chapel.**

Abbey: 9 A.M. to 7 P.M. from June 1 to September 30; 9:30 A.M. to 12:30 P.M. and 2 to 6 P.M. at other times.

Restaurants: *Auberge de l'Abbaye, 8 Avenue des Roches, tel: 4151-7104; closed Tuesday evenings, Wednesdays, February and October. Traditional menu, moderately priced. **Licorne,** Allée Sainte-Catherine, tel: 4151-7249, fax: 4151-7040; closed Sunday evenings and Mondays. Inventive cuisine in wonderfully refined setting, medium-priced.

Hotel-Restaurants: *Croix Blanche, tel: 4151-7111, fax: 4138-1538; closed November and January. Conventional, moderately priced. **Hôtellerie du Prieuré Saint-Lazare,** Fontevraud Abbey, tel: 4151-7316, fax: 4151-7550. Located in the former priory, peaceful, well equipped, good quality, medium-priced.

Private home: **Domaine de Mestré,** tel: 4151-7587 and 4151-7232. Former farm of Fontevraud Abbey, white stone, comfort and quiet, dinner and breakfast available, moderately priced.

Take the D19 down to the Loire and go back towards Saumur on the D947. You will pass **Gratien & Meyer,** an independent winery open daily for those who wish to taste delightful Anjou sparkling wines. They employ the same double fermentation process as champagne (but are much less expensive). As Caroline, the English-speaking PR at Gratien puts it: "We sell happiness!" The **International School of Wine** on their grounds organizes classes in English, two-hour and thirty-minute sessions and all-day sessions.

Go through Saumur and continue on the D751. At **Saint-Hilaire-Saint-Florent** turn left for the **National Riding School.** Visitors may attend training sessions during the season. If you yourself are interested in horseback riding, many possibilities exist in the region. Inquire at any tourist office for information, and ask for the brochure called *Le Cheval en Anjou.*

Just beyond Saint-Hilaire-Saint-Florent on the river road going west is the **Mushroom Museum.** Stop and see mushrooms grow.

Wine tasting: **Gratien-Meyer,** Route de Chinon, 9 A.M. to 12 P.M. and 2 to 6 P.M. In August: 9 A.M. to 6 P.M.
National Riding School: From April 1 to September 30 guided tours every afternoon except Sundays; morning tours on Tuesdays, Wednesdays, Thursdays and Saturdays include training sessions of the Cadre Noir.
Mushroom Museum: 10 A.M. to 7 P.M. from March 15 to November 15.

Stay on the D751. You will pass numerous troglodyte caves and villages carved in the chalk stone of the cliffs. This is a result of a phenomenon which dates from the early Middle Ages when stones were extracted from the cliffsides for the building of churches and fortresses. The inhabitants of the valley quickly realized that the quarries could be transformed into fine homes, already constructed of stone on three sides. All that was required was a facade, door and windows.

Halt at **Cunault** to see its superb Romanesque church. If it is Sunday you will hear Gregorian chants at 11 o'clock mass. Take in the perspective from the top of the steps, then descend into the nave which gradually tightens as you advance. Then up some steps to the choir. As you walk, study the capitals for which Cunault is noted; there are 223 of varying styles, all from the 12th century. Murals covered the church at one time. Those on the left side of the nave are in fairly good condition. Gregorian concerts are held here during July and August.

Cunault's seasonal market draws people from all around. It takes place on the first Sunday of the month from Easter to September.

Look inside the long café near the church on the other side of the parking area. It contains a curved court surface on which a game dating from the Middle Ages, *boules de fort,* a variation of bowling, is played. It is unique to this valley.

Stay on the D751. At the fork of Le Plessis go left. Take your first left for **L'Orbière (Saint-Georges-des-Sept-Voies),** so small a place it seems not to exist. Actually, here and throughout the plain behind the Loire cliffs, many underground villages have existed for centuries. After the Troglodyte caves along the Loire were taken up with homes, wine cellars and the rest, local people had the idea of digging under the soil on the plains until they reached the chalk layer. Once again they quarried stone and sold it, and with the proceeds they would turn the quarries into living quarters.

At L'Orbière stop at **Jacques Warminski's Contemporary Plastic Arts Space.** There where five families lived and formed a village until the beginning of the 20th century, a bombastic sculptor has created what he calls a "sculpture amphitheatre and land propellor," perhaps the largest modern sculpture in Europe. The work defies description: to call it a sculpture is a misnomer for it is an underground universe of passages, miniature auditoriums and grandstands, replete with sound and light effects. Warminski has labored here almost four years, manipulating 3,500 tons of stone with very rudimentary equipment.

From L'Orbières return to the D751 and go left. This road will take you to the N160 a few miles from Angers. Go right across the Loire into the city.

Angers

The history of Angers, city of art, follows the main lines of the rest of the Loire Valley. The first Celtic farmers probably settled in the region during the neolithic period. The reign of the Gauls, then the Romans followed. In the 3rd century A.D. Christians arrived and began the construction of abbeys, of which five have come through the ages. With the decline of Rome in the 3rd century, incursions of invaders increased.

The need for a protective fortress gave rise to the Cité which dominates Angers today.

Various Anjou dynasties reigned during the Middle Ages, the best known being the Plantagenêt family, whose members governed England and much of France. They contributed greatly to the cultural and artistic achievements of the times. It was during their reign that the most famous theological school of France, the Catholic University—known as the "Catho"—was founded in Angers.

The dukes of Anjou reigned until 1475 when the region was definitively taken over by the kingdom of France. The last reigning duke was called "king" René, a poet prince and artist, celebrated for his generosity and kindness.

The city developed as a trading center for fruits and vegetables sold abroad to England and Holland. The making of boat sails and hemp rope for the maritime trade was also a prosperous venture from the 17th century on. Another major activity, that of slate extraction and export endowed Angers with the tag: "the black city of a thousand slates."

Angers suffered as a battleground during the years of the Vendéen counter-revolution. It was heavily bombarded by the Germans in World War II. Fortunately the old neighborhoods were unharmed.

This is a vital city, active in the computer industry, vegetable biotechnology and horticulture. Half the population is under twenty-five years of age.

Tour

The obvious place to start a visit is Place du Président-Kennedy, next to the fortress. The statue in the intersection between Boulevard Général-de-Gaulle and Boulevard du Roi-René is of king René by David d'Angers.

Go to Rue Toussaint, past numerous antique shops. At number 33 is the **David d'Angers Gallery,** a sculpture museum located in a former abbey church. The Gothic edifice having disintegrated over the years, in 1981 the city undertook its restoration. The museum brings together the majority of the works of David d'Angers, a renowned 18th and 19th century sculptor born in Angers. Under a glass roof, the somewhat restricted space literally jumps with personalities and scenes so realistic they come alive. The contrast between republican realism and Gothic spirituality is exciting. Note the busts of Washington and Lafayette.

The next street to the right will take you to the **Beaux-Arts Museum,** known for its primitive art, as well as 18th-century masterpieces by Watteau, Chardin, Fragonard and others.

Back on Rue Toussaint, go up to **Place Sainte-Croix.** Adam's House is 15th-century Gothic, and the oldest house in Angers. His apple tree is carved into the corner. The abundance of sculpture tells us that the house belonged to a well-to-do resident of the city.

Go around to Place Chappoulie and the entrance to **Saint Morris' Cathedral.** The portal is covered with large statues representing biblical personalities, including a braided Queen of Sheba perched on oriental domes. The inside of the church is a single nave without side aisles or bays. It is wide and well proportioned and offers a sense of grandeur. A wrought-iron gallery runs along the walls. The leading feature of Saint Morris is its beautiful stained glass windows; those along the left-hand side date from the 12th century. The rose window of the Apocalypse contains the signs of the zodiac in the upper half of the circles.

Leave the cathedral on the Montée Saint-Maurice. Go down to cobble-stoned **Rue Saint-Aignan.** At Numbers 15 and 17 the knights of the Order of the Crescent, created by king René, were lodged. Notice the use of schist, the local laminar stone from west of Angers, as compared to the white chalk from the east.

Continue on to the **château** or **Cité** as it is known. It is from the outside that it is most spectacular: the seventeen giant towers—certain of them are a hundred feet high—and an odd pentagonal shape. The stone is schist, sandstone and granite.

Actually the City was higher by a floor and a half until the end of the 16th century. Governor Donadieu de Puycharic had received orders from Henry III to raze the fortress. He proceeded with its dismantling at a snail's pace until the death of the king, thereby safeguarding the monument for posterity. Under Louis XIV it became a prison.

Inside the château visit the **Grande Galerie** built for the special purpose of exhibiting the celebrated 14th-century tapestry of the Apocalypse. This extraordinary accomplishment required thirty-five weavers and seven years. It is composed of seventy-five separate scenes of the Apocalypse by Saint John: the struggle of Christ under Satan, the Last Judgment, etc.

Despite the misuse to which the tapestry was put after the Revolution, the colors are surprisingly effective. Split into pieces, it has served both as doormats and horse blankets!

Across the way are the Governor's Lodgings, built into the ramparts. Here too, a number of interesting tapestries are on display. Take the steps up to the ramparts and admire the city from the top.

Leave the château on **Rue Donadieu-de-Puycharic,** turn left at the Montée Saint-Maurice and cross the river to the quarter called the **Doutre.**

The village here grew up around the Ronceray Abbey, which today houses the School of Arts and Trades. Take Rue Beaurepaire to the **Trinity Church** next door to the old abbey. Another lovely, simple church with a long nave: deep recesses line the walls below the window openings which were particularly large for the times.

Turn back towards the bridge and go left on Boulevard Arago for the **Jean Lurçat Museum.** This is a former hospital commissioned by Henry II of England, a member of the Plantagenêt family. It is the oldest in France, dating from 1175. Take time to contemplate the romantic garden, then head for the main ward. This is Plantagenêt Gothic. The roof vaults of flowering sprays are composed of numerous ribs which, despite appearances, are of equal size. The modern stained glass windows are especially delicate, composed of narrow, rectangular layers, one above the other. The color spectrum is all in nuance: darker blues and purples below moving to brighter pinks, reds or mauves above. Despite the notes of fantasy, the general effect of the hall is sobriety.

Around the walls are the modern tapestries of Jean Lurçat called *Song of the World,* intended as the rejoinder to the Apocalypse. The weaving was executed at Aubusson. In the right-hand corner near the entrance is a 17th century apothecary.

Go through the far end to the cloister, a small haven of peace.

Another fine museum in Angers is the **Turpin de Crissé Museum** at the **Hôtel de Pincé.** From Place Sainte-Croix behind Saint Morris' Cathedral take Rue de la Chapelle-Saint-Pierre to Rue Lenepveu. With this 16th-century private manor house as a backdrop, see the fine antiquities section and especially the Japanese print room and the Chinese and Korean fabrics collection.

David d'Angers was born at Number **38 Rue Lenepveu.**

Note too that Angers is an excellent departure point for **river boating.** It is possible to navigate on the Sarthe all the way to Le Mans, on the Mayenne all the way to Mayenne and on the Oudon to Segré. Reservations can be made at Maine Reservations on Place Kennedy. Many types of houseboats are available at widely varying prices.

Tourist Info: Place du Président-Kennedy, 49051 Angers, tel: 4188-6993.

David d'Angers Museum: 37bis Rue Toussaint. 9:30 A.M. to 12:30 P.M. and 2 to 7 P.M. in season; 9 A.M. to 12 P.M. and 2 to 6 P.M. off season; closed Mondays off season.
Beaux-Arts Museum: 10 Rue du Musée, same as above.

Château: 9 A.M. to 7 P.M. from June 1 to September 15; 9 A.M. to 12:30 P.M. and 2 to 6 P.M. from Palm Sunday to May 31 and from September 16 to Palm Sunday.

Jean Lurçat Museum: 4 Boulevard Arago; same as other museums.

de Crissé Museum: 32bis Rue Lenepveu; same as other museums.

Wine Tasting: **Maison du Vin de l'Anjou,** Place Président-Kennedy, 9 A.M. to 1 P.M. and 3 to 6:15 P.M.; closed Tuesdays.

Restaurants: ***Ferme,** 2 Place Freppel, tel: 4187-0990. Simple fare, inexpensive. ***Petit Mâchon,** 43 Rue de Bressigny, tel: 4186-0113. Former butcher's shop, good quality for the price, inexpensive. **Logis,** 17 Rue Saint-Laud, tel: 4187-4415; closed Saturdays and Sundays in summer. Good seafood, moderately to medium-priced.

Hotel-Restaurants: Pavillon le Quéré, 3 Boulevard Foch, tel: 4120-0020, fax: 4120-0620. Grand elegance, superb cuisine by fine chef, rooms decorated tastefully, moderately expensive to expensive. **Anjou** and **Salamandre Restaurant,** 1 Boulevard du Maréchal-Foch, tel: 4188-9955 (R), 4188-2482 (H). Restaurant closed Sundays. Fine regional cuisine, spacious rooms newly renovated, medium-priced.

Accommodations: **Champagne,** 34 Rue Denis-Papin, tel: 4188-7808, fax: 4188-0394. Conventional hotel, medium-priced. **Continental,** 12–14 Rue Louis-de-Romain, tel: 4186-9494, fax: 4186-9660. Well situated, moderately priced. **Mail,** 8 Rue Ursules, tel: 4188-5622. Quiet, moderately priced. **Progrès,** 26 Rue Denis-Papin, tel: 4188-1014, fax: 4187-8293. Convenient location, moderately priced.

Take route N23 to **Saint-Georges-sur-Loire.** Just before the village is the distinguished **Serrant Castle,** built by Hardouin-Mansart. This château was acquired by an Irish nobleman in the 18th century. The interior decoration is lavish. The library contains 12,000 volumes.

Château: 9 to 11:30 A.M. and 2 to 6 P.M; from end of March to November 1; closed Tuesdays except in July and August.

Take the D961 south and cross the Loire. On the other side go right on the D751. You will come to **Montjean-sur-Loire,** beautifully situated on the river. From the end of the 18th century into the 20th this town produced lime in its giant kilns. With the aid of local coal and a fleet of boats that ran the Loire, the city had a heyday. The last limekiln shut down after the Second World War.

The **Ecomusée,** located in an old forge, is particularly interesting. Visit the **Auguste-Paul,** a flatboat that hauled lime on the river between 1910 and 1958. At the **Hemp Farm** you can see how the fiber was prepared. Take the footpath to the limekilns. One of them, **Pincourt,** has been classified a historic monument.

Ecomusée: 10 A.M. to 12 P.M. and 2:30 to 6:30 P.M. from July 1 to September 15.

Continue on the D210 along the left bank of the river. You will arrive at **Saint-Florent-le-Vieil.** The abbey church overlooking the Loire contains the Bonchamps Tomb by David d'Angers. Bonchamps was a Vendéen general. The church, the esplanade and the tomb are well worth the stop.

Hotel-Restaurant: *Hostellerie de la Gabelle, tel: 4172-5019, fax: 4172-5438. Conventional, moderately priced.

Pick up the D751 again. You will pass the remains of the **Bourgonnière castle,** burned during the French Revolution. The 16th-century **chapel,** still intact, is quite lovely and contains a fine retable with an interesting golden Christ on the Cross.

Visit: 9 A.M. to 12 noon and 2 to 7 P.M., 5 P.M. in winter.

Continue on to **Champtoceaux,** magnificently perched on

cliffs. At the time of the Gauls and during the Middle Ages this location was strategic and the town's military role was primary.

Restaurant: **Jardins de la Forge,** 1bis Place Piliers, tel: 4083-5623; closed Sundays, Tuesdays, Wednesday evenings, February and October. Pleasant, regional specialties, medium-priced to moderately expensive.
Hotel-Restaurants: ***Chez Claudie,** Le Cul du Moulin, 1 kilometer ouest on D751, tel: 4083-5043; closed Sunday evenings and Mondays, October and February. Conventional, moderately priced. ***Voyageurs,** tel: 4083-5009, fax: 4083-5381; closed Wednesdays off season. Regional specialties, moderately priced.

Stick with the D751 to **La Varenne.** From the church there is a lovely view over the river and countryside.

At Rezé take the N137 into Nantes.

Nantes

Leaving Anjou, proceed to Nantes, the old capital of Brittany and residence of their reigning dukes. It was only in 1491 that it was captured and taken over by the French.

Its importance as a harbor was recognized by the Gauls and the Romans. From the 16th to the 18th century it was the major European link in the triangular slave trade. Nantes manufactured trinkets, ribbons and fabrics which its shippers traded for human cargo in Africa and transported to the New World. They would load sugar cane in the Indies and bring it to Nantes for refining. The cotton shipped back to Nantes would be turned into the cloth sold in Africa. And so it went round and round . . . The French Revolution outlawed the slave trade, sugar was being produced from beet roots, and Nantes declined. The city at first glance is a hodgepodge of new and old, beauty and ugliness. Don't be put off, Nantes conceals myriad treasures.

Tour

Start the tour of Nantes at the **Château,** residence of the dukes of Brittany. The name most closely associated with the castle is that of Anne of Brittany, the last reigning duchess. She was wed to Charles VIII of France in 1491 at the age of 14, and upon his death to Louis XII, his brother and successor. Upon the marriage of her daughter to Francis I, the union of Brittany and France became total, the independent dukedom relinquishing its particular rights and privileges.

It was here that Henry IV formulated the Edict of Nantes in 1598 which would ensure freedom of worship for Protestants. The castle served as an army barracks between the French Revolution and the First World War.

Walk around the outside of the castle. The moat is supplied with water and ducks and the atmosphere around the back near the bridge is tranquil and romantic. Enter here.

See the royal lodge with its five dormer windows. On one of them is Anne's device, the greyhound, and her motto "I have loved." On another is Louis XII's: the porcupine and "from near and afar." From the tower, royalty and guests surveyed festivities.

There are three museums on the grounds, the most interesting being the **Salorges Museum.** Its collections pay homage to the City of Nantes and recount its history. Among other displays are model boats for river and ocean traffic, fishing schooners, capehorners and whaleboats, a model of the city in 1905. In another section are the artifacts of the slave trade: irons, trinkets, documents and paintings.

On leaving the castle take Rue Henri-IV to the left. **Saint Peter's Cathedral** is practically next door. Built on the foundations of an old Romanesque cathedral of which only the crypt remains, Saint Peter's was begun in 1434. The towers were completed in 1508. If part of the facade is devoid of sculpture it is because the church's backers ran out of money!

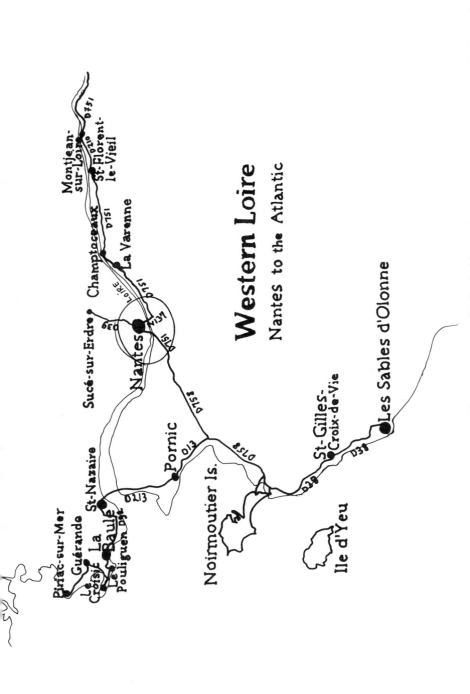

Western Loire

Nantes to the Atlantic

The nave, transept and buttresses were finally finished in the 17th century.

This is an handsome church, all in white stone. The pillars are refined, unbroken by capitals; the extending ribs are but a continuation of the columns. The stained glass windows are some of the finest modern glass you can find: soft colors and good movement. In February a festival of children's choirs takes place in the cathedral.

The recumbent figures are of Francis II, Duke of Brittany, Marguerite of Brittany, his first wife, and Marguerite Foix, his second wife. Note that one of the corner statues is double-faced, that of an old man on one side of the head and a young woman on the other. Leave the church through the side portal. Go through the courtyard and garden with the giant chestnut tree.

Return to Rue Henri-IV. Turn right on Rue Georges-Clemenceau and you will arrive at the **Beaux-Arts Museum,** one of the best in the provinces. In 1801, fifteen museums were created throughout France in order to receive the works of art retrieved from noble and royal domains. The initial endowment was soon enriched with gifts from various local benefactors. This museum is especially known for its paintings by Georges de la Tour, Ingres, Courbet and Monet, but there is much more: a good collection of Italian primitives, 17th, 18th and 19th century painting, Flemish landscapes, impressionists, and very good contemporary art. The presentation of statutory and objects is awesome. A visit not to be missed.

Beyond the Museum on Rue Georges-Clemenceau is a vast and lovely **Plant Garden** created in 1829 on the model of London's Kew Gardens. The hothouses are sublime structures. Of the many parks and gardens in Nantes, it is the most beautiful.

Go back to the castle and take Cours John-F.-Kennedy to the right. At Place Neptune take Cours Franklin-Roosevelt. To your right is the old quarter of the city. Turn right at Place de la Bourse. Take Place du Commerce and Rue de Gorges to **Place Royale,** an elegant square with a lovely fountain.

Leave here on Rue de la Fosse. On your right you will see **Passage Pommeraye,** a well-preserved 19th-century glass-vaulted arcade. Among the interesting shops is the Bellanger bookshop, specialists in old books and prints. At the top of the arcade you will come out on the luxury shopping street, Rue Crébillon, which will take you left to **Place Graslin.** At number 4 is the **Cigale,** a turn-of-the-century restaurant. In perfect condition, its mosaics, stucco, ceramics and mirrors sparkle and energize a pleasant table with an inexpensive luncheon special.

Just behind Place Graslin is **Cours Cambronne,** an elegant 19th-century square closed at night to non-residents. In the center of the square, General Cambronne surveys. When summoned to surrender at Waterloo, history books and this statue inform us of his retort: "the guard dies but does not surrender." Any Nantais will tell you that this is a truncated version of the single word he used: "merde."

Turn right at the end of Cours Cambronne. At Rue Voltaire to your right is the **Museum of Natural History.** It occupies the former mint, a neo-classic structure of the early 19th century, one of the first to employ metal: see the dome of the conference hall. Visually a live museum, the exhibits are varied and eminently didactic, covering minerology, zoology, paleontology, etc.

Immediately to the right on leaving the Museum of Natural History, you will come to the **Dobrée and Archaeological Museums.** The Dobrée is an eclectic collection put together by Thomas Dobrée, a wise, lifelong collector. You will find objects of all sorts: religious art, illuminated manuscripts, Anne of Brittany's reliquary, historical pieces from the Vendéen war, etc. The Archaeological Museum exhibits Egyptian statutory and funerary objects, a large number of local archaeological finds and some Latin American and Asian artifacts.

Nantes is at the crossroads of two rivers: the Loire and the **Erdre.** The latter merits mention. It is a beautiful river bordered by châteaux, woods and fields. And it is navigable. Boat trips are available from Quai de Versailles in Nantes (inquire at the Tourist Office). Houseboats are for hire in **Sucé-sur-Erdre,** just a few miles upstream.

Tourist Info: Place du Commerce, 44000 Nantes, tel: 4089-5077.

Château: 10 A.M. to 12 P.M. and 2 to 6 P.M., 10 A.M. to 6 P.M. in July and August; closed Tuesdays.
Beaux-Arts Museum: 10 A.M. to 12 P.M. and 1 to 5:45 P.M.; Sundays, 11 A.M. to 5 P.M.; closed Tuesdays.
Museum of Natural History: 10 A.M. to 12 P.M. and 2 to 6 P.M.; 2 to 6 P.M. on Sundays; closed Mondays.
Dobrée/Archaeological Museums: 10 A.M. to 12 noon and 2 to 6 P.M.; closed Tuesdays.

Restaurants: **Atlantide,** 16 Quai Renaud, tel: 4073-2323, fax: 4073-7646; closed August. Excellent cuisine, creative, medium-priced. **Auberge du Château,** 5 Place de la Duchesse Anne, tel: 4074-0551; closed Sundays and Mondays, August and Christmas week. Lovely setting, pleasant food, medium-priced. **Cigale,** 4 Place Graslin, tel: 4069-7641, fax: 4073-7537. Regional specialties in extraordinary Art Nouveau setting, medium-priced. ***Pont-Levis,** 1 Rue du Château, tel: 4035-1020. Pretty restaurant and terrace, traditional menus, moderately priced. **Torigaï,** Ile Versailles, tel: 4037-0637, fax: 4093-3429; closed Sundays. Japanese chef, trained by one of France's best, inventive cuisine, moderately expensive. ***Vieux Quimper,** 10 Rue Bâclerie, tel: 4020-4609. Briton pancake house for crêpes, lovely old house, inexpensive.

Accommodations: **Amiral,** 26bis Rue Scribe, tel: 4069-2021, fax: 4073-9813. Modern hotel, pleasant décor, medium-priced. **l'Hôtel,** 6 Rue Henri-IV, tel: 4029-3031, fax: 4029-0095. Pretty rooms with view on château or garden, medium-priced. **Jules Verne,** 3 Rue Couëdic, tel: 4035-7450, fax: 4020-0935. Well located, medium-priced.

Out-of-town Restaurants: **Auberge du Vieux Gachet,** Le Gachet, *Carquefou,* 11 kilometers north on D178, tel: 4025-1092. Lovely dining room with view on river Erdre, traditional cuisine, medium-priced. **Châtaigneraie,** Delphin, 156 Route de Carquefou, *Sucé-sur-Erdre,* 16 kilometers north on D69, tel: 4077-9095, fax: 4077-9008. Beautiful manor on the Erdre, refined cuisine and atmosphere, expensive. **Vié, Sucé-sur-Erdre,* 16 kilometers north on D69. Great terrace on the water and in the village, traditional menus, moderately priced.

Out-of Town Accommodations: **Abbaye de Villeneuve,** Route des Sables d'Olonne, *Les Sorinières,* 10 kilometers south on N137, tel: 4004-4025, fax: 4031-2845. Elegant hotel in 13th-century abbey, comfort and tranquility, pool, expensive. **Plauderie,** Madame Mignen, 1 Rue du Verdelet, *44680 Sainte-Pazanne,* 25 kilometers from Nantes taking D750 and D758 towards Bourgneuf-en-Retz, tel: 4002-4508. Lovely 19th century private residence located near village church, moderately to medium-priced.

Noirmoutier

Go off to Noirmoutier on the D751 to Port-Saint-Père where you pick up the D758. Pass through vineyards of white Muscadet and Gros Plant wines, ideal with fish in general and oysters in particular. You will arrive in Bourneuf-en-Retz and notice that the air is balmy. And as you leave Bourneuf, you will know the sea is over the dunes from the way the wind blows on the grass, the stumpiness of the trees and bushes. It may well be around the next bend in the road.

Through Bouin you will pass between alignments of simple, low white houses. The farmhouses in the fields are also close to the ground, white with red tile roofs.

As you near Noirmoutier, road signs will inform you of the

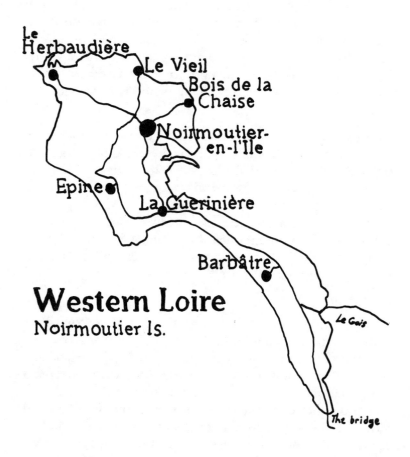

Le Herbaudière

Le Vieil

Bois de la Chaise

Noirmoutier-en-l'Île

Epine

La Guérinière

Barbâtre

Le Gois

The bridge

Western Loire

Noirmoutier Is.

tides. This is important for there are two roads to the island: one is over a bridge and the other literally through the sea. The latter is only usable during the ninety minutes preceding low tide and the ninety minutes following it. If you are within the limits, take the sea road out, but *only* if you are within the time limits; it is called the **Passage du Gois.** You can take the bridge road back.

The intensity of the colors in the sky is striking: shades of strong azure blue, almost mauve. The barrier you see in the heavens is not a cliff lodged in paradise but vapor from the evaporation of salt beds creating a screen that chases the clouds.

When you come up from the sea floor to terra firma, you may want to stop and watch the tide come in. You may think you have arrived at the end of the world, but in actual fact Noirmoutier has shielded mankind from the sea since at least the paleolithic era. Dolmens indicate the passage of early inhabitants. Later the Gauls, then the Romans occupied the island. In the 7th century Saint Philibert came here with monks and built a monastery. In 836, however, the Normans invaded and dispersed them. A second abbey was built at the end of the 12th century: Notre Dame de la Blanche.

From the 15th to the 18th century, the island was subjected to invasion off and on from England, Spain and Holland. Noirmoutier was purchased by the king of France in 1767. Producer of wheat and of salt, the island prospered. It was taken over by the Vendéens after the French Revolution. Retaken a few months later, the Vendéen general d'Elbée was executed here.

Today Noirmoutier has planted its wheat fields with potatoes and is known for its early crop. Salt is still dried though not in the quantities of earlier times. Oysters and other shellfish are cultivated; lobster and crab pots dot the coast; fishing for sole and other delicacies also provides a livelihood. In recent years, the island has developed its aquaculture industry to become the leading producer of cultivated turbot in the world. A well-known sailmaker supplies the sailing elite in many countries, including for the America's Cup.

The major industry, however, is tourism. The population of Noirmoutier year round is 9,000 people. During the summer months it can receive 150,000 visitors. Accommodations vary from camp grounds to three-star hotels. Noirmoutier is, above all, a family vacation spot with 3,000 house rentals available.

While the island is one of my favorites, I should warn the visitor against the peak period of July 14 to August 15. Since this region benefits from a delightful microclimate the off-seasons are wonderful: try it anytime between Easter and July or in September and October after the summer rush.

Tour

A visit to the island begins with **Barbâtre:** village, then forest, then dunes, beach and sea, in that order. Fig trees, bougainvillaea, rosemary, lavender, cypress, pines, and mimosa distribute their colors and scents everywhere. The small whitewashed houses are adorned with red tile roofs and blue shutters. You are not daydreaming; this is not the Riviera and that is not the Mediterranean!

Drive on to **La Guerinière** where there is a charming local museum of popular and traditional arts. Now and again you will pass a windmill. Then to **Epine** for a look at the salt beds. The water comes through small canals to the beds and actually meanders for six miles within a small patch. As the water evaporates, crystals form. The salt is pushed into piles with wooden shovels and left to dry. The following day it is stocked. This is a totally natural process requiring salt and water only. You can purchase coarse grain salt most anywhere on the island as well as salt flakes. The latter form on the surface of the water on windy days, becoming the only naturally refined salt in existence.

Except for one protected part of the island facing the "continent," all construction is low level. Nothing higher than six meters is now permitted.

Noirmoutier-en-l'Ile is the historic center of the island. The long buildings you will see here are salt attics. The stone of varying colors which served for their construction, as of other buildings on the island, arrived here as the ballast of ships. It was then exchanged for salt before the outward journey.

The **Museum of Naval Construction** on Rue de l'Ecluse is lodged in a former salt warehouse which later became a shipbuilding location. The museum displays the equipment of the shipbuilder under a spectacular framework of wood as it was until it stopped operating in 1979.

Drive around the harbor and come around to the central square to visit the **Romanesque church;** its crypt is all that remains of the old abbey. This is a wide church with three naves and a wood ceiling. That of the central nave suggests an upturned boat.

The medieval **château** next door is very much as it was in the Middle Ages. The donjon tower has a small **museum of local history** containing mainly ship models and navigation equipment. Note the sculpted female torsos of the prows and the fine picture frames containing ship models tossing with the sea. There is a good view from the tower.

A walk through the little streets of the old town to the left of the square is pleasant. Regular tours are organized to visit the nearby bird sanctuary. See the Tourist Office for exact times.

Take the dyke road through the forest to **Bois de la Chaise,** a turn-of-the-century resort area of elegant villas among the oaks and mimosa.

Go on to **le Vieil** where there is a small community of artists which organizes exhibits in the summer season. The water off shore is rich turquoise blue. On the first weekend of July over one hundred painters meet here for a painting holiday.

La Herbaudière is an active fishing port for fish and shell-fish. The morning's catch is marketed here on the docks every afternoon. Boats from Noirmoutier make daily trips to **l'Ile d'Yeu,** another lovely island, a more natural haven, with very few accommodations for tourists.

Tourist Info: Located near arrival point of Passage du Gois, 85330 Ile-de-Noirmoutier, tel: 5139-8071, fax: 5139:5316.

Museum of Island Traditions: La Guérinière. 10 A.M. to 12 noon and 2:30 to 6:30 P.M. from June 15 to September 15; 2:30 to 5 P.M., except Mondays, from September 16 to November 15.
Museum of Naval Construction: Rue de l'Ecluse, Noirmoutier-en-l'Ile. 10 A.M. to 7 P.M. from June 15 to September 15; 10 A.M. to 12:30 P.M. and 2:30 to 6 P.M., except Mondays, from April 1 to June 14 and September 16 to November 15.
Château: Noirmoutier-en-l'Ile, 10 A.M. to 7 P.M. from June 15 to September 15; 10 A.M. to 12:30 P.M. and 2:30 to 6 P.M., except Tuesdays, from February 1 to June 14 and September 16 to November 15.

Restaurants: *Côté **Jardin,** 1bis Rue du Grand-Four, Noirmoutier-en-l'Ile, tel: 5139-0302; closed Sunday evenings and Mondays off season. Wonderful décor for fine cuisine, moderately priced. *Etrier, Route de l'Epine, tel: 5139-1028; closed Wednesdays off season. Seafood specialties, moderately priced.
Hotel-Restaurants: **Général d'Elbée,** Place des Armes, Noirmoutier-en-l'Isle, tel: 5139-1029, fax: 5139-6912; closed November 1 to March 31. Charm, each room individually decorated, inside garden, pool, half-pension required in season, medium-priced. **Prateaux,** Bois-de-la-Chaise, tel: 5139-1252, fax: 5139-4628; closed October 1 to March 14. Charming hotel surrounded by trees and garden, good table, pension required in season, medium-priced. **Punta Lara,** chemin de la Noure, La Guérinière, tel: 5139-1158, fax: 5139-6912;

closed November 1 to March 31. Bungalow-style, all rooms face the sea, half-pension required during season, medium-priced to moderately expensive.

Hotel: **Bord à Bord,** 6 Rue de la Linière, l'Herbaudière, tel: 5139-2792. Open all year. Pretty hotel facing harbor, simple charm, kitchenettes in rooms, moderately priced.

From Noirmoutier one can go south to the seaside resort of Les Sables-d'Olonne or north the La Baule, a chic resort created at the turn-of-the-century.

Les Sables d'Olonne

The road south, the D38, passes numerous turn-offs for isolated swims and walks on the beaches. It goes through **Saint-Gilles-Croix-de-Vie,** a nice town with an active port. After Saint-Nicholas-de-Brem, the road traverses a refreshing forest.

Les Sables, as the local population calls the town, is not an artificial creation. It is a real, throbbing city with an active fishing harbor, a harbor for pleasure boats, and small-boat shipyards. It also has a long, ever-inviting beach covered with the finest sand I have ever trod.

A port since Gallo-Roman times, Les Sables was a leading harbor for whalers and then for cod in the 16th and 17th centuries. Staunchly Republican, Les Sables resisted the Vendéens following the French Revolution. In the early 18th century, it became one of France's first seaside resorts.

Today Les Sables is a fishing port, a commercial harbor for the export of wheat and wine and the import of wood and other merchandise. It is above all a family vacation beach.

Tour

Any visit to Les Sables begins with the **beach,** a languidly curving protective expanse of sand. After a first breath of sea and its atmosphere, a visit to the city center would be in order. From the Justice Palace on the beach, go right and right again on Rue des Halles. The minute **Rue de l'Enfer** on the left is advertised as the narrowest street in the world, you have to sidle in.

Continue on Rue des Halles to the **Church of Our Lady of Good Port,** a church of the Counter Reformation. Les Sables held out against the Huguenots, and a grateful Louis XIII, encouraged by Richelieu, endowed the city with a grand church. It is well proportioned, contains a long nave and no transept. Its bays, decorated with stars and crosses against a sky of blue and wine, contain several fine paintings and statues. As is normal for a port town, ship models find their place here too.

Next door to the church is a covered **market place** designed by Baltard.

Take Rue Bisson to the right until you reach the **port.** Go right and left on Avenue Nicot and Boulevard de l'Ile-Vertime, then left over the bridge to the area called **La Chaume.** An island before a sand bar united it to the mainland; this was the fishermen's quarter. Les Sables and its notables supported the Church during the Reformation, la Chaume supported the Protestant Reform.

From the top of **Arundel Tower,** there is an excellent view of the region. Go past the tower to **Fort Saint Nicholas.** The priory, built in the 11th century, was damaged by the Huguenot army in 1622 and then redone by Richelieu in flamboyant Gothic. The acoustics are particularly good and a number of concerts are held here during the season. Along the esplanade notice the old World War II blockhouses.

The neighborhood is especially interesting for its low, well-kept whitewashed houses. Take Rue Saint-Nicholas and Rue du Docteur-Canteleau and the little offshoots from them for a pleasant walk.

Back in town, at the far end of the beach corniche, is the **Thalassotherapy Institute,** a very special seawater universe for treatment of ailments such as obesity, stress, muscular reeducation, nutritional imbalance, circulatory problems, etc.

The French are great believers in the benefits to be derived from seawater therapy and such centers are very popular. The one in Les Sables d'Olonne is modern, well-equipped, and enjoys an excellent reputation.

Just behind the Institute is a casino replete with one-arm bandits, black jack and roulette. There is also a zoo. In front of the Institute is the Creps Sailing School.

The interesting museum at the **Saint Cross Abbey** on Rue de Verdun contains a large collection of works by Victor Brauner, always quizzical. The 17th-century oak-roofed upper exhibition hall is amazingly intricate with its supporting beams lined up from floor to ceiling for its entire length. In the maritime collection are wonderful naive paintings of ships by Gilbert and Paul-Emile Pajot, as well as other artifacts of the sea.

In 1992 the round-the-world sailing competition left from Les Sables. Harbor and sea excursions are organized by the Tourist Office on a regular basis.

There are five excellent **golf courses** in the area: Saint-Jean-de-Monts, Les Fontonelles at L'Aiguillon-sur-Vié, La Domangère in Nesmy, Les Olonnes in Olonne-sur-Mer, and Port Bourgenay in Talmont-Saint-Hilaire. A golf pass enables players to switch from one to the other. The Fontonelles is an agreeable, relatively easy course; Saint-Jean-de-Monts along the sea is a more difficult one.

Tourist Info: Rue du Maréchal-Leclerc, 85104 Les Sables-d'Olonne, tel: 5132-0328.

Saint Cross Abbey Museum: 10 A.M. to 12 P.M. and 2:30 to 6:30 P.M. from June 15 to September 30; 2:30 to 5:30 P.M. rest of year. Closed Mondays.

Restaurants: *Au Capitaine, 5 Quai Guiné, tel: 5195-1810; closed Sunday evenings and Mondays off season and February. Fresh seafood on the harbor, moderately priced. *Clipper, 19bis Quai Guiné, tel: 5132-0361; closed Wednesdays except in season, Tuesday evenings and February. Local fare, seafood with view of port, moderately priced. **Navarin,** 18 Place Navarin, tel: 5121-1161; closed Sunday evenings and Mondays, except July and August. Sidewalk restaurant with view on the sea, fresh seafood, moderately to medium-priced.

Hotel-Restaurants: **Atlantic** 5 Promenade Godet, tel: 5195-3771, fax: 5195-3730. Restaurant closed Fridays from October to April and November 15 to December 15. Pleasant hotel on the beach, medium-priced to moderately expensive, restaurant moderately priced. **Beau Rivage,** 40 Promenade Georges-Clemenceau, tel: 5132-0301, fax: 5132-4648. Les Sables' best, excellent "master chef" (an official title awarded only to the most qualified), pretty dining room facing the sea, comfortable rooms, medium-priced to moderately expensive. **Mercure,** Zone Tranchet, tel: 5121-7777, fax: 5121-7780. Adjacent to the Thalassotherapy Institute, modern, comfortable, quiet, expensive, restaurant on the sea, moderately priced.

Hotels: **Résidence,** 36 Promenade Georges-Clemenceau, tel: 5132-0666. On the sea, comfortable, medium-priced. **Roches Noires,** 12 Promenade Georges-Clemenceau, tel: 5132-0171, fax: 5195-3730. Modern hotel facing the sea, medium-priced.

Out-of-town: **Château de la Millière,** 85150 *Saint-Mathurin,* 8 kilometers on N160, tel: 5122-7329 et 5136-1308; closed from October to Easter. Lovely 19th-century château with extended grounds, private residence, medium-priced.

From Les Sables take the D38 into the D758. From Noirmoutier pick up the D758 on hitting the continent. At Bourgneuf-en-Retz go left on the D13 to **Pornic.** This is a pleasant little port and tourist center with a miniature casino in town on the little harbor.

Tourist Info: Quai L'Herminier, 44210 Pornic, tel: 4082-0440.

Restaurant: **Amphitrite,** 4 Quai Le Tay, tel: 4082-0511. Fresh seafood on the quay, moderately priced. *****Grilladin,** 4 Escalier Galipaud, tel: 4082-4034; closed Wednesdays. Inventive cuisine with local products, moderately priced. **Jade,** Quai Leroy, Old Port, tel: 4082-6050. Fresh seafood, moderately priced.

Hotel-Restaurants: **Alliance,** Plage de la Source, tel: 4082-2121, fax: 4082-8089; closed January. Thalassotherapy center with view on the ocean, moderately expensive, restaurant, medium-priced. **Relais Saint-Gilles,** 7 Rue François-de-Mun, tel: 4082-0225, restaurant open evenings only. Comfortable hotel, moderately priced.

La Baule

The D213 will take you along the coast, over the longest bridge in France to **Saint-Nazaire,** a spectacular ride. This city, known for its ship docks and naval construction, was practically totally destroyed during the Second World War. Rebuilt, it prospered again in the post-war years. Today, however, the shipbuilding industry faces economic recession. A free port is being organized in Saint-Nazaire which, it is hoped, will profit the city's maritime traffic.

After Saint-Nazaire get on the D92 into **La Baule,** whose claim to fame is the most perfect beach on the Atlantic coast of France. This is a "new" city, created from nothing at the end of the 19th century. Situated among the modern constructions which line the coastline are elegant Art Nouveau villas. They are also very much in evidence behind the front-row hotels in the areas called **Quartier des Oiseaux** and **Quartier des Arbres.** At the beginning of this century, La Baule was known for the chic clientele which lined the extraordinary fine-sand beach facing south. While the resort town has become much more democratic over the years, it has not been abandoned by artists, celebrities and movie stars. The local casino has a large slot-machine area.

A number of excursions are possible from La Baule: along the coast to **Le Pouliguen, Le Croisic** and **Guérande** with its salt beds, up to **Piriac-sur-Mer.** In the interior is a wonderful natural park, the **Grande Brière.** In addition to sea sports, horseback riding, golf and tennis are easily available. Inquire at Tourist Office.

Tourist Info: 8 Place Victoire, 44500 La Baule, tel: 4024-3444.

Restaurants: **Marcanderie,** 5 Avenue Agen, tel: 4024-0312, fax: 4060-5596; closed Mondays except evenings in July and August. Pretty restaurant in former private residence, good local fish specialties, medium-priced. **Voile d'Or,** Pouliguen, tel: 4042-3168; closed Sunday evenings, Mondays and January. Creative cuisine on the seaside, medium-priced to moderately expensive.

Hotel-Restaurants: **Castel Marie-Louise,** 1 Avenue Andrieux, tel: 4060-2060, fax: 4042-7210. La Baule's best cuisine in a lovely hotel with magnificent grounds on the edge of the sea, hotel: luxury prices, restaurant: expensive. **Christina,** 26 Boulevard Hennecart, tel: 4060-2244, fax: 4011-0431; restaurant closed November to April. Modern hotel on the sea, medium-priced. **Palmeraie,** 7 Allée des Cormorans, tel: 4060-2441, fax: 4042-7371; closed November to Easter. Charming villa with a Mexican flavor, comfortable, tranquil, half-pension available, medium-priced. **Saint-Christophe Gardenia,** 1 Avenue Alcyons, tel: 4060-3535, fax: 4060-1174. Half-pension available. A 1900s residence on pretty grounds, comfortable, welcoming, medium-priced.

Hotels: **Manoir du Parc,** 3 Allée Albatros, tel: 4060-2452, fax: 4060-5596. Comfortable, quiet, pretty grounds, turn-of-century villa, medium-priced.

Some Useful Words and Phrases

Africa	**Afrique** (f)
bay	**baie** (f)
crab	**crabe** (m)
cross	**croix** (f)
family	**famille** (f)
farm	**ferme** (f)
harbor	**port** (m)
haven	**havre** (m)
insurance	**assurance** (f)
lobster	**homard** (m), **langouste** (f)
New World	**Nouveau Monde** (m)
oyster	**huître** (f)
pepper	**poivre** (m)
salt	**sel** (m)
shellfish	**coquillage** (m)
slave	**esclave** (f/m)
tide	**marée** (f)
trade	**commerce** (m)

Passez-moi le sel, s'il vous plaît. (Pass the salt, please.)

J'aimerais une douzaine d'huîtres. (I would like a dozen oysters.)

A marée basse, on peut chercher des coquillages. (At low tide, we can look for shellfish.)

Nantes a fait sa fortune avec le commerce des esclaves. (Nantes made its fortune with the slave trade.)

Nous avons acheté du miel à la ferme. (We bought some honey at the farm.)

Ils vont voir leur famille à Angers ce weekend. (They are going to see their family at Angers this weekend.)

Est-ce que je peux aller au port avec toi. (Can I go to the harbor with you?)

Nous nous sommes baignés ce matin. (We went swimming this morning.)

CHAPTER 20

Grammar

Pronunciation Table

a, à, â   like the **a** in **part**
Examples: **tarte, voilà** (there is, there are),
château

b   same as English

c, ç   c is pronounced hard as in **card**
Example: **café**

ç is pronounced as the **s** in **sun.** The **cédille,**
or comma attached to the bottom of the let-
ter, indicates that the sound is soft. When
capitalized, the cedilla does not appear
Example: **leçon** (lesson)

ch   **ch** is pronounced softly like the **sh** in show
Example: **chéri** (darling)

d   same as English

e, è, ê   like the **e** in **met**
Examples: **demi** (half), **après** (after), **arrêter**
(to stop, to arrest)
e at the end of a word is mute
Example: **étudiante** (woman student)

é, er, ez   like the **a** in **date**

	Examples: **né** (born), **rester** (to stay), **allez** (you go)
f	same as English
g	pronounced hard, except before **e** and **i** when it is pronounced softly like the **z** in **azure.**
	Examples: **garde** (guard), **guerre** (war) = hard sound
	gentil (nice), **général** (general) = soft sound
h	always silent
i	like the **double e** in **meet**
	Examples: **ami** (friend)
j	pronounced softly, like the **z** in **azure**
	Example: **je** (I)
k, l, m, n	same as English
o, ô	at the end of a word or a syllable, like the **o** in **rose**
	Within a syllable **o** (but not **ô**) resembles the **o** in **ton**
	Examples: **opéra, côte** (coast), **sonnette** (bell)
oi	pronounced **wa**
	Examples: **soie** (silk), **oiseau** (bird)
ou	pronounced **oo** like in **food**
	Example: **beaucoup** (a lot)
p, q	same as English
r	pronounced deep in the throat and slightly gargled

	Examples: **numéro** (number), **réserver** (to reserve)
s	same as English except when between two vowels; it is then pronounced **z** Examples: **fraise** (strawberry), **choisir** (to choose)
t	same as English
th	same as English **t** Example: **thé** (tea), **théâtre**
u	no English equivalent. Purse your lips and pronounce the word **you,** without the **y** sound that precedes it in English, in the upper part of the mouth Examples: **une** (one), **musée** (museum), **jupe** (skirt)
v	same as English
w	pronounced **v** Examples: **wagon** (carriage or wagon), **w (double u)** = double v
x, y, z	similar to English

Nasal sounds:
an, en, am, em, ain, ein, ian, ien, im, in, om, on, un are nasalized. The final **n** or **m** is barely pronounced.

Verbs

Present tense (regular verbs ending in **er** and **ir**)

aimer (to like, to love)	**finir** (to finish)
j'aime = I like, I love	je finis = I finish

tu aimes	tu finis
elle, il aime	elle, il finit
nous aimons	nous finissons
vous aimez	vous finissez
elles, ils aiment	elles, ils finissent

Perfect tense (regular verbs ending in **er** and **ir**)

j'ai aimé = I (have) loved	j'ai fini = I (have) finished
tu as aimé	tu as fini
elle, il a aimé	elle, il a fini
nous avons aimé	nous avons fini
vous avez aimé	vous avez fini
elles, ils ont aimé	elles, ils ont fini

NOTE: past participle of all **er** verbs ends in **é,** whereas past participle of **ir** and **re** verbs can end in **i, is, t, u.**

Future tense (regular verbs ending in **er** and **ir**)

j'aimerai = I shall, will love	je finirai = I shall, will finish
tu aimeras	tu finiras
elle, il aimera	elle, il finira
nous aimerons	nous finirons
vous aimerez	vous finirez
elles, ils aimeront	elles, ils finiront

Conditional tense (regular verbs ending in **er** and **ir**)

j'aimerais = I should, would love	je finirais = I should, would finish
tu aimerais	tu finirais
elle, il aimerait	elle, il finirait
nous aimerions	nous finirions
vous aimeriez	vous finiriez
elles, ils aimeraient	elles, ils finiraient

Essential irregular verbs

être (to be)

present tense
je suis = I am
tu es
elle, il est
nous sommes
vous êtes
elles, ils sont

future tense
je serai = I shall, will be
tu seras
elle, il sera
nous serons
vous serez
elles, ils seraient

conditional tense
je serais = I should, would be
tu serais
elle, il serait
nous serions
vous seriez
elles, ils seraient

imperfect tense
j'étais = I was
tu étais
elle, il était
nous étions
vous étiez
elles, ils étaient

past participle: été
j'ai été = I have been

avoir (to have)

present tense
j'ai = I have
tu as
elle, il a
nous avons
vous avez
elles, ils ont

future tense
j'aurai = I shall, will have
tu auras
elle, il aura
nous aurons
vous aurez
elles, ils auront

conditional tense
j'aurais = I should, would
        have

imperfect tense
j'avais = I had

tu aurais
elle, il aurait
nous aurions
vous auriez
elles, ils auraient

tu avais
elle, il avait
nous avions
vous aviez
elles, ils avaient

past participle: eu
j'ai eu = I have had

aller (to go)

present tense
je vais = I go, do go, am going
tu vas
elle, il va
nous allons
vous allez
elles, ils vont

future tense
j'irai = I shall, will go
tu iras
elle, il ira
nous irons
vous irez
elles, ils iront

conditional tense
j'irais = I should, would go
tu irais
elle, il irait
nous irions
vous iriez
elles, ils iraient

imperfect tense
j'allais = I was going
tu allais
elle, il allait
nous allions
vous alliez
elles, ils allaient

past participle: allé
je suis allé(e) = I went

faire (to do, to make)

present tense
je fais = I do, make, do make,
        am making

future tense
je ferai = I shall, will do,
        make

tu fais
elle, il fait
nous faisons
vous faites
elles, ils font

tu feras
elle, il fera
nous ferons
vous ferez
elles, ils feront

conditional tense
je ferais = I should, would do, make
tu ferais
elle, il ferait
nous ferions
vous feriez
elles, ils feraient

imperfect tense
je faisais = I was doing, making
tu faisais
elle, il faisait
nous faisions
vous faisiez
elles, ils faisaient

past participle: fait
j'ai fait = I did, have done, I (have) made

Possessives

Possessive adjectives

ma/mon/mes — **ma malle/mon père/mes invités**
my trunk/my father/my guests

ta/ton/tes — **ta poupée/ton magasin/tes cheveux**
your doll/your store/your hair

sa/son/ses — **sa raquette/son café/ses affaires**
his-her racket/his-her coffee/his-her affairs

notre/nos — **notre maison/nos rêves**
our house/our dreams

votre/vos — **votre femme/vos clés**
your wife/your keys

leur/leurs   **leur cousin(e)/leurs paquets**
their cousin/their packages

ma, ta and **sa** qualify feminine nouns.

Possessive pronouns

singular	plural	
mien(ne)	**mien(ne)s**	mine
tien(ne)	**tien(ne)s**	yours
sien(ne)	**sien(ne)s**	his, hers, its
nôtre	**nôtres**	ours
vôtre	**vôtres**	yours
leur	**leurs**	theirs

ne indicates that the object's gender is feminine.

Disjunctive pronouns

moi	**chez moi**	at my house
toi	**avec toi**	with you
soi	**pour soi**	for oneself
nous	**près de nous**	near us
vous	**après vous**	after you
eux	**par eux**	by them

CHAPTER 21

Glossary: English—French

(f) = feminine noun
(m) = masculine noun
(e), (le), (ne), (ue) = feminine
endings for adjectives (singular)

able (to be): pouvoir
about, approximately: environ
according to: selon
address: adresse (f)
advise (to): conseiller
affair: affaire (f), liaison (f)
Africa: Afrique (f)
after: après
afternoon: après-midi (m/f)
age: âge (m)
agreement: accord (m)
airplane: avion (m)
airport: aéroport (m)
alive: vivant(e)
all: tout(e)
alone: seul(e)
also: aussi, également
always: toujours
American: américain(e)
ancient: ancien(ne)
angel: ange (m)
antique: antiquité (f), antique
apartment: appartement, logement
   (m)

apartment house, building:
   immeuble (m)
apostle: apôtre (m)
appointment: rendez-vous (m)
April: avril (m)
archbishop: archevêque (m)
architecture: architecture (f)
arena: arène (f)
arm: bras (m)
army: armée (f)
around: autour
arrest (to): arrêter
arrival: arrivée (f)
arrive (to): arriver
arrow: flèche (f)
ash: cendre (f)
ashtray: cendrier (m)
Asian: asiatique
ask (to): demander
attend (to): assister
August: août (m)
average: moyen(ne)
bad: mauvais(e)
badly: mal
bag: sac (m)
bakery: boulangerie (f)
balcony: balcon (m)
bank: banque (f)

bath: bain (m)
bathe (to), take a bath (to): se baigner
bathroom: salle de bains (f)
battle: bataille (f)
bay: baie (f)
be (to): être
beach: plage (f)
beam: poutre (f)
beautiful: beau/belle
beauty parlor: salon de beauté (m)
become (to): devenir
bed: lit (m)
bed and breakfast: chambre d'hôte (f)
bedroom: chambre (f)
beer: bière (f)
beet: betterave (f)
before: avant
begin (to): commencer
beginning: début (m)
behind: arrière (m), derrière (m)
Belgium: Belgique (f)
bell: sonnette, sonnerie (f)
belt: ceinture (f)
best: mieux
better: meilleur(e)
between: entre
big: grand(e)
bike: vélo (m)
bill: facture (f), addition (f)
bird: oiseau (m)
birth: naissance (f)
bishop: évêque (m)
black: noir(e)
blue: bleu(e)
boat: bateau (m)
bombing: bombardement (m)
book: livre (m)
bookseller: bouquiniste (m)
bookshop: librairie (f)
born: né(e)

born (to be): naître
boss: patron(ne)
bottle: bouteille (f)
box: boîte (f)
box office: guichet (m)
boy: garçon (m)
brake: frein (m)
brandy: cognac (m)
bread: pain (m)
break (to): casser
breakdown: panne (f)
breakdown service: dépannage (m)
breakfast: petit déjeuner (m)
brick: brique (f)
bridge: pont (m)
bring (to): apporter
brother: frère (m)
brotherhood: fraternité (f)
brown: marron, brun (m)
bubble: bulle (f)
build (to): bâtir, construire
bullfight: course de taureaux, corrida (f)
Burgundian: bourguignon(e)
burn (to): brûler
bury (to): enterrer
bus: autobus (m), car (m)
business: affaire (f)
but: mais
butter: beurre (m)
buy (to): acheter
by: par
cabbage: chou (m)
cake: gâteau (m)
call: appel (m)
call (to): appeler
call back (to): rappeler
camp: colonie (f), camp (m)
camp ground: camping (m)
Canadian: Canadien(ne)
canvas: toile (f)
capital: chapiteau (m)

car: voiture (f)
cashier: caisse (f)
castle: château (m)
cat: chat(te)
cave: caverne (f), grotte (f)
celebrate (to): célébrer, fêter
celebration: fête (f)
cellar: cave (f)
cemetery: cimetière (m)
center: centre (m)
century: siècle (m)
certain: certain(e)
chair: chaise (f)
chambermaid: femme de chambre (f)
Chamber of Deputies: Chambre des députés (f)
character: caractère (m)
characteristic: caractéristique
charming: charmant(e)
cheap: bon marché
cheaper: meilleur marché
check: chèque (m), addition (f)
check (to): vérifier
cheek: joue (f)
cheese: fromage (m)
cherry: cerise (f)
chicken: poulet (m)
child: enfant(e)
China: Chine (f)
choice: choix (m)
choose (to): choisir
Christianity: christianisme (m)
Christmas: Noël (m)
church: église (f)
circus: cirque (m)
citrus fruit: agrumes (m)
city: ville (f)
cliff: falaise (f)
climb (to): monter
clock: horloge (f)
close: proche

close (to): fermer
cloth: tissu (m)
coast: côte (f)
coffee: café (m)
coin: pièce (f)
coke: coca (m)
cold: froid(e)
college: université (f)
colony: colonie (f), camp (m)
column: colonne (f)
come (to): venir
comma: virgule (f)
conquest: conquête (f)
construct (to): construire
consult (to): consulter
contain (to): contenir
convent: couvent (m)
cooking: cuisine (f)
corkscrew: tire-bouchon (m)
corner: coin (m)
cost: coût (m)
cost (to): coûter
costly: coûteux/coûteuse
cotton: coton (m)
council: conseil (m)
counter: guichet (m)
country: pays (m), campagne (f)
countryside: campagne (f)
court: cour (f), tribunal (m)
courtyard: cour (f)
cover (to): couvrir
cow: vache (f)
crab: crabe (m)
craftsman: artisan (m)
cross: croix (f)
cross (to): traverser
crossroads: croisement (m), carrefour (m)
crowd: foule (f)
crown: couronne (f)
crusader: croisé (m)
currency: monnaie (f)

custom: coutume (f)
customs: douane (f)
damage (to): endommager
dancer: danseur/danseuse
dangerous: dangereux/dangereuse
dark: foncé(e)
darling: chéri(e)
date: date (f)
date (to): dater, sortir
daughter: fille (f)
day: jour (m), journée (f)
day after tomorrow: après-demain
    (m)
day before yesterday: avant-hier
    (m)
daybreak: lever du jour (m)
daytime: journée (f)
December: décembre (m)
department store: grand magasin
    (m)
departure: départ (m)
despite: malgré
devotion: dévouement (m)
die (to): mourir
dining room: salle à manger (f)
dinner: dîner (m)
discovery: découverte (f)
dish: plat (m)
divide (to): diviser
do (to): faire
doctor: docteur, médecin (m)
dog: chien(ne)
doll: poupée (f)
door: porte (f)
draw (to): dessiner
dream: rêve (m)
dress (to), dressed (to get):
    s'habiller
dressmaker: couturier/couturière
dressmaking: couture (f)
drink: boisson (f)
drink (to): boire

drive (to): conduire
drug: drogue (f)
drugstore: pharmacie (f)
dry: sec/sèche
duck: canard (m)
duke: duc (m)
during: pendant
dust: poussière (f)
dye: teinture (f)
each: chaque
east: est (m)
Easter: Pâques (f)
eat (to): manger
efficiency apartment/house:
    gîte rural (m)
egg: oeuf (m)
elevator: ascenseur (m)
embrace (to): embrasser
embroidery: broderie (f)
end: fin (f)
engagement: fiançailles (f)
engineer: ingénieur (m)
England: Angleterre (f)
English: anglais(e)
engraving: gravure (f)
enough: assez
enter (to): entrer
entrance, entry fee: entrée (f)
equal: égal(e)
era: ère, époque (f), âge (m)
errand: course (f)
establish (to): établir
evening: soir (m)
event: événement (m)
everyone: tous/toutes
everywhere: partout
example: exemple (m)
excavation: fouille (f)
exchange: change (m)
excursion: tour (m)
excuse (to): excuser, pardonner
executioner: bourreau (m)

exercise: exercice (m)
exhibition: exposition (f)
exit: sortie (f)
expensive: cher/chère
fabric: tissu (m)
factory: usine, fabrique (f)
fair: foire (f)
fairy: fée (f)
faithful: fidèle
fall: automne (m)
false: faux/fausse
fame: renommée (f)
family: famille (f)
far: loin
farm: ferme (f)
farmer: paysan(ne), fermier/
  fermière
fashion: mode (f)
father: père (m)
February: février (m)
feudal: féodal(e)
fever: fièvre (f)
few: peu, peu de
field: champ (m)
fight (to): lutter
film: pellicule (f)
find (to): trouver
fine: amende (f)
fine arts: beaux-arts (m)
finger: doigt (m)
finish (to): finir
fire: feu (m)
fireworks: feu d'artifice (m)
fish: poisson (m)
fishing: pêche (f)
flight: vol (m)
float (to): flotter
floor: étage (m)
flower: fleur (f)
follow (to): suivre
foot: pied (m)
footstep: pas (m)

for: pour
foreigner: étranger/étrangère
forest: forêt (f)
forget (to): oublier
forgive (to): pardonner, excuser
fort: fort (m)
fortress: forteresse (f)
fountain: fontaine (f)
free: libre
free-of-charge: gratuit(e)
freedom: liberté (f)
French: français(e)
French fries: frites (f)
fresco: fresque (f)
Friday: vendredi (m)
friend: ami(e)
friendly: sympathique, amical(e)
full: complet/complète, plein(e)
furniture: meuble (m)
Gallic: gaulois(e)
garden: jardin (m)
Gaul: Gaule (f)
German: allemand(e)
Germany: Allemagne
get up (to), rise (to), stand up
  (to): se lever
gift: cadeau (m)
gilt: doré(e)
girl: fille, jeune fille (f)
give (to): donner
glass: verre (m)
go (to): aller
go down (to): descendre
go out (to): sortir
goat, goat cheese: chèvre (f)
gold: or (m)
good: bon(ne), bien
goodbye: au revoir
good day, good morning: bonjour
good evening, good afternoon:
  bonsoir
Gothic: gothique

government: gouvernement (m)
grape: raisin (m)
gray: gris(e)
Great Britain: Grande-Bretagne (f)
green: vert(e)
green light: feu vert (m)
grocery: épicerie (f)
grotto: grotte, caverne (f)
ground floor: rez-de-chaussée (m)
guest: invité(e)
hairdresser: coiffeur/coiffeuse
half: demi(e), moitié (f)
half-past: demie
ham: jambon (m)
hand: main (f)
happy: heureux/heureuse,
  content(e)
harbor: port (m)
hard: dur(e)
harm: dommage (m)
harvest: récolte (f)
hat: chapeau (m)
have (to): avoir
haven: havre (m)
head: tête (f)
headlight: phare (m)
headquarters: quartier général (m)
heart: coeur (m)
heat: chauffage (m)
here: ici
here is, here are: voici
hide (to): cacher
high: haut(e)
high school: lycée (m), collège (m)
hill: colline (f)
holiday: fête (f)
home: maison (f), chez
honey: miel (m)
hope (to): espérer
horse: cheval (m)
horse race: course de chevaux (f)
hospital: hôpital (m)

hot: chaud(e)
hour: heure (f)
house: maison (f)
how: comment
how much, how many: combien
humanity: humanité (f)
hunt (to): chasser
husband: mari (m)
ice, ice cream: glace (f)
idea: idée (f)
ill: mal (m), malade
immediately: immédiatement, tout
  de suite
in: dans
increase (to): augmenter
independent: indépendant(e)
India: Inde (f)
indicate (to): indiquer, signaler
information: information (f),
  renseignement (m)
inn: auberge (f)
insurance: assurance (f)
intersection: croisement (m),
  carrefour (m)
interview: entrevue, interview (f)
introduce (to): introduire
Ireland: Irlande (f)
iron: fer (m)
island: île, isle (f)
Italian: italien(ne)
Italy: Italie (f)
itinerary: itinéraire (m)
jam: confiture (f)
January: janvier (m)
jewel: bijou (m)
jeweler: bijoutier (m)
Jewish: juif/juive
July: juillet (m)
June: juin (m)
key: clé, clef (f)
kill (to): tuer
kind: gentil(le)

king: roi (m)
kingdom: royaume (m)
kiss: baiser (m)
kiss (to): embrasser
knitting, knitted fabric: tricot (m)
know (to): savoir
know (to): acquainted with (to
   be): connaître
known: connu(e)
lady: dame (f)
lake: lac (m)
lamp: lampe (f)
land: terre (f)
language: langue (f)
last: dernier/dernière
last (to): durer
laugh (to): rire
laugh, laughter: rire (m)
law: droit (m)
law courts: palais de justice,
   tribunaux (m)
layout: maquette (f)
lead (to): conduire (f)
leather: cuir (m)
leave (to): partir, quitter
left: gauche (f)
left bank: rive gauche (f)
legend: légende (f)
lemon: citron (m)
less: moins
lesson: leçon (f)
letter: lettre (f)
level: niveau (m)
life: vie (f)
light: lumière (f), feu (m)
light: clair(e)
lighting: éclairage (m)
like (to): aimer
limestone: calcaire (m)
line: ligne (f)
linen: lin (m)
listen (to): écouter

little: petit(e)
lively: vif/vive
liver: foie (m)
live in (to): habiter
living room: salon (m), salle de
   séjour (f)
lobby: hall (m)
lobster: homard (m), langouste (f)
lock: serrure (f)
lock (nautical): écluse (f)
lodgings: logement (m)
long: long(ue)
long time: longtemps
look at (to): regarder
look for (to): chercher
lose (to): perdre
love (to): aimer
low: bas(se)
luck: chance (f), fortune (f)
luggage: bagage (m)
lunch: déjeuner (m)
luxury: luxe (m)
madam: madame (f)
main street: rue principale (f)
make (to): faire
man: homme (m)
map: carte (f)
marble: marbre (m)
market: marché (m)
marriage: mariage (m)
marry (to), married (to get): se
   marier
March: mars (m)
marsh, marshland: marais (m)
mass: masse, messe (f)
masterpiece: chef-d'oeuvre (m)
May: mai (m)
meat: viande (f)
medicine: médicament (m)
meet (to): rencontrer
meet again (to): revoir
member: membre (m)

memory: mémoire (f)
menu: carte (f), menu (m)
merchandise: marchandise (f)
Middle Ages: moyen âge (m)
midnight: minuit (m)
milk: lait (m)
mill: moulin (m), usine (f)
millenium: millénaire (m)
mind: esprit (m)
minus: moins
mirror: miroir (m)
miss: mademoiselle (f)
missionary: missionnaire (m)
mix (to): mélanger
model: modèle, mannequin (m),
  maquette (f)
Monday: lundi (m)
money: argent (m)
month: mois (m)
more: plus, encore, davantage
morning: matin (m)
mother: mère (f)
motor: moteur (m)
motorcycle: moto (f)
mountain: montagne (f)
movies: cinéma (m)
Mr., Messrs.: monsieur, messieurs
  (m)
much: beaucoup
museum: musée (m)
music: musique (f)
musician: musicien(ne)
name: nom (m)
name (to), nominate (to): nommer
National Assembly: Assemblée
  nationale (f)
nationality: nationalité (f)
nature: nature (f)
nave: nef (f)
near: près, près de
necessary: nécessaire
neighbor: voisin(e)

neighborhood: quartier (m)
nerve: nerf (m)
never: jamais
new: neuf/neuve
New World: Nouveau Monde (m)
next: prochain(e)
nice: gentil(le)
night: nuit (f)
no: non
noon: midi (m)
north: nord (m)
nose: nez (m)
nothing: rien
novel: roman (m)
November: novembre (m)
now: maintenant
number: numéro (m)
ocean: océan (m)
October: octobre (m)
offer (to): offrir
office: bureau (m)
often: souvent
oil: huile (f)
okay: OK, d'accord
old: vieux/vieille
on: sur
one: un(e)
only: seulement
open: ouvert(e)
open (to): ouvrir
or: ou
orchard: verger (m)
orchestra: orchestre (m)
order (to): commander
organic produce: culture
  biologique (f)
other: autre
outskirts: environs (m)
oven: four (m)
over: dessus
over there: là-bas
owner: propriétaire, patron(ne)

oyster: huître (f)
package: paquet (m)
painting: peinture (f), tableau (m)
pair: paire (f)
palace: palais (m)
palm tree: palmier (m)
panel: panneau (m)
parade: défilé (m)
paradise: paradis (m)
pardon: pardon (m)
pardon (to): pardonner
parent: parent (m)
parking lot: parking (m)
parkway: autoroute (f)
pass (to): passer
passenger: passager/passagère
passport: passeport (m)
past: passé (m)
pastry, pastry shop: pâtisserie (f)
pay (to): payer, régler
peach: pêche (f)
pear: poire (f)
pedestrian: piéton(ne)
people: peuple (m)
pepper: poivre (m)
percent: pour cent
perfume: parfum (m)
permanent: permanent(e)
person: personne (f)
person-in-charge: responsable (m/f)
pharmacist: pharmacien(ne)
pharmacy: pharmacie (f)
picnic: pique-nique (m)
picture: tableau (m), photo (f)
piece: morceau (m)
pig: cochon (m)
pill: pillule (f), comprimé (m)
pillar: colonne (f)
pink: rose
pity: dommage (m), pitié (f)
place: lieu (m)

plaster: plâtre (m)
platform: quai (m), plate-forme (f)
play (to): jouer
playing card: carte de jeu (f)
pleasant: agréable, plaisant(e),
    sympathique
please: s'il vous plaît
pleased to meet you: enchanté(e)
pleasure: plaisir (m)
plum: prune (f)
poet, poetess: poète, poétesse
police station: commissariat (m)
policeman: agent de police (m)
pool: piscine (f)
pope: pape (m)
post office: poste (f)
poster: affiche (f)
poultry: volaille (f)
pound: livre (f)
power: puissance (f)
praise (to): louer
prefer (to): préférer
present (to): présenter
present-day: actuel(le)
present time: actuellement
pretty: joli(e)
price: prix (m)
print: gravure (f)
priority: priorité (f)
problem: problème (m)
produce (to): produire
product: produit (m)
progress: progrès (m)
prohibited: défense de, interdit(e)
projector: projecteur (m)
property: propriété (f)
prosperous: prospère
purple: pourpre, violet (m)
put (to): mettre
quarter: quart, quartier (m)
queen: reine (f)
quick: rapide

quickly: vite, rapidement
race course: champ de course (m)
racket: raquette (f)
rain: pluie (f)
rain (to): pleuvoir
raincoat: imperméable (m)
raisin: raisin sec (m)
rampart: rempart (m)
raspberry: framboise (f)
rate of exchange: taux de change
  (m)
read (to): lire
ready-to-wear: prêt-à-porter (m)
receive (to): recevoir
reception: réception (f)
recipe: recette (f)
recruit (to): recruter
reduce (to): réduire
red: rouge
red light: feu rouge (m)
relative: parent (m)
remain (to): rester
remember (to): se rappeler
rent (to): louer
reply (to): répondre
representative: représentant(e)
reservation (to): réservation (f)
reserve: réserver
return (to): retourner
Rhine: Rhin (m)
rice: riz (m)
right: droite (f)
right bank: rive droite (f)
ring: bague (f)
river: fleuve (m), rivière (f)
road: route (f)
Roman: romain(e)
Romanesque: roman(e)
roof: toit (m)
room: chambre (f)
round trip: aller-retour (m)
rule: règle (f)

sacred: sacré(e)
sad: triste
safe box: coffre (m)
sail: voile (f)
sale: solde (m)
salesperson: vendeur/vendeuse
salt: sel (m)
same: même
Saturday: samedi (m)
sausage: saucisse (f)
say (to): dire
schedule: horaire (m)
school: école (f)
Scotland: Ecosse (f)
Scottish, Scots: écossais(e)
sea: mer (f)
season: saison (f)
seat: siège (m), place (f)
security: sécurité (f)
see (to): voir
sell (to): vendre
September: septembre (m)
serve (to): servir
settle (to): coloniser, s'installer
several: plusieurs
sewing: couture (f)
shellfish: coquillage (m)
shirt: chemise (f)
shoe: chaussure (f)
shop: boutique (f)
shopping: courses (f)
show: exposition (f), spectacle
  (m), présentation (f)
show (to): montrer
shower: douche (f)
shower (to), take a shower (to):
  se doucher
shrimp: crevette (f)
sick: malade
side: côté (m)
sign: pancarte (f)
silk: soie (f)

silver: argent (m)
since: depuis
sister: soeur (f)
sit (to): s'asseoir, siéger
skin: peau (f)
skirt: jupe (f)
slave: esclave (f/m)
small: petit(e)
smooth: doux/douce
snow: neige (f)
snow (to): neiger
soap: savon (m)
sock: bas (m)
soft: doux/douce
sold out: complet/complète
soldier: soldat (m)
something: quelque chose (f)
song: chanson (f)
son: fils (m)
sorry: désolé(e)
sound: son (m)
south: sud
Spain: Espagne (f)
Spanish: espagnol(e)
sparkling: mousseux/mousseuse
speak (to): parler
spectator: spectateur/spectatrice
spinning mill: filature (f)
spirit: esprit (m)
springtime: printemps (m)
square: place (f), carré(e)
stable: écurie (f)
stained glass window: vitrail (m)
stamp: timbre (m)
star: étoile (f)
state: état (m)
state (to): déclarer
station: gare (f)
stay (to): rester
steel: acier (m)
steeple, spire: flèche (f)
step: pas (m)

stocking: bas (m)
stone: pierre (f)
stop: arrêt (m)
stop (to): arrêter
store: magasin (m)
straight: droit(e)
straight ahead: tout droit
strawberry: fraise (f)
street: rue (f)
strength: puissance, force (f)
strike: grève (f)
strong: fort(e)
struggle (to): lutter
student: étudiant(e)
studio: atelier (m)
study (to): étudier
style: style (m)
suburbs: banlieue (f)
subway: métro (m)
success: succès (m)
suffer (to): souffrir
sugar: sucre (m)
suitcase: valise (f)
summer: été (m)
sun: soleil (m)
Sunday: dimanche (m)
sunrise: lever du soleil (m)
sunset: coucher du soleil (m)
suntanned: bronzé(e)
Superintendent: concièrge (f/m)
sure: sûr(e)
surrender: reddition (f)
swan: cygne (m)
swim (to): nager
talent: don
talk (to): parler
tall: grand(e)
tan: beige, bronzage (m)
tapestry: tapisserie (f)
taste: goût (m)
tasting: dégustation (f)
tax: impôt (m)

taxi: taxi (m)
tea: thé (m)
tea room: salon de thé (m)
telephone: téléphone (m)
telephone booth: cabine
 téléphonique (f)
temporary: provisoire
thank you: merci
theater play: pièce (f)
theater: théâtre (m)
then: alors, puis
there is, there are: voilà, il y a
there: là
this, that: ça, cela, ce/cette
Thursday: jeudi (m)
ticket: billet (m)
tide: marée (f)
time: temps (m), heure (f)
timetable: horaire (m)
tip: pourboire (m)
tire: pneu (m)
tobacco, tobacco shop: tabac (m)
today: aujourd'hui
toilet: toilette (f), WC (m)
toll: péage (m)
tomb: tombeau (m)
tomorrow: demain (m)
tongue: langue (f)
too, too much: trop
tool: outil (m)
tooth: dent (f)
tournament: tournoi (m)
towards: vers
tower: tour (f)
town hall: hôtel de ville (m),
 mairie (f)
trace (to): tracer
trade: commerce (m)
trade union: syndicat (m)
traffic: circulation (f)
training: formation (f)
tranquility: tranquillité (f)

transportation: transport (m)
traveler: voyageur/voyageuse
traveler's check: traveller (m)
treaty: traité (m)
tree: arbre (m)
tremendous: formidable
tribe: tribu (f)
trip: voyage (m)
trousers: pantalon (m)
trunk: malle (f)
try (to): essayer
Tuesday: mardi (m)
turn (to): tourner
UN: ONU (f)
under: underneath: dessous, sous
understand (to): comprendre
uniform: uniforme (m)
union: syndicat (m), union (f)
United Nations: Nations unies (f)
United States: Etats-Unis (m)
university: université (f)
unknown: inconnu(e)
until: jusque
upkeep: maintenance (f)
use (to): utiliser, user
vacation: vacances (f)
veal: veau (m)
vegetable: légume (m)
veil: voile (m)
velvet: velours (m)
very: très
view: vue (f)
vineyard: vignoble (m)
virgin: vierge (f)
visit (to): visiter
visitor: visiteur/visiteuse
wait for (to): attendre
waiter: garçon, serveur (m)
waitress: serveuse (f)
walk (to): marcher
wall: mur (m)
want (to): vouloir

war: guerre (f)
warehouse: entrepôt (m)
wash (to): se laver
watchman, night: veilleur de nuit,
  gardien de nuit (m)
water: eau (f)
wax: cire (f)
wealth: richesse (f)
weather: temps (m)
wedding: mariage (m)
Wednesday: mercredi (m)
week: semaine (f)
weight: poids (m)
welcome: bienvenu(e)
well: bien
west: ouest
what: que, quoi
wheat: blé (m)
when: quand
where: où
which: quel(le), lequel(le)
while: pendant que
white: blanc/blanche
who: qui
whole: entier/entière
why: pourquoi
wife: femme, épouse (f)
windmill: moulin à vent (m)
window: fenêtre (f)
wine: vin (m)

wine bar: bar à vin (m)
wing: aile (f)
winter: hiver (m)
with: avec
without: sans
woman: femme (f)
wool: laine (f)
word: mot (m)
work: travail (m)
work (to): travailler, marcher
work of art: oeuvre d'art (f)
worker: ouvrier/ouvrière;
  travailleur/travailleuse
workshop: atelier (m)
world: monde (m), mondial(e)
World War I: Première Guerre
  mondiale (f)
World War II: Seconde Guerre
  mondiale (f)
worldwide: mondial(e)
write (to): écrire
writer: écrivain (m)
wrong: tort (m)
year: an (m), année (f)
yellow: jaune (m)
yes: oui
yesterday: hier (m)
young: jeune
youth hostel: auberge de la
  jeunesse (f)
zero: zéro (m)

CHAPTER 22

Glossary: French-English

(e), (le), (ne), (ue) = feminine
endings for adjectives (singular)
(f) = feminine noun
(m) = masculine noun

abbaye (f): abbey
accepter: to accept
accord (m): agreement
d'accord: OK, all right
acheter: to buy
acier (m): steel
actuel(le): present-day
actuellement: at the present time
addition (f): check, bill, addition
adresse (f): address
aéroport (m): airport
affaire (f): affair, business
affiche (f): poster
Afrique (f): Africa
agent (m): policeman
âge (m): age
agréable: agreeable, pleasant
agrumes (f): citrus fruit
aile (f): wing
aimer: to like, to love
alcool blanc (m): fruit brandy
Allemagne (f): Germany
allemand(e): German
aller: to go

aller-retour (m): round trip
alors: then
amende (f): fine
américain(e): American
ami(e): friend
an (m): year
ancien(ne): ancient, old
ange (m): angel
anglais(e): English
Angleterre (f): England
année (f): year
antiquité (f): antique
août (m): August
apôtre (m): apostle
appel (m): call
appeler: to call
apporter: to bring
après: after, then
après-demain (m): day after
    tomorrow
après-midi (f/m): afternoon
arbre (m): tree
archevêque (m): archbishop
architecture (f): architecture
arène (f): arena
argent (m): money, silver
armée (f): army
arrêt (m): stop
arrêter: to stop, to arrest

arrière (m): behind
arrivée (f): arrival
arriver: to arrive
arrondissement (m): district
artisan (m): artisan, craftsman
artiste peintre (m/f): artist, painter
ascenseur (m): elevator
asiatique: Asian
Assemblée nationale (f): National Assembly
assez: enough, rather
assister: to attend
assurance (f): insurance
atelier (m): studio, workshop
attendre: to wait (for)
auberge (f): inn
auberge de jeunesse (f): youth hostel
augmenter: to increase
aujourd'hui: today
aussi: also
autobus (m): bus
automne (m): autumn, fall
autoroute (f): turnpike, parkway
autour: around
autrefois: in the past
autre: other
avant: before
avant-hier: day before yesterday
avec: with
avion (m): airplane
avoir: to have
avril (m): April
bagage (m): luggage, baggage
bague (f): ring
baie (f): bay
baigner, se baigner: to bathe, to take a bath
bain (m): bath
baiser (m): kiss
balcon (m): balcony
banlieue (f): suburbs

banque (f): bank
bar à vin (m): wine bar
bas/basse (a): low
bas (m): sock, stocking
bataille (f): battle
bateau (m): boat
beau/belle: beautiful
beaucoup: a lot, much, a great deal
beaux-arts (m): fine arts
beige, bronzage (m): tan
Belgique (f): Belgium
betterave (f): beet
beurre (m): butter
bienvenue (f): welcome
bien: well, good
bière (f): beer
bijou (m): jewel
bijoutier (m): jeweler
billet (m): ticket
blanc/blanche: white
bleu(e): blue
blé (m): wheat
boire: to drink
boisson (f): drink
bois (m): wood, woods
boîte (f): box
bombardement (m): bombing
bon/bonne: good
bonjour: good day, good morning, hello
bonsoir: good evening, good afternoon
bon marché: cheap
boulangerie (m): bakery
bouquiniste (m): bookseller
bourguignon(ne): Burgundian
bourreau (m): executioner
bouteille (f): bottle
boutique (f): shop
brasserie (f): beer-hall, restaurant
bras (m): arm
brique (f): brick

bronzé(e): suntanned
broderie (f): embroidery
brûler: to burn
bulle (f): bubble
bureau (m): office
ça, cela: this, that
cabine téléphonique (f): telephone booth
cacher: to hide, to conceal
cadeau (m): gift
café (m): coffee, café
caisse (f): cashier
calcaire (m): limestone
Cambodge (m): Cambodia
campagne (f): country, countryside
camping (m): camp ground
Canada (m): Canada
canadien(ne): Canadian
canard (m): duck
car (m): bus
caractère (m): character
caractéristique: characteristic
carrefour (m): intersection, crossroads
carte (f): map, menu
carte de jeu (f): playing card
casser: to break
caverne (f): cave
cave (f): cellar
ce/cette: this, that
ceinture (f): belt
célébrer: celebrate
cendre (f): ash
cendrier (m): ashtray
centre (m): center
cerise (f): cherry
certain(e): certain
César: Caesar
chaise (f): chair
chambre (f): room, bedroom
Chambre des députés (f): Chamber of Deputies
chambre d'hôte (f): bed and breakfast
champ (m): field
champ de course (m): race course
chance (f): luck
change (m): exchange
chanson (f): song
chapeau (m): hat
chapiteau (m): capital
chaque: each
charmante(e): charming
chasser: to hunt, to chase
chat(te): cat
château (m): castle
chaud(e): hot
chauffage (m): heat
chaussure (f): shoe
chef-d'oeuvre (m): masterpiece
chemise (f): shirt
chèque (m): check
cher/chère: expensive, dear
chercher: to look for, to search for
chéri(e): darling
cheval (m): horse
chèvre (f): goat cheese
chez: at the home of, at home
chien(ne): dog
Chine (f): China
choisir: to choose
choix (m): choice
chou (m): cabbage
christianisme (m): Christianity
cimetière (m): cemetery
cinéma (m): movies, movie theater
circulation (f): circulation, traffic
cire (f): wax
cirque (m): circus
citron (m): lemon
clair(e): light
clé (or clef) (f): key
coca (m): coca-cola
cochon(ne): pig

coeur (m): heart
coffre (m): safe box
cognac (m): brandy
coiffeur/coiffeuse: hairdresser
coin (m): corner
collège (m): high school
colline (f): hill
colonie (f): colony, camp
coloniser, s'installer: to settle
colonne (f): column, pillar
combien: how much, how many
commander: to order
comme: like, as
commencer: to begin, to commence
comment: how
commerce (m): trade
commissariat (m): police station
complet/complète: full, sold out
composter: to stamp
comprendre: to understand
comprimé (m): tablet, pill
concièrge (m/f): superintendent
conduire: to drive, to conduct, to lead
confiture (f): jam
connaître: to know, to be acquainted with
connu(e): known
conquête (f): conquest
conseil (m): council, advice
conseiller: to advise, to counsel
construire: to build, to construct
consulter: to consult
contenir: to contain
content(e): happy, pleased
coquillage (m): shellfish
côte (f): coast
côté (m): side
coton (m): cotton
coucher du soleil (m): sunset
cour (f): court, tribunal, courtyard

couronne (f): crown
cours (m): rate of exchange
course (f): errand, race
courses (f): shopping, races
course de taureaux (f): bullfight
course de chevaux (f): horse race
coût (m): cost
coûter: to cost
coûteux/coûteuse: costly
coutume (f): custom
couture (f): dressmaking, sewing
couturier/couturière: couturier, dressmaker
couvent (m): convent
couvrir: to cover
crabe (m): crab
crevette (f): shrimp
croix (f): cross
croisé (m): crusader
cuir (m): leather
cuisine (f): cooking, kitchen
culture biologique (f): organic produce
cygne (m): swan
dame (f): lady
dangereux/dangereuse: dangerous
danseur/danseuse: dancer
dans: in
date (f): date
dater: to date
début (m): beginning
décembre (m): December
déclarer: to declare, to state
découverte (f): discovery
défense de: prohibited
défilé (m): parade
dégustation (f): tasting, sampling
déjeuner (m): lunch
demain (m): tomorrow
demander: to ask
demi(e): half, half past
dent (f): tooth

dépannage (m): breakdown service
départ (m): departure
depuis: since
dernier/dernière: last
derrière (m): behind
descendre: to go down, to descend
désolé(e): sorry
dessiner: to design, to draw
dessous: under, underneath
dessus: over
devenir: to become
dévouement (m): devotion
dimanche (m): Sunday
dîner (m): dinner
dire: to say
diviser: to divide
docteur (m): doctor
doigt (m): finger
dommage (m): harm
don (m): gift, talent
donner: to give
doré(e): golden, gilt
douane (f): customs
douche (f): shower
doucher, se doucher: to shower, to
 take a shower
doux/douce: soft, smooth, mild
drogue (f): drug, drugs
droit (m): law
droit(e): straight
droite (f): right
duc (m): duke
dur(e): hard
durer: to last
eau (f): water
éclairage (m): lighting
écluse (f): lock (nautical)
école (f): school
écossais(e): Scotch, Scots, Scottish
Ecosse (f): Scotland
écouter: to listen
écrire: to write

écrivain (m): writer
écurie (f): stable
égal(e): equal, even
également: also
église (f): church
embrasser: to embrace, to kiss
enchanté(e): pleased to meet you
encore: still, more
endommager: to damage
enfant (m/f): child
enterrer: to bury
entier/entière: entire, whole
entre: between
entrée (f): entrance
entrepôt (m): warehouse
entrer: to enter
entrevue (f): interview
environs (m): outskirts
environ: about, approximately
épicerie (f): grocery
époque (f): epoch, era
escalier (m): staircase
esclave (f/m): slave
Espagne (f): Spain
espagnol(e): Spanish
espérer: to hope
esprit (m): spirit, mind
essayer: to try
est (m): east
étable (m): animal shed
établir: to establish
étage (m): floor
Etats-Unis (m): United States
état (m): state
été (m): summer
étoile (f): star
étranger/étrangère: foreigner
être: to be
étudiant(e): student
étudier: to study
événement (m): event
évêque (m): bishop

excuser: to excuse, to forgive
exemple (m): example
exercise (m): exercise
exposition (f): show, exhibition
faire: to do, to make
falaise (f): cliff
famille (f): family
(il) faut: must, have to, need
faux/fausse: wrong, false
fée (f): fairy
femme (f): woman, wife
femme de chambre (f): chambermaid
fenêtre (f): window
féodal(e): feudal
fer (m): iron
fermer: to close
fête (f): holiday, celebration
fêter: to celebrate
feu (m): fire, light
feu d'artifice (m): fireworks
feu rouge, feu vert (m): red light, green light
février (m): February
fiançailles (f): engagement
fidèle: faithful
fièvre (f): fever
filature (f): spinning mill
fille (f): daughter, girl
fils (m): son
fin (f): end
finir: to finish
flèche (f): arrow, steeple, spire
fleur (f): flower
fleuve (m): river
flotter: to float
foie (m): liver
foire (f): fair
foncé(e): dark
fontaine (f): fountain
forêt (f): forest
formation (f): training

formidable: tremendous
fort (m): fort, fortress
fort(e): strong
forteresse (f): fortress
fouille (f): excavation
foule (f): crowd
four (m): oven
fraise (f): strawberry
framboise (f): raspberry
français(e): French
fraternité (f): brotherhood, fraternity
frein (m): brake
frère (m): brother
fresque (f): fresco
frites (f): French fries
froid(e): cold
fromage (m): cheese
garçon (m): boy, waiter
gardien de nuit (m): night watchman
gare (f): station
gâteau (m): cake
gauche (f): left, awkward
Gaule (f): Gaul
gaulois(e): Gallic
gentil(le): nice, kind
gîte rural (m): efficiency apartment or house
glace (f): ice, ice cream
gothique: Gothic
goût (m): taste
gouvernement (m): government
grand(e): tall, big, large
Grande-Bretagne (f): Great Britain
grand magasin (m): department store
gratuit(e): free-of-charge, gratuitous
gravure (f): engraving
gris(e): gray
grotte (f): grotto, cave

guerre (f): war

guichet (m): ticket office, box office

habiller, s'habiller: to dress, to get dressed

habiter: to live in

halle (f): market

hall (m): lobby, hall

haut(e): high, tall

havre (m): haven

hectare (m): 2.471 acres

heure (f): hour, time

hier (m): yesterday

hiver (m): winter

homard (m): lobster

homme (m): man

hôpital (m): hospital

horaire (m): timetable, schedule

horloge (f): clock

hôtel de ville (m): town hall

hôtel particulier (m): private mansion

huile (f): oil

huître (f): oyster

humanité (f): humanity

ici: here

idée (f): idea

il y a: there is, there are

île, isle (f): island

immeuble (m): building, apartment house

imperméable (m): raincoat

impôt (m): tax

inconnu(e): unknown

Inde (f): India

indépendant(e): independent

indiquer: to indicate

ingénieur (m): engineer

interdit(e): prohibited

introduire: to introduce

invité(e): guest

irlandais(e): Irish

Irlande (f): Ireland

Italie (f): Italy

italien(ne): Italian

itinéraire (m): itinerary

jamais: never

jambon (m): ham

janvier (m): January

jardin (m): garden

jaune (m): yellow

jeudi (m): Thursday

jeune fille (f): girl

jeune: young

joli(e): pretty

joue (f): cheek

jouer: to play

journée (f): day, daytime

jour (m): day

journal (m): newspaper

juif/juive: Jewish

juillet (m): July

juin (m): June

jupe (f): skirt

jusque: until

là-bas: over there

lac (m): lake

laine (f): wool

lait (m): milk

lampe (f): lamp, light

langouste (f): lobster

langue (f): tongue, language

là: there

laver, se laver: to wash

leçon (f): lesson

lecture (f): reading

légende (f): legend

légume (m): vegetable

lettre (f): letter

lever, se lever: to raise, to get up, to rise, to stand up

lever du jour (m): daybreak

lever du soleil (m): sunrise

liberté (f): freedom

librairie (f): bookshop
libre: free
lieu (m): place
ligne (f): line
lin (m): linen
lire: to read
lit (m): bed
livre (f): pound
livre (m): book
logement (m): housing, lodgings, apartment
loger: to lodge, to live (in)
loin: far
long(ue): long
longtemps: long time
louer: to rent, to praise
lumière (f): light
lundi (m): Monday
lutter: to fight, to struggle
luxe (m): luxury, wealth
madame (f): madam, Mrs.
mademoiselle (f): Miss
magasin (m): store
main (f): hand
maintenance (f): maintenance, upkeep
mai (m): May
maintenant: now
maison (f): house
mais: but
maison de couture (f): couture house
mal: bad, badly
malade: sick, ill
malgré: despite
malle (f): trunk
manger: to eat
mannequin (m): model
maquette (f): layout, model
marais (m): marsh, marshland
marbre (m): marble
marchandise (f): goods, merchandise
marcher: to walk, to work or function
marché (m): market
mardi (m): Tuesday
marée (f): tide
mari (m): husband
mariage (m): marriage, wedding
marier, se marier: to marry, to get married
marron, brun (m): brown
mars (m): March
matin (m): morning
mauvais(e): bad
médecin (m): doctor
médicament (m): medicine
meilleur(e): better
meilleur marché: cheaper
mélanger: to mix
membre (m): member
même: same
mémoire (f): memory
mer (f): sea
merci: thank you
mercredi (m): Wednesday
mère (f): mother
messe (f): mass
métro (m): subway
mettre: to put
meuble (m): piece of furniture
midi (m): noon
miel (m): honey
mieux: better
millénaire (m): millenium
minuit (m): midnight
miroir (m): mirror
missionnaire (m/f): missionary
mode (f): fashion
moins: less, minus
mois (m): month
moitié (f): half

monde (m): world, people
mondial(e): world, worldwide
monnaie (f): change, currency, mint
monsieur, messieurs (m): Mr., Messsrs.
montagne (f): mountain
monter: to climb, to go up
montrer: to show
morceau (m): piece
moteur (m): engine, motor
moto (f): motorcycle
mot (m): word
moulin (m), usine (f): mill
moulin à vent (m): windmill
mourir: to die
mousseux/mousseuse: sparkling
moyen(ne): average, medium
moyen âge (m): Middle Ages
mur (m): wall
musée (m): museum
musicien(ne): musician
musique (f): music
nager: to swim
naissance (f): birth
naître: to be born
nationalité (f): nationality
Nations unies (f): United Nations
nature (f): nature, natural
né(e): born
nécessaire: necessary
nef (f): nave
neige (f): snow
neiger: to snow
nerf (m): nerve
neuf/neuve: new
nez (m): nose
niveau (m): level
Noël (m): Christmas
noir(e): black
nom (m): name
nommer: to name, to nominate

non: no
nord (m): north
note (f): bill
novembre (m): November
nuit (f): night
numéro (m): number
océan (m): ocean
octobre (m): October
oeuf (m): egg
oeuvre d'art (f): work of art
offrir: to offer
oiseau (m): bird
ONU (f): UN
on: one, they, people
or (m): gold
orchestre (m): orchestra
ouest (m): west
outil (m): tool
ouvert(e): open
ou: or
oublier: to forget
oui: yes
ouvrier/ouvrière: worker
ouvrir: to open
où: where
pain (m): bread
paire (f): pair
palais (m): palace
palais de justice (m): law courts
palmier (m): palm tree
pancarte (f): sign
panne (f): breakdown
panneau (m): panel, sign, board
pantalon (m): trousers
pape (m): pope
Pâques (f): Easter
paquet (m): package
paradis (m): paradise
pardon (m): pardon
par: by
pardonner: to pardon, to forgive
parent(e): relative, parent

parfum (m): perfume
parking (m): parking lot
parler: to speak, to talk
partir: to leave, to go
partout: everywhere
passeport (m): passport
pas (m): step, footstep
passer: to pass
passé (m): past
pâtisserie (f): pastry, pastry shop
patron/patronne: boss, owner
pays (m): country
paysan/paysanne: peasant, farmer
péage (m): toll
peau (f): skin
pêche (f): peach, fishing
peinture (f): painting
pellicule (f): film
pendant: during
pendant que: while
perdre: to lose
père (m): father
permanent(e): permanent
personne (f): person
petit déjeuner (m): breakfast
petit(e): little, small
peuple (m): people
peu: little, few
phare (m): headlight, beacon, lighthouse
pharmacie (f): pharmacy, drug store
pharmacien(ne): pharmacist
pièce (f): coin, theater play
pied (m): foot
pierre (f): stone
piéton(ne): pedestrian
pique-nique (m): picnic
piscine (f): pool
place (f): square, place, seat
plage (f): beach
plaisir (m): pleasure

plat (m): dish
plâtre (m): plaster
plein(e): full
pleuvoir: to rain
pluie (f): rain
plus: more
plusieurs: several
pneu (m): tire
poète/poétesse: poet, poetess
poids (m): weight
poire (f): pear
poisson (m): fish
poivre (m): pepper
police (f): police
pont (m): bridge
port (m): harbor, port
porte (f): door
poste (f): post office
pot-pourri (m): stew, medley, mixture
poulet (m): chicken
poupée (f): doll
pourboire (m): tip
pour cent: percent
pour: for
pourpre, violet (m): purple
pourquoi: why
poussière (f): dust
poutre (f): beam
pouvoir: to be able
préférer: to prefer
premier/première: first
Première Guerre mondiale (f): World War I
prendre: to take
prénom (m): first name
préparer: to prepare
présentation (f): show, presentation
présenter: to present
près: near
prêt-à-porter (m): ready-to-wear

printemps (m): springtime
priorité (f): priority
prix (m): price
problème (m): problem
prochain(e): next
proche: close, near, nearby
produire: to produce
produit (m): product
progrès (m): progress
projecteur (m): projector
propriété (f): property, estate
prospère: prosperous
provisoire: temporary, provisional
prune (f): plum
puissance (f): power, strength
quai (m): platform
quand: when
quart (m): quarter, one-fourth
quartier (m): neighborhood,
    quarter
quartier général (m): headquarters
que: that, which, than, what
quel(le): which, what
quelque chose (f): something
quitter: to leave
qui: who
quoi: what
raisin (m): grape
raisin sec (m): raisin
rapide: rapid, quick
rappeler: to call back, to remember
raquette (f): racket
réception (f): reception
recette (f): recipe
recevoir: to receive
récolte (f): harvest
recruter: to recruit
reddition (f): surrender
réduire: to reduce
regarder: to look at
régler: to settle, to pay
règle (f): rule

reine (f): queen
rempart (m): rampart
rencontrer: to meet
rendez-vous (m): appointment,
    date
renommée (f): fame, renown
renseignement (m): information
répondre: to reply
représentant(e): representative
réservation (f): reservation
réserver: to reserve
responsable (m/f): person in
    charge, responsible
rester: to stay, to remain
retourner: to return, to turn over
rêve (m): dream
revoir: to meet again
au revoir: goodbye
rez-de-chaussée (m): ground floor
Rhin (m): Rhine
richesse (f): wealth, riches
rien: nothing
rire (m): laugh, laughter, to laugh
rive droite (f): right bank
rive gauche (f): left bank
rivière (f): river
riz (m): rice
roi (m): king
romain(e): Roman
roman (m): novel
roman(e): Romanesque
rose (f): rose
rouge: red
route (f): road, route
royaume (m): kingdom
rue (f): street
rue principale (f): main street
s'il vous plaît: please
sac (m): bag, sack
sacré(e): sacred
saison (f): season
salle à manger (f): dining room

salle de bains (f): bathroom
salon (m): salon, lounge, living room
salon de beauté (m): beauty parlor
salon de thé (m): tea room
samedi (m): Saturday
sans: without
saucisse (f): sausage
savoir: to know
savon (m): soap
sec/sèche: dry
Seconde Guerre mondiale (f): World War II
sécurité (f): security
sel (m): salt
selon: according to
semaine (f): week
septembre (m): September
serrure (f): lock
serveur/serveuse: waiter, waitress
service (m): service, service charge
servir: to serve
seul(e): alone
seulement: only
siècle (m): century
siège (m): seat
siéger: to sit, to be located
signaler: to indicate, to signal
soeur (f): sister
soie (f): silk
soir (m): evening
soldat (m): soldier
solde (m): sale
solder: to put on sale
soleil (m): sun
sonnette (f): bell
son (m): sound
sortie (f): exit
sortir: to exit, to go out
souffrir: to suffer
sous: under
souterrain(e): underground

souvent: often
spectacle (m): show, sight
spectateur/spectatrice: spectator
style (m): style
succès (m): success
sucre (m): sugar
sud (m): south
suivre: to follow
sur: on, upon
sûr(e): sure
sympathique: nice, pleasant, friendly
synagogue (f): synagogue
syndicat (m): trade union
tabac (m): tobacco, tobacco shop
tableau (m): painting, picture
tapisserie (f): tapistry
taux de change (m): exchange rate
taxi (m): taxi
téléphone (m): telephone
temps (m): time, weather
teinture (f): dye
terre (f): land
tête (f): head
TGV (m): high-speed train
thé (m): tea
théâtre (m): theater
timbre (m): stamp
tire-bouchon (m): corkscrew
tissu (m): fabric, material, cloth
toile (f): canvas
toilette (f): toilet, outfit, cleaning
toit (m): roof
tombeau (m): tomb
tort (m): fault, wrong
toujours: always
tour (f): tower
tournoi (m): tournament
tour (m): turn, excursion, tour
tourner: to turn
tous/toutes: everyone, all
tout(e): all, whole

tout de suite: at once, immediately
tracer: to trace
traité (m): treaty
tranquillité (f): tranquility
transport (m): transport, transportation
travail (m): work
travailler: to work
traveller (m): traveler's check
traverser: to cross
très: very
tribu (f): tribe
tribunal (m): tribunal, law court
tricot (m): knitted fabric, knitting, jersey
triste: sad
trop: too much
trouver: to find
tuer: to kill
un(e): one, a
uniforme (m): uniform
université (f): university, college
usine (f): factory
utiliser: to use, to utilize
vacances (f): vacation
vache (f): cow
valise (f): valise, suitcase
veau (m): veal
veilleur de nuit (m): night watchman
velours (m): velvet
vélo (m): bike, cycle
vendeur/vendeuse: salesman, saleswoman
vendredi (m): Friday
vendre: to sell

venir: to come
verger (m): orchard
vérifier: to verify, to check
verre (m): glass
vers: towards
vert(e): green
viande (f): meat
vie (f): life
vierge (f): virgin
vieux/vieille: old
vif/vive: lively
vignoble (m): vineyard
ville (f): city
vin (m): wine
virgule (f): comma
visiter: to visit
visiteur/visiteuse: visitor
vite: quickly
vitrail (m): stained glass window
vivant(e): alive, living
voici: here is, here are
voilà: there is, there are
voile (f): sail
voile (m): veil
voir: to see
voisin(e): neighbor
voiture (f): car, carriage
vol (m): flight
volaille (f): poultry
vouloir: to wish, to want
voyage (m): trip
voyageur (m): traveler, passenger
vue (f): view
wagon (m): wagon, carriage
WC (m): toilet
zéro (m): zero, nought

Key to Price Information on Hotels and Restaurants

Accommodations:

Suggestions for hotels and other accommodations are provided at the end of each itinerary. Pricing corresponds to the following categories:

Inexpensive: under 150 francs
Moderately priced: from 150 to 300 francs
Medium-priced: from 300 to 500 francs
Moderately expensive: from 500 to 700 francs
Expensive: from 700 to 1000 francs
Luxury prices: over 1000 francs

Restaurants:

Suggestions for restaurants are provided at the end of each itinerary. The asterisk (*) preceding an address indicates that the establishment offers a fixed price menu for 100 francs or less. Restaurant pricing in this guide corresponds to the following categories for full meal and one-half bottle of wine:

Inexpensive: under 100 francs
Moderately priced: from 100 to 200 francs
Medium-priced: from 200 to 300 francs
Moderately expensive: from 300 to 400 francs
Expensive: from 400 to 600 francs
Luxury prices: over 600 francs

NOTE: For suggestions on hotels, restaurants, tearooms, wine bars, pastry shops, etc., in Paris, see Hippocrene *Insider's Guide to Paris*.

Index

*Names of places are indicated in **bold**.*